So Cranes May Dance

A
RESCUE
FROM
THE
BRINK
OF
EXTINCTION

Barbara Katz

CHICAGO
REVIEW
PRESS

Library of Congress Cataloging-in-Publication Data
Katz, Barbara, 1956–
So cranes may dance : a rescue from the brink of extinction /
Barbara Katz : [foreword by Roger Tory Peterson]. — 1st ed.
   p. cm.
  Includes index.
  ISBN 1-55652-171-5 : $19.95
  1. International Crane Foundation—History. 2. Cranes
(Birds) 3. Birds, Protection of. I. Title.
QL696.G84K385 1993
639.9'7831—dc20 92-44904

A portion of the proceeds from the sale of this book will be donated to the International Crane Foundation.

Illustrations © 1993 by Diane Pierce

Published by Chicago Review Press, Incorporated
814 North Franklin Street
Chicago, Illinois 60610
1 2 3 4 5 6 7 8 9 10
ISBN 1-55652-171-5
Printed in the United States of America on recycled paper

For my parents

Contents

Foreword

Several birds have slipped into the void of extinction in recent years in spite of frantic and costly attempts to save them. The passenger pigeon and the Carolina paroquet plummeted from abundance to zero before the environmental movement really got under way after the turn of the century. Others such as the heath hen and the ivory-billed woodpecker faded away more recently because of environmental pressures that they could not cope with. Bachmans warbler may now be gone but we are not sure; it is somewhat of a mystery bird. The latest loss, the dusky seaside sparrow, was officially declared extinct in 1990 after vast amounts of money and effort had been spent to safeguard it. Eventually the crosscurrents of bureaucratic bungling and mismanagement sealed its fate. Extinction is forever.

On the credit side of the ledger is the story of the cranes, which Barbara Katz details so vividly in this fascinating book. Due to the passionate leadership and hardball tactics of two men, George Archibald and Ron Sauey, at least one species of crane, and perhaps others, have been turned back from almost certain extinction. It was by a stroke of fortune that these two like-minded men crossed paths when they were involved with research at Cornell. It was there, at the Laboratory of Ornithology in Sapsucker Woods near Ithaca, where I first met them. As I remember, George had some sandhill cranes in a makeshift cage.

Little did we know that these two young men, loners in a way, more attuned to the natural world than most of their brethren, would have a world-wide influence on wildlife conservation through the International Crane Foundation, which they initiated and nurtured to its present status.

Of course, there were many others who played a part: the late Owen Gromme, the wildlife artist, and his wife Anne who gave early support; Ron Sauey's own parents, who made available their property at Baraboo for the facilities in which the cranes would be housed; and a host of volunteers and students, including Barbara Katz, the author of this book, who, like her mentors, gained such deep insights into crane behavior that she almost thinks like a crane.

Sadly, Ron Sauey died of a brain hemorrhage at the untimely age of 37, but George Archibald carries on, spending much of his time in India, Siberia, and other far parts of the world with exotic cranes and crane people. He is the most internationally connected man I know. George spends the other half of the year at Baraboo, actually dancing with his favorite cranes, which accept him as one of their own.

The drawings in these pages are by the celebrated bird artist Diane Pierce who has selflessly given of her own time to the work at Baraboo as have so many others.

Read the following chapters and be better informed about cranes and the people who keep them dancing.

—Roger Tory Peterson

Acknowledgments

The genesis of this book was in an article I wrote for *Birder's World* magazine, "A Dream Realized." That article convinced me to pursue my own dream, a book about the International Crane Foundation. Before I got around to pitching the idea to ICF, I received a letter from George Archibald informing me that trustee Chappie Fox was interested in putting together a little history book about ICF and inquiring whether I was interested in the project. Was I ever! In our first meeting I talked them into a big history book, and without so much as an outline to show them, Chappie and George agreed to support my endeavor.

George Archibald's encouragement, confidence, friendship, and trust was a lifeline throughout the writing of this book. He patiently submitted to hours of taped interviews and provided many leads and names of people when I was trying to track down information for which there was no written record. George read every page of this manuscript and offered many valuable insights. His support went far beyond his responsibilities as director of ICF.

Jim Harris always took time from his hectic schedule to give me whatever assistance I needed. If I had a crisis, Jim made it go away.

Jack Puelicher provided financial support for various expenses. The Crane Foundation also provided funds.

Diane Pierce overwhelmed me with her generosity when she offered to contribute the stunning illustrations that grace this book.

I owe a great deal of gratitude to all of the photographers who graciously allowed me to use their pictures.

The people who consented to interviews, most of whom are identified within the text, helped create this book as surely as they helped build the Crane Foundation. For many it was a challenge to open their memories of five, ten, and twenty years ago. But Norman and Claire Sauey also opened their hearts during our three-hour meeting and, at the conclusion, told me to call them anytime for anything at all. I often did.

Milly Zantow, Marge Winski, and Mini Nagendran allowed me access to their personal papers.

Drs. F. Josh Dein and Doug Docherty provided technical advice for chapter 7. The information in chapter 12 about satellite transmitters and their deployment on cranes is courtesy of Dr. David Ellis of the United States Fish & Wildlife Service and the National Space and Aeronautics Administration.

The entire staff of the International Crane Foundation offered support and friendship and extended themselves to ensure my visits were always productive. I relied heavily on secretaries Rosanne Blada and Teresa Searock, and it was always reassuring to hear their voices at the other end of the phone line. Portions of the manuscript were reviewed by Jim Harris, Claire Mirande, Scott Swengel, Marianne Wellington, Ann Burke, Julie Langenberg, and Jeb Barzen. Jim Harris helped choose the photos and Dave Thompson assisted. Terry Brooks, Gordon Dietzman, Bob Hallam, Patty McCourt, Dave Chesky, and Rich Beilfuss were also part of this amazing network. Eric Scott was an essential link between myself and the rest of the staff. I pestered these people a lot and they're all still speaking to me.

Konrad Liegel and Mini Nagendran also read parts of the manuscript.

Kyoko Archibald translated communications between myself and Masahiro Wada.

In Baraboo, Joanne and Joe Burke opened their home and saved me from many lonely nights in a motel. They welcomed me as one of their family.

Susie and Roy Quiriconi and their entire staff made Susie's Restaurant my oasis in the Baraboo Hills.

Bonnie Jacobs and Donna Eyre-Polk were part of my support crew in Chicago and, on behalf of Audubon and Bagel, their patience and dedication was greatly appreciated.

Also, thanks to Mark Lefebvre.

My agent, Lyle Steele, and his project editor, Jim Kepler, believed in this book before I had even written one word.

The people at Chicago Review Press added immeasurably to the fun of producing this book. I would like to especially thank my editor, Amy Teschner. Her suggestions added clarity and strength to the manuscript.

Finally, it's important to know there are people who love you no matter what you do. Writing this book has been one of the saner things I've done in my life. Ann, Louise, Shelly, Howard, Joshua, Nate, Eli, and Sara hold my safety net.

That net was woven by Philip and Muriel Katz. Without their love, friendship, talent for editing, home-cooked meals, and shoulders to lean on, this book would not exist.

Introduction

When I attended Beloit College in the late 1970s, there was no way to get released from the place unless you completed your field term, a period during which you had to be away from the college and your home and practice being part of the real world. I sought out positions related to my major interests, biology and conservation, and ended up with three options: the regional Audubon office in Red Wing, Minnesota, which would have paid a small stipend; the prestigious Library of Natural Sounds at the Cornell Laboratory of Ornithology; or a volunteer stint at an upstart four-year-old organization located on a horse farm in rural Baraboo, Wisconsin, with the audacity to declare itself the "world center for the study and preservation of cranes."

I chose the International Crane Foundation, where for eight months, January through August, I studied the breeding biology of the Hooded Crane, assisted with artificial insemination, raised the chicks, fed and watered the adult birds, gave tours, and even partied once or twice. I met cranes that I loved and cranes that I feared. I met people from places around the world that, at the time, I couldn't even find on the map. I was welcomed into the family of ICFers, the volunteers who helped build the foundation.

Two people in particular made an impression on me that year, George Archibald and Ron Sauey. Many of the people you will meet in this book were introduced to me by Ron and George—famous people and fast friends. Though my tenure at the Crane Foundation ended in 1977, my association with ICF did not. My visits in the ensuing years allowed me to witness ICF's evolution into the world-renowned institution it is today and introduced me to each succeeding generation of ICFers. But mostly I kept coming back for the cranes, to hear them call, to see them dance.

So Cranes May Dance

ONE

Birdmen

W hen he was seven years old, Ron Sauey proudly marched into his home in Baraboo, Wisconsin, dragging an opossum by the tail behind him. It was so big he could barely lift it. The possum, naturally, played dead. Ron discovered the animal while he and his twin brother, Don, were exploring the woods near their home. Convinced it was dead, the boys brought it home for a proper burial. No doubt their mother would have been satisfied with a bouquet of dandelions. As it was, she had a difficult time convincing them the possum was alive. Ron finally let go of the tail, and the critter beat a hasty retreat to the woods.

It was just another sign that Ron, the third of Norman and Claire Sauey's four children (by five minutes after his twin brother), was not destined to enter the family plastics business.

As far back as anyone can remember, including Ron, he was always interested in anything that "slithered, crawled, or flew." The possum incident only reinforced Don's growing realization that his brother had his own agenda.

"We had a childhood friend nearby named Phil Effinger. We were always playing cowboys and Indians or playing with toy trucks. We'd start out playing together and suddenly Ron was no longer with us. He was down by the river taking water up in his hands and looking at the things that lived in the river.

"Or we'd look up and there would be Ron in the field with a homemade butterfly net. He took a broom pole and attached a net on the end. He'd capture butterflies, look at them, and let them go. Later on he had a tremendous collection."

Ron's dad bought him a real butterfly net and gave up an old toolbox so Ron could safely store his specimens. In his room late at night, long after Don was under the covers, Ron labored to carefully preserve the beauties he had collected.

Baraboo was Ron's playground and laboratory. He walked out his back door and immersed himself in birds, bugs, rocks, and the river the way most kids walk down to the neighborhood park and lose themselves in sandlot baseball and pickup basketball games.

The Sauey family's previous home was in Melrose Park, a Chicago suburb. Ron's father, Norman, had moved there in 1938. He took a job at a plastics factory where he discovered his talent as a toolmaker and his future wife, Claire Femali. Six years later Norman bought three tooling machines and with his sixteen-year-old brother-in-law established the A-1 Tool & Die Company in the basement of the home he and Claire rented. It became one of the largest independent tool companies in the nation. In 1950 Norman accepted his brothers' invitation to join them in a plastics manufacturing business and moved the family to Baraboo. Ron was two years old.

For Norman, moving to Wisconsin was a homecoming of sorts. He and his nine brothers and sisters grew up on an eighty-acre farm near Kennan, scraping a living from the fields. Life would be much different this time around. The family lived on the south side of town on Effinger Road, named for Phil's ancestors. The Baraboo River flowed behind Phil's home, across the street from Ron's house. In 1959 Norman relocated the family to a custom-built home on a ridge overlooking the town. Though only minutes from downtown Baraboo, the area was essentially rural. On the western portion of the sixty-five-acre spread, Norman and Claire built a stable and fenced pastures for their Arabian horses. They named the horse farm by combining the first two letters of their children's names. Nodoroma stood for Norman, Jr., the twins Don and Ron, and Mary Anne. Between the Sauey home and the Wisconsin Dells ten miles north lay rolling hills and farms. To the south, three miles past town, is Devil's Lake State Park with its quartzite bluffs looming five hundred feet above the pristine landlocked lake.

The Sauey children went to a Catholic elementary school that provided a solid foundation for Ron's education but didn't do much for the budding naturalist within. Years later Ron related a story to a magazine writer about discovering the word *ornithologist* in the dictionary and realizing that he wanted birds to be his life's work.

"Asked by his parish priest what he would 'like to be,' [Ron] responded, 'an ornithologist.'

'And what might that be, son?'

'One who studies birds, Father.'

'Well,' the priest replied, 'I suppose we have to have some of those, too.' "

But his primary-school education did release another latent talent in young Ron Sauey. Music. His curriculum was rich with the classical composers. The piano and Chopin made a lasting impression—he never gave up either of them.

With his father's business thriving and the family firmly ensconced in a comfortable lifestyle, Ron was free to indulge his intellectual curiosity. Though his parents didn't share his interest, they never hindered his desires. Ron pursued his bugs and butterflies and birds while his brother Don developed a passion for sports.

Norm, Jr., even reaped a benefit from his little brother's hobby, a benefit that brought Ron a bit of notoriety. Like all students at Baraboo High School, young Norman had to take biology. He had the good fortune (from Ron's perspective) to be assigned to Gerald Scott's sophomore science class. Gerald's teaching methods, for his time and place, were a bit unorthodox.

Gerald recalls his homespun curriculum that inspired generations of students. "I had developed this departure from book learning. I got the idea that if you studied all winter the book gets kind of stale. So why not put some of this into practical knowledge. Let's see what they learned from the book." So he set up a system whereby his students earned points by collecting bugs and plants and stuff.

"But if they brought in something that was protected by law, they got points taken off. So they had to know what they were doing."

Norm, Jr., had no interest in the assignment. Ron, eleven years old, was up to the challenge. He collected Norm's points. Rumor has it he collected for the neighborhood. Ron made the most of his first opportunity to be a working field biologist.

Twenty-five years later he recalled the moment he actually met Gerald Scott for the first time.

It was "on a Friday night, in the fall of 1963. I was a freshman at a Baraboo High School dance hosted by the Foreign Student Committee. Mr. Scott, the club's longtime advisor, was one of the two adults supervising the dance. . . . I remember carefully examining him as he stood, facing east as I recall, by the refreshment stand. The moment is so indelibly impressed on my brain, I suppose, because Gerald Scott was already a hero to me, and had been ever since my older brother Norm had taken biology from him three years earlier. At the time, I had joyfully collected "biology points" for Norm. At my tender age, it seemed well-nigh miraculous that an adult could make a living at studying living things."

Ron's youthful study of living things continued to expand. He became interested in owls and pheasants and asked his father if he could raise some pheasants. Norman granted Ron's request and realized this wasn't a phase his son would grow out of: "I encouraged his brothers to go into the business, but I knew Ron was already slanted towards nature."

They designed a coop and built it just west of the driveway entering the horse farm. Then father and son drove around Wisconsin picking up birds from breeders. It was Ron's first attempt at aviculture. Some of the birds died. He felt awful and vowed not to make the same mistakes again. Ron kept those pheasants all through high school. They, along with Chopin, became a lifelong interest.

Never one to limit himself, even as a teenager, Ron hooked up with wildlife biologist Dr. Francis Hammerstrom and her research project on Harriers, a type of hawk. Ron and the rest of the volunteers arrived at Hammerstrom's home by 6:30 in the morning. Fran recalls a quiet boy, about thirteen or fourteen at the time, who "really put his mind on the birds." In the book that Hammerstrom wrote about the research, she acknowledges all of the volunteers who toiled the requisite number of hours. Among the names listed is Ron Sauey. Long after the field project was concluded, Fran Hammerstrom and her husband remained part of Ron's life. It didn't matter that decades of living, experience, and knowledge separated him from the Hammerstroms. Ron easily reached across the years.

Ron with a kestral. *Photo by Gerald Scott.*

In the meantime Ron found himself in Gerald Scott's biology class. Gerald recalls that "people said, 'Wait till you get this Ron Sauey.' It didn't mean much to me because I had a bunch of new kids every year. But when Ron did come, why, we really hit it off."

Ron delighted in the field trips. The class often went to the Aldo Leopold Memorial Reserve only a few miles away. The reserve is private, but Gerald had permission to take his classes there. It was one of Gerald's treasured spots for birding, and it became one of Ron's as well. Their favorite birding trail began at the old shack where Leopold, a pioneer conservationist and University of Wisconsin professor, lived with his family on their weekend retreats from Madison. On one memorable trip to the reserve, they found a Barred Owl by the side of the road. Ron just about jumped out of the car. They took it to a vet, who couldn't find any injuries. The bird was just sick. Ron put it in his pheasant coop and nursed it back to health.

It was Gerald who took Ron to see his first wild Sandhill Cranes. In the early 1960s Gerald visited a bog not far from Baraboo where a flock of Greater Sandhill Cranes gathered. He didn't know much about cranes at the time but thought it would be an ideal site for photography. He went there several times and spent hours watching the birds from blinds that he built himself. Later he took Ron with him.

Ron and several classmates developed powerful friendships with each other and with Gerald and his wife, Gladys, an elementary school teacher, that went beyond the classroom. Ron and Jim Greenhaulgh had been friends since they were five years old. Along with Bea Wenban, Jim Epstein, Sue Premo, and Jim's cousin, Peter, they spent hours with the Scotts, both on field trips and at their home, sometimes gathering for taffy pulls (homemade by Gladys) until the wee hours of the morning. If they were with the Scotts, their parents didn't worry. They were smart, driven teenagers but not without a typical adolescent sense of humor. They called themselves SMA. Years later Gerald found out it stood for Sex Maniacs Anonymous.

Gerald and Gladys took Ron on his first camping trip. Bea went along. The first leg of the expedition was a two-hundred-mile drive north to the Bad River Indian Reservation. There, on the Wolf River a few miles shy of Lake Superior, they put their canoes in the water. The Scotts paddled one canoe, Bea and Ron were in a second, and food and gear were in a third canoe tied up to the Scotts' lead boat. They made their way to the lake and followed the shoreline northwest to Chequamegon Point. Madeline Island in the Apostle Islands was only four miles away. As they unloaded the gear a Bald Eagle flew overhead, screaming. They watched it for a while and then realized there was a nest a few hundred feet away. Ron was ecstatic. After moving their campsite further away so they wouldn't disturb the birds, Ron proceeded to spend more time looking at the nest than unloading supplies. When an eaglet's head popped up over the rim of the nest, he could barely contain his excitement and certainly couldn't be bothered with unloading cooking pots.

Gerald Scott nurtured Ron's interest in birds and biology. The friendship between teacher and pupil deepened through hours of birdwatching, photography, and long conversations. But Gerald was worried. Was he causing trouble for Ron at home by encouraging his naturalist bent? Gerald knew that Norman had a business to run and that his two other sons were probably going to join their father in the corporate world. So Gerald asked Norman if perhaps he, Gerald, shouldn't support Ron's desire to pursue ornithology as a field of study.

But Norman replied, "If that's what he wants, then that's what he shall have."

By the time Ron was a junior in high school he was an avid birder and could often be seen wandering the roads near his home, binoculars hanging from his neck. In 1965, while out birding, he met someone else who was to have a profound influence on his life.

"I didn't meet Ron. Ron met me," recalls Chappie Fox. "Our houses were about a mile apart. I had known his father. I was running the Circus World Museum at the time, and through that you meet a lot of people. So Ron would have no qualms about coming onto my property. It was kind of a casual meeting. And then all we talked about was birds. What did he see? What did I see? What was nesting on my land? And he kept coming. He might have come many times when I wasn't even there. We had forty acres and lots of areas to parade around in. I enjoyed talking to Ron. We just kind of hit it off."

Chappie and Ron had more in common than their interest in birds. Both had broken ranks from the family business. In Ron's case, manufacturing. For Chappie, it was medicine. His father and grandfather had been surgeons, chiefs of staff no less. His brother was a surgeon, as was an uncle. But Chappie wasn't interested in medicine.

"I had an interest in animals, particularly horses. As a kid I used to be intrigued with draft horses. When the circus came to town with hundreds of draft horses I was out there and began to photograph the horses. Before I knew it I became intrigued with the whole idea of these enormous circuses coming to town for one day—unloading the trains and setting up these tents, putting in seats for ten thousand people, putting on two shows, tearing it all down, loading it in the wagon and back on the train, and going a hundred miles to another town. And it was all done with these big six- and eight-horse teams of draft horses. I became obsessed with the circus."

After graduation from high school in 1932, Chappie joined others struggling through the Depression and searched for a job.

"I went down to the Milwaukee Public Museum to see if I could get a job there. All I was offered was a volunteer position in the taxidermy department. I didn't know a damn thing about taxidermy. But I knew the animals and birds. I worked there for a year and a half before I finally did get a job for forty bucks a month. Owen Gromme was head of that department. Owen and I became very close friends."

An artist and illustrator all his life, Gromme retired as a curator of the museum in 1965 to devote all his time to painting. He became one of the finest wildlife artists in the world. It was Chappie who later introduced Ron to Owen.

And when Ron, after graduating from the University of Wisconsin, turned his sights toward Cornell University, Chappie extended himself on behalf of his young friend and asked Walter Scott (no relation to Gerald Scott), a prominent biologist with the Wisconsin Department of Natural Resources, and Owen Gromme to write letters of recommendation. In a letter to Chappie written from Cornell, Ron stated his belief that "these letters were the final and timely boost to my application, which resulted in acceptance at Cornell" and expressed his heartfelt gratitude to his friend the birdwatching circus man.

At Cornell, Ron was assigned Dr. William Dilger as his major advisor. He was all set to study pheasants. In fact, Ron planned to house his study subjects in his old coop back home in Baraboo. But then he met one of Dilger's other graduate students, a guy who had a thing for cranes.

Actually George Archibald's first passion was for chickens. When he was about five or six years old, his parents bought some chickens for their small farm in rural Nova Scotia. But they never laid eggs because George kept disturbing them.

"I felt sorry for them because they couldn't fly. So I'd climb way up on the scaffold in the barn, put them up there, and plop." A quick descent to the barn floor always ended the research.

"But I'd watch these chickens for hours. I'd wait for them to go to roost, and I knew each perch that each one had."

Much to George's dismay the chickens ended up on the dinner table. But they were replaced by others that equally held his fascination.

George, born in 1946 in New Glasgow, was the second of Donald and Lettie Archibald's six children. His parents were also born in

Nova Scotia, and its rural countryside was home for George, brothers Don, Sandy, and Peter, and sisters Anne and Heather. They lived on a poor isolated farm in Rockfield, near New Glasgow. To make ends meet Donald taught in rural schools. Donald had been teaching ever since he finished high school in an accelerated program. He was fifteen years old when he faced his first class, which was in fact the entire school. There were forty kids in the one room. Some of the students were older than he was. Lettie also taught until she had children to raise.

George attended a one-room school until grade seven, when he went to the consolidated school. He walked to school and took the long route so he could pass by Lily Monroe's place. Lily had ducks. George came to know each duck and its family history. And when he asked his parents if he could have some (for pets) they bought three, two females and a male.

Then the tranquility of the Archibald family's life was shattered when their house burned down in 1954. They moved to nearby Stillwater and rented an old farmhouse from a close friend of George's parents. The Archibald children called him Grandpa McKeen, and George fondly remembers the old man's paternal feelings toward him and his siblings. The ducks had survived the fire, and George fixed up a new pen and shelter for his birds and carried them, one by one, to their new home a quarter of a mile away. Their rented house was nestled in a small valley along the St. Mary's River. An island in the river was known as Turtle Island, and the kids could wade out and catch the river reptiles. Sometimes they brought one home, but Lettie always made them take it back the next day. When the turtles were laying low, they could always fish in the nearby brook. Donald Archibald remembers their Stillwater home as a beautiful spot. They lived there for two years while he taught at the high school and the family looked for a place to build a new home.

The Archibalds built that new home in 1956 about a mile downriver from Stillwater. Donald and Lettie still live there. The house sits on 150 acres overlooking the St. Mary's. There are no houses between their home and Stillwater and only one neighbor downriver until the town of Sherbrooke two miles away. George lived here for the next eight years until he went away to Acadia University. A picture of his childhood home next to the river and nestled among the trees hangs today in George's Baraboo home.

George (far right) with his father, Ann, and Donnie. *Photo courtesy of George Archibald.*

By this time, George had several species of ducks and a Canada Goose as well. Some he bought, and some he traded with several local people he met who had an interest in birds. His collection grew. The riverfront location proved to be a boon. Every now and then there would be a flood and someone's barn would end up in the river. George and his dad would haul it out. They were just small structures. George partitioned them, cut holes in the walls so the birds could get outside, and fenced in their outdoor yards.

No one else in the family shared his fascination with the birds. George's younger sister Heather considered his hobby to be a nuisance. "He was always building a pen or a coop and it got in our way."

Heather and brother Donnie teased the ducks at every opportunity. It bothered George more than the birds, and that, after all, was their point. Heather remembers one climactic episode.

"My mom and dad were away one day and George was looking after us. We were bothering the birds and he kept telling us not to do it, and finally he just got really mad. He came after us, but we had an escape route all planned. We went running to our tree house in the woods. George chased us but we had set little traps for him. We put a cord across the trail and of course he tripped on that. We went flying up into the tree house and pulled up the rope ladder and shut the door. We had to stay in that tree house the whole afternoon until Mom and Dad got home because we were scared to come out."

It wasn't long before George was confronted with his first "problem bird." His male Canada Goose took a liking to one of the female mallards. So George arranged for a female Canada Goose to join the group. But the female had no interest in her arranged pair bond. To encourage the geese to socialize with each other, George banished the mallard to a pen down by the pond. Still the geese went their separate ways. The gander stayed by his incarcerated mallard hen. The female built a nest on the path between the house and the barn, protected it fiercely, and forced everyone to take another route in order to milk the cow. She left her nest only to get a drink from the pond. But somehow George's geese managed to work things out because two of her eggs hatched.

When he was still in high school, George helped the local government wildlife office with their pheasant program. He bought an incubator to hatch Ring-necked Pheasants and put it in his bedroom. By the time he had it working properly, the water tray for controlling the humidity left a mark on the wooden floor. The stain is still there, thirty years later.

For people in rural areas, the Archibalds included, nature and wildlife were more often obstacles than marvels. No one had binoculars to look at birds. Not many people thought to wonder about what the first migration wave would bring. Spring meant planting time. Autumn meant precious few days before a killing frost.

Donald Archibald had a small log cabin in a wilderness area about ten miles from home. All of his sons were interested in fishing; all except George. But he went along. While his brothers and father fished, George set off on his own to explore. Much to his brothers' bewilderment, George spent hours wandering through the surrounding expanse. He skirted the lake, respectful of its deep, dark water. If the dense forest's thick, towering trees didn't swallow him up, there were always the bogs. But there were also water lilies and loons, Black Ducks, and Ring-necked Ducks. George was discovering a new way to look at the natural world.

"I enjoyed the wilderness and always loved seeing the birds. But I found it rather overwhelming and frightening because there were stories of people getting lost. As a child I wasn't familiar with conservation because wilderness was what we lived in. It wasn't until later that I learned about conservation. When I worked in Alberta in 1966 and saw lovely wetlands and heard the wild cranes, I saw the wilderness through new eyes, a place of life."

That Alberta wetland set George to questioning his future plans. After graduating high school in 1964, he attended Acadia University for one year before transferring to Dalhousie University in Halifax so he could better prepare for medical school. He and his friends planned to open a clinic together. But then George heard about a game farm in western Canada. He wrote a letter to the director, Dr. Al Oeming, and was invited to work there during the summers of 1966 and 1967. Despite the long hours and seven-day workweek, George remembers those two summers as "a great experience because I could work with a diversity of mammals and birds. And that's where I met cranes." George recalls Oeming telling him to specialize in cranes because "they're special birds. Different from all [the] other birds."

In November 1967, George and some friends went to Expo '67 in Montreal. Tired of the congestion and hassle of getting to the exhibits, George hitchhiked down to Ithaca, New York, to visit Cornell University. He had read about the Cornell Laboratory of Ornithology in *National Geographic* magazine and wanted to see it. It was the first time he saw a professional ornithological organization.

George vividly remembers that first visit.

"There was an open door at the end of the corridor, and I could hear all these birds calling. I walked in and there were all these cages of lovebirds and larger parrots. In another room was Professor William Dilger. He invited me to come in and talk. He asked me who I was, and I told him about the cranes I'd been working with. He was interested and listened to me. He was so unusual."

Dr. Dilger was an associate professor of ethology, the study of animal behavior. He recalls his first meeting with George amid the clamor of nearly one thousand lovebirds; "I was sold on him right away. He was an enthusiastic, determined young fella."

George returned to Dalhousie University and announced to his friends, " 'I'm giving up pre-med and going to Cornell to study birds.' I had a wonderful scholarship from the National Research Council that would have paid for medical school, but the scholarship office said you could use it for graduate school or medical school or whatever you want."

After graduating from Dalhousie in 1968, George spent the summer as a naturalist in Fundy National Park on the Bay of Fundy. The job kept him outdoors and gave him valuable experience speaking in front of people, something he had never done. Meanwhile he wrote a letter to the National Research Council requesting that his financial aid be paid to Cornell University. He was in fine spirits until he received a reply informing him that his scholarship could only be applied to a Canadian school. He immediately called Dr. Dilger, who confidently told him to come anyway and that they'd find some support, somewhere.

So with less than one thousand dollars to his name, George headed off to prestigious Cornell University. He believed that, somehow, things would work out.

Ron Sauey and George Archibald, two men from vastly different socioeconomic strata, already united by an insatiable curiosity about the natural world, thus plotted their way to Ithaca, New York.

On the day that Ron and George met for the first time, George had just received an eagerly awaited movie from Europe on courting Eurasian (Common) Cranes. Ron joined other students and professors in a darkened room to watch the graceful cranes leap and bow on the screen before them.

Since 1968 George had studied the taxonomic relationship of cranes based on their unison call (a territorial and pair bonding vocalization). He persuaded zoos, game farms, the state of Michigan, and even the federal government to loan him cranes for the project. Eventually fifty-six cranes of nine species (there are only fifteen in the whole world) came to live in an old mink barn with George. There were endangered White-naped Cranes, African Crowned Cranes with luxurious golden headdresses, stately and exotic Wattled Cranes, diminutive Demoiselle Cranes, elegant Blue Cranes, Indian Sarus Cranes (at more than five feet the tallest flying bird in the world), Greater and Canada Sandhill Cranes from North America, and the ubiquitous Common Crane. Although cranes are sensitive birds difficult to breed in captivity, one pair of White-naped Cranes hatched five chicks during their second year with George. He had plans to study additional crane species, both in zoos and in the wild, but the Cornell project was coming to an end.

The Common Cranes stopped dancing. Someone turned the lights on and the students and professors dispersed. But Ron and George discovered they had much to talk about: the regal displays, the unison call that could enable researchers to distinguish males from females, the unexpected breeding successes of the White-naped Cranes in George's study group, and the sorry state of the crane family with nearly half the species listed as endangered. There were many more discussions as Ron and George became friends and shared their ideas and passion for birds. They agreed that someone ought to do something for the cranes. And they agreed that they would be that "someone," sometime in the future.

Ron still had his heart set on studying pheasants. George was determined to observe more cranes in the United States and abroad. The Crane Trust, as they already called their dream, would have to wait.

And what did their professor think about two inexperienced students planning to save the world's cranes?

"I took them seriously," Dilger says. "I knew George and I knew Ron and I knew they'd do it."

Three months later, Ron and George ran out of patience. They were participating in a winter waterfowl count at Lake Cayuga. George recalls that day.

"It was so cold we decided we would only count what we could see from the car. But the waves were so high we couldn't see much, so we gave up and went to a local pub for some hot coffee."

Over that cup of coffee the two friends talked once more about their dream. George knew of some land in Nova Scotia that could be the site of the Crane Trust. Ron thought maybe his father would buy it for them. At Christmas break Ron approached his father.

Norman remembers well his son asking him if he would be interested in buying some land in Nova Scotia. And he remembers his reply: "What the hell do I want with land in Nova Scotia?" Ron explained about the endangered cranes and the need to study captive management and thus ensure that there will always be cranes even if their wild habitats are bulldozed into oblivion. Norm listened to his son and quietly answered, "What's wrong with here? All the horses have been moved to Florida."

Ron's eyes brightened. "You mean you'd let us . . . ?"

"Sure. You can do it all here. I think it'll work out great."

Ron called George in New York, and that evening George was in the Sauey living room. The next morning George had his first look at the Baraboo Hills and the Sauey horse farm. It was late December and a deep snow covered the ground. Despite the bright sun it was bitter cold, and they donned blue snowmobile suits before setting off from the house to inspect the farm. Snow crunched beneath their cross-country skis as they crossed the sprawling lawn. They passed an oval paddock stretched east to west with a neat wooden fence painted white. Ron showed George his old pheasant coop. Maybe they could use that for all the young crane chicks they were sure to have. They entered the stable at the south end. Comfortable box stalls lined each side. The rafters were high above their heads. It felt big. It would seem even larger with cranes in residence instead of horses. Halfway down the aisle, on the right, a short stairway led down to a small room with a low ceiling. This was the tack room where the saddles, bridles, and other equipment had been stored. Maybe they could put the incubators in here for all of the crane eggs they were sure to have.

Standing outside the north barn door, Ron and George contemplated the pasture that stretched from the barn all the way out to County A Road at the western edge of the property. A wonderful place for colts to gambol. Soon it would happen again because crane chicks are called colts. At the bottom of the hill, on the northeast corner of the property, they envisioned pens and yards for the precious breeding pairs. Every species would eventually be represented. That had never been done before. Maybe fifteen pairs of each. Wouldn't it be something if the call of the Whooping Crane, last heard in Wisconsin almost one hundred years ago, could once again cry out across the state?

Norman and Claire leased the farm to them for one dollar a year (ten years later they finally paid it!). They were in business.

Ron and George knew their Crane Trust had to be more than just a place for captive cranes, even more than just a place for research. Together they decided upon five goals for their new enterprise:

Research. Little was known about the breeding biology of most of the fifteen crane species. Why did some species number only in the hundreds and others in the tens of thousands? Where did they breed? Where did they winter? How did they get there? What did they eat?

Education. Few people knew anything about the crane family. How can they care about saving something they don't know exists? North America's Whooping Crane enjoyed a certain amount of name recognition built from nearly three decades of conservation work on its behalf, and people along the migration flyways knew about Sandhill Cranes, but most probably didn't know that other crane species all over the world also faced obstacles to their survival.

Conservation. Saving cranes means habitat protection and restoration. Most cranes are wetland birds. Wetlands had been historically perceived as useless swamps and drained for farmland or shopping malls. That attitude would have to change. Wetlands contribute to flood control by absorbing and slowly releasing snowmelt and excess water from heavy rains. They are natural filter systems that cleanse heavily fertilized water of chemicals that can harm rivers and lakes. Saving crane habitats would save entire ecosystems.

Captive propagation. The Crane Trust would eventually house all fifteen species of cranes, refine captive management techniques, and thus ensure that cranes will always be with us. No other institution in the world was devoted solely to cranes, but many zoos maintained cranes in their collections, often with limited breeding success. Why? What could the Crane Trust do differently that would encourage the cranes to breed?

Restocking. Use captive-bred birds to replenish depleted wild crane populations. How? When? Which species would be the first?

Restocking seemed almost futuristic to Ron and George in 1971. They had no cranes. And a good thing, too. They didn't have a pen to put them in anyway.

TWO

A Home in the Hills

B araboo, Wisconsin, birthplace of the Ringling Brothers Circus and now home for the fledgling International Crane Trust. Ten miles up the road the Wisconsin Dells attracted thousands of tourists each summer to its amusement park rides, air and water show, traffic jams, and spectacular rock formations along the Wisconsin River. Closer to town, Devil's Lake State Park tested aspiring rock climbers on its towering bluffs. The Sauey horse farm, Nodoroma, was an ideal place for the new Crane Trust because Ron and George had little choice in the matter. They had no money. Baraboo might have seemed an unusual setting for this novel enterprise, but then where do you put a crane research and breeding institution the likes of which had never been seen before?

Baraboo's population in 1970 was barely eight thousand. It's not much more than that today. There were no traffic lights in 1972. Now there are five. The people are friendly. More than a dozen churches of almost as many denominations dot the town. Fourteen buildings and two historic districts have been nominated for inclusion in the National Register of Historic Places. In 1884, the Ringling brothers began their circus career in Baraboo. The town remained their winter home until 1907. Al, the eldest, built a theater in 1915 modeled after the opera hall at the Palace of Versailles, and the theater still stands at 136 Fourth Avenue. The

Baraboo News Republic, the town's newspaper, traces its roots back to a county periodical first published in 1855.

The county is Sauk, named for the Sauk or Sac Indians that lived along the Wisconsin River where today you'll find Sauk City and Prairie du Sac. Baraboo is the county seat and the county courthouse on the square is the center of the Downtown Baraboo Historic District.

Historians generally agree that a French-Canadian trader named Jean Baribault established a trading post on the Baraboo River in the early 1700s and the town sprouted from there. When the first settlers arrived in the 1800s, they had trouble pronouncing the name (so the theory goes), and early maps identify the place as Bonibau, Beribeau, and Barabeau. Eventually everyone agreed on Baraboo. You can travel around the world and not find another place so named.

But the story of the Baraboo area begins long before Jean Baribault set up shop on the river.

It begins two million years ago during the Pleistocene epoch, North America's Ice Age, when four glaciers advanced and retreated. Each one tore up bedrock as it crept along and loaded up with loose pebbles, rocks, and immense boulders. Some of the boulders were pulverized into fine sand that flattened and polished the earth as the glacier inched forward. Debris was pushed along at the front. Small hills were leveled. When the glacier met a mountain range it was forced into the valleys, where it scraped and cut the mountainsides. Sometimes mighty rivers were forced to take new routes. Small creeks ceased to exist. Then, four different times, the earth warmed up. As a glacier melted, the debris that had been carried, sometimes for thousands of miles, was left where the ice made its last stand. And there were glacial dumps. Geologists call them moraines. Terminal moraines in the form of long ridges mark the outer edges of a glacier, the spot where the shovel that was the ice stopped pushing tons of dirt, gravel, and rocks. Some low areas were filled with additional glacial garbage by the retreating ice and never drained completely. Those areas became marshes, bogs, and lakes.

So it was that the Wisconsin Glacier, the fourth and final one of the Ice Age, left its mark. For sixty thousand years it shaped all but the southwestern corner of Wisconsin. More accurately, four fingers, or lobes, of the glacier reached into the state and down its eastern half. The final retreat was a mere ten thousand years ago.

But there was already a unique topographical feature on the land when the Wisconsin Glacier first encroached, a formation much older than even the oldest glacier. It was born about a billion years ago when Wisconsin was a vast inland sea. Rivers had drained into that sea and deposited sand. The sand accumulated, the waters receded, and sandstone was formed. Over the millennia the sandstone compacted into quartzite, one of the hardest rocks in the world. Those quartzite hills are still standing. They are the Baraboo Bluffs. The bluffs form an irregular oval rim around the Baraboo Valley. The town of Baraboo sits in the middle. The bluffs are the first thing you notice upon arrival in these parts and the last image in your rearview mirror when leaving.

The ancient Wisconsin River once flowed through the bluffs. On the sunset side of Portage, thirteen miles east of Baraboo, it cut a channel into the quartzite west of present-day Interstate 94 and flowed south-southwest before running up against the southern rim of the bluffs. With time on its side the river carved a gorge or gap, Devil's Lake Gap, eight-hundred-feet deep through the rocks before continuing on to the Mississippi. But then came the glacier. One of its lobes, the Green Bay, spanned across the Baraboo Range. It pushed against the river. The water backed up and formed Glacial Lake Wisconsin. When the ice mass finally retreated, the glacier dumped its meltwater and debris into the gap and left a moraine at either end. The gap was sealed. The gorge was almost half full. Devil's Lake was born. And the Wisconsin River was forced into a new channel a few miles east of the Baraboo Bluffs.

But follow the old river channel. Pick up Highway 33 off the interstate and head toward Baraboo. Cross the Baraboo River once. Those hills that began to crop up about twenty miles back now provide a steady escort as the road wends its way west. You are in the Baraboo Range. Be careful on the narrow two-lane bridge that takes you over the meandering Baraboo River for the second time. It's easy to be distracted by the towering tree-covered bluff directly ahead. For a moment you wonder if you're going to drive right into it. Fortunately the road grabs your attention in the nick of time and you follow it south around the bluff. Highway 33 will take you straight into town, but don't go there just yet. A scant mile after you avoided driving headlong into the bluff, a quiet little road on the right angles gently but quickly off the main highway. There's no sign so be alert. It just appears. Take it. There's a stop sign just ahead. Turn right and follow the road as it rises and curves left, taking you west again. This is City View Road. And though you can't see Baraboo even when you get parallel to the town some miles ahead, you'll have an exhilarating view to the south of the five-hundred-foot quartzite bluffs at Devil's Lake State Park, four miles away.

The vista becomes obscured from time to time by rolling hills and scattered homes and farms along the road, but another singular feature of this land is coming up. You won't miss it. This time there is a sign. Man Mound Park. Stop and pay tribute to an ancient culture unique to the Midwest, the Effigy Mound Builders. They were part of the Woodland Culture that flourished from a few hundred years B.C. into the 1200s. Like many other prehistoric people they built round and linear mounds that were often used for burial sites. But unlike any other group in the world, the Effigy Mound Builders also built animal mounds that were often used for ceremonial purposes. There were thousands of Indian mounds in Wisconsin when white settlers arrived in the 1800s. Most were obliterated by the plow. Man Mound remains though City View Road cut him off at the knees before the park was established in 1908.

One site surveyed in 1955 by Dr. E. G. Bruder in northeastern Dodge County, about an hour's drive east of Baraboo, contained three crane effigies. The first one measured 117 feet long with a wingspan of 85 feet. As Bruder and his crew stood at the mound, a lone Sandhill Crane flew over heading west. Bruder surmised the bird was headed for nearby Horicon Marsh.

It was a lonely flight. The best estimate of Wisconsin's Sandhill population in 1955 was a meager two hundred birds. That was an improvement over the twenty-five pairs believed to have nested in the state in 1936. Drainage of wetlands, hunting, and fire suppression (fires keep woody plants such as willow from encroaching on the prairies and marshes) all contributed to the Sandhill's decline. Slowly, with the advent of waterfowl management and the acquisition and protection of wetlands, the Sandhill Crane began to recover. By the early 1970s there were not quite one thousand of the stately gray birds.

ICF on City View Road. *Photo courtesy of International Crane Foundation.*

In 1972, as you leave Man Mound Park and continue west as the crane flies on City View Road, the Greater Sandhill Crane is still listed as endangered in Wisconsin, and endangered cranes all over the world are forming a crowded club. In 1950 Lawrence Walkinshaw estimated the Cuban Sandhill population at two hundred birds. No American biologist had been allowed in to study them since. The Mississippi Sandhill had just been classified as a distinct subspecies and within a year would be added to the federal list of endangered species. Only about fifty birds survived in the wild in 1972, and a small captive breeding population resided at the government's Patuxent Wildlife Research Center in Maryland. The Whooping, Siberian, and Red-crowned Cranes were also in trouble. Fewer than one hundred Whoopers appeared each winter on the Texas Gulf Coast. No one even knew how many Siberian Cranes existed. And who, except for a few zoo people and ornithologists, had even seen the Wattled Crane from South Africa? The White-naped Crane found in Japan and China flirted with survival by wintering on the Demilitarized Zone (DMZ) between North and South Korea. The Eastern Sarus, that giant flier, stood tall among the cranes but needed as much help as any of them, its habitat devastated by the Vietnam War. And the mysterious Black-necked Crane was presumed to be holding on in Tibet and neighboring areas, remote lands inaccessible to most ornithologists.

Few people in the world outside the scientific community knew about the plight of the crane. Around the globe a handful of dedicated scientists worked to census and understand their birds. Just up the road on your right, three miles past Man Mound, two more were about to join the effort.

The International Crane Trust got off to a rousing start in 1972. Ron returned to Cornell and George went to Japan.

George had planned to go to India and study the wintering Siberian Cranes, but India's conflict with Pakistan convinced him to change his itinerary. He spent most of his time in Japan observing Red-crowned Cranes in the wild, in various zoos, and at the Kushiro Crane Park in Kushiro on the island of Hokkaido. Japan also hosts wintering populations of Hooded and White-naped Cranes, and George made sure he saw them.

George and Ron's absence from Baraboo may have delayed the start of the International Crane Trust, but it didn't weaken their resolve. George thrived on the wild cranes, and he shared it all with Ron through his letters. On February 23, 1972, George watched 280 White-naped Cranes begin their migration from the Izumi Valley to South Korea:

"It was one of the most spectacular ornithological experiences I have ever had. The day was clear, a warm breeze blew from the south. By 9:30 A.M., the cranes had fed and were standing in the morning sun, preening. Suddenly several pairs flew from the flock. They soared in huge spirals, climbing higher and higher. Other pairs and family groups followed. Soon the air above the Izumi Valley was alive with glistening White-napeds."

Being with the birds fed George's creative drive. From Japan he sent back suggestions complete with drawings for letterhead for the trust, which he found out later could not be called the International Crane Trust. Under Wisconsin law, only an actual trust company can use the word *trust* in its name. George was dismayed because he was talking about their endeavor to his Japanese colleagues and they along with the Japanese press were already familiar with the name International Crane Trust.

Meanwhile Ron wondered how to fund their enterprise. The original plan to be a private research institution closed to public visitation was already showing its shortcomings. Norman and Claire Sauey had promised the boys capital to begin their work, but they needed a way to cover operational expenses. Ron questioned whether they should cash in on the tourist trade in Baraboo, which was already a considerable source of revenue for the town thanks to Devil's Lake State Park and the Circus World Museum. Or maybe they should become a nonprofit organization and rely on member-ships to support their work. They were leery of public visitation, which might disturb the birds and possibly the tranquility of the Sauey family home next door. They also treasured their freedom and wondered if they could work with a board of directors. Even so, the nonprofit format seemed to be their best chance.

But how to survive until they had enough five- and ten-dollar memberships to support the trust? Ron had an idea that he shared with Owen Gromme: a commissioned painting just for the newly named International Crane Foundation would be used to produce a limited number of prints as premiums for memberships. Out of their discussion came the vision of "Salute to the Dawn." It became the largest canvas that Owen ever painted. Against a background of early morning mist rising from the marsh of Wood Buffalo National Park in Canada's Northwest Territories, two Whooping Cranes stand on their nest in a triumphant unison call. At their feet are two chicks, one newly hatched and still too weak to stand and a second one just pipping its shell.

In March, Ron wrote George to apprise him of the plan and ask his opinion. He couldn't have been too surprised at George's response, for surely it reflected his own feelings on the issue. George's answer read like a debate.

"We both want it like our lifeblood.

"We should wait until we're on our feet [financially].

"But it is an investment.

"I want to say yes.

"If you want to invest your own money, that's your decision. I just hope you decide to do it.

"Talk it over with your father [and a few other people]. Get their opinions. Disregard ours.

"But we shouldn't let other people make up our minds.

"I can just see that glorious piece of art hanging above our fireplace. We must have it!"

And they did. Ron used his personal funds for the commission. Each print was signed and numbered by Owen and given to anyone who donated at least $1,000 to the foundation. Owen subsequently painted another canvas to help with fundraising. "Sacred Cranes over Hokkaido" depicts seven Red-crowned Cranes flying above the clouds in a blue sky over Japan. He was inspired by George's pictures and stories of the wild cranes in Hokkaido. Owen's signature in Japanese was added to the canvas before the limited print edition was issued. The prints, signed and numbered by Owen, became premiums for donations of between $500 and $999. A smaller version, unsigned, was given in appreciation for memberships between $100 and $499. The money the prints brought in was important, but so was Owen Gromme's association with the Crane Foundation. He and his wife, Anne, became steadfast supporters, advisors, and friends.

While Ron was busy trying to build crane pens in Baraboo, George was trying to find some birds for the foundation. In the same breathless letter to Ron about the Gromme painting, George broke the news that he had permission to export Red-crowned Cranes to the United States. He was ecstatic. He thought he had only a few bureaucratic hurdles to clear to complete the arrangements. In the meantime he needed pictures of Nodoroma and diagrams of the pens and shelters that would house the cranes so he could show the authorities exactly where their birds were going. The Red-crowned Crane is a treasured bird in Japan—an important cultural and traditional symbol of long life and good luck. Getting all the necessary parties to approve the exportation would prove to be not such a simple matter after all.

Japanese zoos had been trying for years to obtain the few Red-crowned Cranes already in captivity. The government, which has jurisdiction over the birds in the same way the United States government has over endangered species within its borders, was wary of seeming partial to a few zoos at the expense of others. So the birds remained at the Crane Park in southeastern Hokkaido, next to the vast Kushiro Marsh. The park was established in 1961 with the capture of five cranes, all of whom later proved to be males. A few years later wild females flew in to join the captive males and reared young. The females return each year to nest, and the young cranes are free to join the wild flock. In 1968 the park staff pulled one egg from two-egg nests and hand-reared the chicks. In his effort to export some of these birds, along with six Hooded Cranes and a lone Siberian Crane at the Kagoshima Zoo that was blown to the island during a storm in 1969, George was about to enter a maze of Japanese politics that would consume his energy for the next several months.

Ron returned to Baraboo in late spring of 1972. With his parents' financial backing, he was able to tackle the job of building the breeding unit that he and George had already designed. Each pair of birds would have access to a house for protection against inclement weather and an adjacent yard to roam in at will. The pens would be situated in a rectangular fashion so the birds could see other pairs on the opposite side of the complex and be encouraged to "defend" their territory. A vacant zone in the middle would be off-limits to both birds and people. Visual barriers would prevent adjacent pairs from fighting through the fence and injuring themselves.

But contractors can't offer competitive bids from ideas, and sketches are not blueprints. Ron had no more ever built a holding facility for birds than George had ever imported endangered cranes. Over the next several months, Ron arranged for blueprints to be drawn, hired a contractor, and supervised the construction. The final product of that initial effort became the basic model for all future construction.

Each of the fifteen pens contained a 15' × 15' house built with weather-resistant cedar boards and siding. There were clear plastic windows and skylights. A door enabled them to lock a crane inside if necessary. This was especially important to protect cranes native to warm habitats during Wisconsin's harsh winters. The outdoor grass-covered yards came in three different sizes: 40' × 60', 60' × 60', and 80' × 80'. An eight-foot-high galvanized steel fence buried one foot in the ground established the perimeter of each yard. A gravel service road encircled the U-shaped breeding unit. One critical feature added to the complex a few years later was the nylon mesh stretched across the top of each pen, "flight netting." It meant the Crane Foundation could house full-winged cranes who could perform the ritualized dancing of leaps and bows so important in the establishment of the pair bond. Full-winged birds were also more likely to copulate successfully. They put the complex "down below" at the bottom of the hill and away from the traffic on City View Road so the cranes would have more privacy and fewer disturbances. North of the unit was a cornfield that belonged to a neighbor. To the east and west were wooded areas. The birds were thus effectively isolated from unnecessary intrusions.

With the breeding unit construction proceeding and George busy in Japan doing whatever he was doing at the moment to get cranes for ICF (his letters never quite kept pace with his activities), Ron drove into town late one morning and headed for the courthouse for a special errand. He found the courtroom he needed and took a seat at the back. The judge adjourned the proceedings at noon and the attorneys packed files into briefcases and walked down the aisle to leave. Ron fixed his gaze on Forrest Hartmann, mid-30s, slight build, a Baraboo lawyer since he passed the bar a half-dozen years ago. As Forrest approached the rear of the courtroom he saw a pleasant young man in his mid-20s with an engaging smile rise to greet him. He wasn't sure where he'd seen him before.

Red-crowned Crane flying over the nonbreeder field. *Photo by George Archibald.*

But Ron remembered their first meeting on a Saturday five years before in May 1967. The young attorney took Ron and his good friend Bea Wenban to the marsh near Sauk City and the bluffs beyond. Bea's mother, Katie, worked at Forrest's law firm and had arranged the outing for the three self-confessed nature enthusiasts. Then Ron and Bea showed Forrest the Aldo Leopold Memorial Reserve and visited Leopold's shack. A couple of years later Ron and Forrest met again at a party hosted by Bea's parents. Ron reintroduced himself to Forrest, who remembered the outing but not Ron's name.

In the courtroom that late spring afternoon Ron extended his hand and yet another introduction. It was the last one Forrest would need. As they walked out together Ron explained that he and a friend were setting up an organization to save the world's cranes. Since Forrest was interested in nature and he was a lawyer, would he be interested in joining them? The reply was immediate, and positive.

The International Crane Foundation could not have been established without Forrest Hartmann's guidance and legal expertise. Problems were already waiting for him when he finished his brief conversation with Ron in the courthouse lobby. Ron and George knew nothing of the rules governing nonprofit organizations. They didn't know much about anything except birds. Forrest had to do a lot of teaching, and "they weren't good students." Forrest shouldered the organizational and legal responsibilities, while Ron and George's hearts and energies were with the cranes.

George was still trying to get the necessary permits to obtain some birds in Japan and nearly exhausting himself in the process. No sooner was he assured by one official that the Crane Foundation could export the Red-crowned Cranes than he found out that he still had to secure approval from additional authorities. Local governments had control over the birds in their area, so even if officials in Tokyo and fellow biologists approved the export, George still had to clear hurdles with the local people. It seemed there was no end to the meetings, letters, and slide presentations. The situation was constantly changing. On April 1, George wrote that they had permission (again)—pending a successful June 20 presentation about the foundation complete with visuals of a place that did not yet exist—to export not only the Red-crowned Cranes but also Hooded Cranes and the lone Siberian Crane at the Kagoshima Zoo.

While all the negotiations were taking place, George continued his behavioral studies of the wild cranes and became embroiled in the effort to save the Kushiro Marsh and Japan's only nesting population of Red-crowned Cranes. That Red-crowned Cranes wintered in Japan was a well-known fact. Farmers and schoolchildren had been feeding them corn for years. George began his study, accompanied by ornithologist Tamaka Kitagawa, from a small two-man tent near Akan with the winter flock of one hundred sixty cranes. In spring the cranes left the winter area and returned to the marshes to breed. Japanese ornithologists had always thought that most of the birds migrated to Siberia and that only a few remained in Japan. George left the winter area in spring, too. He and Kitagawa traveled north by motorbike, camping when they stopped, and searched the marshes for what was supposed to be a few breeding pairs. Instead, they discovered a sizeable population of fifty-three breeding pairs. But only three were on protected wetlands. Most were on land threatened with imminent industrial development.

George, Kitagawa, and Dr. Hiroyuki Masatomi conducted a five-hour aerial survey in a small airplane of the marshes of eastern Hokkaido on May 19. Flying several hundred feet above the wetlands, they located eighteen crane pairs in the Kushiro Marsh, nine pairs in a smaller coastal marsh, five pairs along a river, and thirteen pairs on other small marshes. This confirmed that the population was not migratory. If the nesting habitat was developed, it would mean the end of Japan's sacred cranes.

George embarked on a series of meetings with officials from numerous ministries. He gave slide talks and even went on Japanese television and radio. Government officials and local people became alarmed, and the government pledged to investigate the crisis. By summer's end, George had attained something of a celebrity status in Japan, and the International Crane Foundation, though still only a vacant green field and an empty horse barn, was known as the organization that saves cranes and their habitats.

All of this made it a bit easier for George to negotiate for the exportation of cranes, but he still had to produce proof of the foundation. Shortly after the successful aerial survey of the marsh in May, George wrote Ron that he was "in dire need" of pictures. Ron had received a number of George's letters while still at Cornell, including some with requests for pictures of the farm. By the time Ron returned to Baraboo, George was asking for pictures of the pens and Ron was barely at the blueprint stage. The slow international mail only accentuated the frantic nature of George's requests. A letter from Japan written on the fifth of the month might reach Ron on the fifteenth. George's deadline for the needed material would be the thirtieth. Then George would follow up that letter with an apology for his previous impossible request but reiterate that he still needed the stuff. In June, Ron sent a package to George that contained pictures of the farm and main barn and blueprints for the breeding unit. All of these materials were used in the endless presentations George was making in an effort to secure cranes for the Crane Foundation.

On George's twenty-sixth birthday, July 13, he wrote that local officials in Kushiro, home of the Crane Park, had narrowly approved by a four-to-three vote the shipment of Red-crowned Cranes to the

Crane Foundation. Six days later he learned the shipment was off. The local department of education objected to the removal of their birds. George was crushed. He was tired, and frustration overcame him for the first time. He didn't know that the department of education was involved and never gave a slide presentation to them. But he soon bounced back and began another round of meetings with anyone who would listen. In August, he sent Ron a telegram with an urgent request to "get 4 pens and associated houses up, photograph, and get the crap off to Tokyo." Certain he would still get the birds, George asked Ron to put off his return to Cornell in the fall. Someone had to take care of the cranes (he was also hoping to get a few of his Cornell birds from the New York Zoological Society) because George was off to Australia to trap Brolga Cranes.

After years of correspondence that George initiated in 1968 before a crane research facility was even a blip in his dreams, the Crane Foundation received permits to trap three pairs of Brolga Cranes and export them to Wisconsin. It wasn't possible for the Crane Foundation to get captive cranes. There simply weren't any available. The science of breeding cranes was still in its infancy. Brolga Cranes live only in Australia. These would be the first Brolgas ever exported legally and, except for an old male in a North American zoo, the only ones outside Australia. The expedition was made possible by the financial support of Norman Sauey and Dan Southwick of Southwick Animal Farm.

George and his Australian colleagues spent two grueling months in the scorching Gibson Desert of western Australia before they caught the cranes. These Brolgas are unusual in that they are not wetland birds. Their arid habitat is a harsh contrast to the rich marshes that most cranes inhabit.

During the nine-month dry season, hundreds of Brolgas congregate at agricultural stations where sorghum fields are maintained with extensive irrigation systems. George's base of operations was the Ord River Agricultural Development Site, where the Brolgas (along with Magpie Geese, Plumed Tree Ducks, and Corella Cockatoos) feast in the fields. In addition to fifty-eight square miles of sorghum and cotton fields, there is an eight-hundred-square-mile reservoir thanks to a dam that traps immense quantities of rain during the brief wet season.

After George captured four Brolgas, he and the cranes endured a harrowing drive through the desert with frequent stops so he could water the birds. Not wanting to take any chances under such stressful conditions, George tube-fed the water directly into their stomachs. His destination was the northern port city of Darwin. All the birds arrived safely. However, the United States Department of Agriculture had imposed an import ban on all exotic birds because of Newcastle's, a poultry disease. So the birds were flown from Darwin, on the north coast, to Perth, in the extreme southwest, practically the length of the continent. At the South Perth Zoo, director Tom Spence took the birds in until such time that they could enter the United States. No one knew when that would be.

The Crane Foundation also had permits to capture six Eastern, or Sharpe's, Sarus Cranes from northeastern Queensland. Despite the import ban, George continued on to the Queensland wetlands for another two months. He had no assurance he'd ever have the money to return if he canceled the trip. About two hundred Eastern Sarus, a separate subspecies from the more plentiful and larger Indian Sarus, made up the entire Australian population. The bird's historic range included Burma, Cambodia, Vietnam, Thailand, the Philippines, and Malaysia. Only recently had they colonized Australia. Australian ornithologists first recorded their presence in 1964. A population of Brolgas also resided in northeastern Queensland, and George planned to capture two for comparative studies with the western birds.

As with the Brolgas, capturing the Sarus was only half the headache. Their final destination was the Taronga Zoo in the southeast coastal city of Sydney, more than one thousand miles away. The nearest town to the capture site was Atherton. At four o'clock in the morning, a farmer George befriended drove George and the birds south sixty-four miles to Cairns, where they caught separate planes to Brisbane down the coast. The cranes left first and were waiting when George arrived in Brisbane. Then George flew on to Sydney followed an hour later by the birds, who were scheduled to arrive in the early evening. Kerry Muller from the Taronga Zoo met George at the airport and they waited for the birds . . . And waited . . . Ten-thirty . . . Midnight. No birds. No information. At three in the morning, they called it a night. Later that day, the cranes finally arrived. The plane had engine trouble and never left Brisbane the previous afternoon.

Back in Baraboo, construction of the breeding unit was finally completed. In October, Ron sent pictures and a detailed description of ICF to the director of the Yamashina Institute for Ornithology in Tokyo. Enclosed with the information was a copy of the United States Department of the Interior's permit for the foundation to import the Red-crowned Cranes.

The reluctance of the Japanese to export their treasured Red-crowned Cranes was understandable when you realize that all ICF had to show for itself so far was a glut of enthusiasm. From another perspective, how would the United States Fish & Wildlife Service, the agency responsible for conservation of the Whooping Crane, react if foreigners wanted to "do something about the Whooper problem"? When George went to Australia in August, the offer on the table in Japan had been reduced to one pair of Red-crowned Cranes on a trial basis with a second pair to follow if all went well at the foundation. Even so, George assured Ron the pens would be filled two weeks after his return. But George came back to Baraboo in December 1972 alone. The Red-crowned Cranes were still at the Crane Park. The Hooded Cranes and lone Siberian were still at their respective zoos. The Brolgas were waiting at Australia's South Perth Zoo, and the Sarus and two additional Brolgas were in Sydney, on the opposite side of the Australian continent.

It had been a frenzied, challenging, yet exhilarating year for Ron, George, Forrest, and their International Crane Foundation. No, they didn't import any cranes, but they did build the breeding unit. And they didn't have any financial backers except for Ron's parents, but people in Japan, Australia, and the United States Department of Agriculture at least knew they existed.

Ron was waiting when George returned home to the two-story white frame house two-tenths of a mile down the road from the Crane Foundation. Ron's parents purchased the house and he laid out the welcome mat. On the first floor, the back door led to the kitchen, which opened into the living room. Off the living room was a bathroom and a bedroom. Another bathroom and three more bedrooms were upstairs. Furnishings were spare and old. Mattresses were lumpy with craters in the middle where too many bodies had spent the night over too many years. Behind the house was an old white barn. Next to it was a small field that separated Ron's house from his neighbors' next door. This was base camp, Baraboo, and everybody connected with the Crane Foundation passed through sooner or later. The white house was soon christened the White House.

One of the earliest White House dinners was a meeting of the new board of directors: Ron, George, and Forrest. After a gourmet meal (Ron's culinary talents were already legendary), they sat on the kitchen floor and planned the foundation's development, growth, and survival. Forrest sent the articles of incorporation to Wisconsin's secretary of state in early March of 1973.

The normal way to set up a new organization is probably to establish a financial base and perhaps write a five-year plan. The ICF way was to hatch a dream, go after it, and hope you didn't wake up too soon.

THREE

By Plane and Truck the Cranes Arrived

. . .

Except for Stella, Who Made Her Own Arrangements

Despite a paucity of cranes when George returned to ICF at the end of 1972, the physical development of the Crane Foundation continued. The main horse barn was prepared to hold cranes. Dirt floors were covered with cement and then a thick layer of wood shavings. Horse-sized doors leading from stalls to outdoor yards were latched tight and small crane-sized openings with doors controlled by pulleys were installed. One stall was converted into an office. The tack room was cleaned out and readied for the incubators and hatchers. Outside, in front of the lounge, the paddock was modified to provide housing for a pair of Demoiselle Cranes. And the old pheasant coop was turned into a chick-rearing facility. (Ron wouldn't be needing it anymore. After long discussions with Dr. Dilger and careful examination of the logistical and financial problems of studying pheasants in captivity and the wild, Ron realized a dissertation on pheasants was not to be. With George's encouragement Ron decided to take over the study of the Siberian Cranes in India.)

ICF still looked like the horse farm it once was. Only a close inspection revealed the various modifications to accommodate the cranes. Visitors accustomed to viewing animals in a zoo setting where aesthetics were paramount could be forgiven their initial surprise. Undoubtedly some were shocked, and a stroll down the hill to the breeding unit probably didn't ease their stress. A bunch of dark green sheds connected to outdoor yards enclosed by a steel fence and set in a rectangle was the pride and joy of the International Crane Foundation. This, then, was the world center for the study and preservation of cranes.

The ICF's struggle for recognition was fought on two fronts: with both the scientific community and the general public.

"I'm a volunteer at the International Crane Foundation," a nineteen-year-old English literature major from a nearby university would say to her Aunt Sara.

"Can you handle all that heavy equipment, dear?"

Then there was the matter of explaining just what manner of beast a crane was. Not everyone who volunteered or donated money was a birder. And that was fine with Ron and George. They wanted to involve anyone with even the faintest flicker of interest in birds, wetlands, or conservation.

But they did stress that cranes were a special group, one of the most endangered families of birds in the world. The rarest ones have highly specialized diets or perilous migration routes, sometimes both. All fifteen species suffer from development pressures to some extent on their native lands. Wetlands are drained, rivers diverted, and roads laid down. Cranes are indicator species, symbols of a healthy environment by virtue of their rank at the top of the food chain. If something goes awry in the marsh deep among the grasses and breaks the chain, a slight decrease in water level or a new toxin from agricultural runoff, we may notice it only when it finally affects a large, easily observed animal, one whose absence is immediately felt. Picture a house of cards. Each card in the precariously balanced structure must be secure in order to support the one on top. Special, indeed.

Different, too. Much different than the herons people often mistake for cranes. Herons, storks, ibises, and flamingos are each other's closest relatives. Cranes are, literally, a whole different family.

Cranes have a vocal bravado few other birds can match. They have an extended convoluted trachea of varying complexity depending on the species. The Whooping Crane's trachea measures five feet in length and its resonating trumpet can be heard from two miles away. The Crowned Cranes have a booming sound that permeates the savannah. A Siberian Crane's mournful, flutelike song is as amazing for its unbelievably high register as the Sarus Crane's ear-splitting, heart-thumping yell is for its decibel level, which tests your bladder control if you're standing within thirty feet of one.

Only the cranes dance with leaps, bows, and pirouettes, garnished with a stick tossed high into the air. They dance to establish and maintain a pair bond. But young unmated cranes and downy chicks dance, too. A flock may be feeding quietly and then suddenly one bird will explode off the ground into a weightless aerial ballet and be followed by another, then a third, maybe several. Some observers swear the birds do it out of sheer exuberance.

Cranes nest on the ground, while herons, ibises, and storks nest in trees (or an occasional rooftop in the last case). And while it's true that flamingos nest on the ground (or close to it—their single egg sits upon a hardened pile of muck), there are no pink cranes to confuse the issue.

The birds that came to live in the Baraboo Hills were the dancing, trumpeting, ground-nesting kind. Cranes.

Barely one year after they conceived the idea of the International Crane Foundation, Ron and George were ready to receive the world's cranes. Unfortunately, the world wasn't ready for Ron and George. They had letters of support for their endeavor from respected scientists including Dr. S. Dillon Ripley, Jr., and the late Sir Peter Scott, but ultimately ICF had to stand by itself. If they could just get a few cranes and hatch a few chicks, the Crane Foundation would be real enough that zoos might loan their birds. To get started, George turned to an old friend.

That friend was William Conway, general director of the New York Zoological Society and the Bronx Zoo. George had first sought Conway's advice and cranes in the late 1960s when he was designing his research project at Cornell. Had George been aware of Conway's mindset regarding cranes, he probably wouldn't have worried so much about his sales pitch.

According to Conway, "We were convinced that a great deal needed to be done to help the cranes and that somewhere there had to be someone who had the vision and the compelling interest to do it. Out of the blue here came George, who was more than anybody could ever have hoped for. He was suitably crazy."

So Conway loaned George the White-naped Cranes that produced five chicks at Cornell. When George went back to Conway, this time to request birds for the new International Crane Foundation, Conway was not surprised.

"I knew he was going to do something with cranes. I think that wonderful thing was the connection with Ron, whose family made the Crane Foundation possible."

The population of the Bronx Zoo's cranes in 1972 included two surplus White-naped Cranes. Both were chicks from the Cornell study. Unfortunately, both chicks were blind. Fortunately, Conway didn't mind parting with them. So the International Crane Foundation proudly accepted two members of an endangered species as their first cranes, even if they weren't quite what George and Ron had in mind. Conway sent the White-naped Cranes to Baraboo in 1972 while George was still in Australia, so Ron was stuck with the housing problem. These particular birds needed a secure confine, not too large or they wouldn't be able to find their food and water (cranes, like nearly all birds, have no sense of smell). And it couldn't be too small because then they would be constantly bumping into the sides of their pen. Neither the breeding unit nor the main barn was suitable, so Ron settled them into the small barn behind the White House. He put thick wire mesh across the front so he could open the door to let in fresh air and sunshine.

Even without knowing the birds were blind you couldn't help but be drawn to their faces, bare except for a few black bristlelike feathers called filoplumes on the forehead and cheeks. Bare but not boring. A White-naped Crane's face is a tantalizing red-orange. The orange appears to lay just beneath the dominant red, waiting to burst forth. Look around the eye. You see a hint of flame. Gray feathers cover the ear openings, the front of the neck, and the body. The long white nape may give the bird its name, but it's the face that captivates your eye.

In December 1972, on his way back to Baraboo from Australia, George had paid a visit to the Honolulu Zoo and met its director, Jack Throp. The Honolulu Zoo had two of the four Red-crowned Cranes in the United States. They'd been at the zoo for years, but no one knew for certain their sexual identity. It wasn't unusual for a zoo not to know whether its cranes were male or female. Size and behavior often provide clues for a trained observer, but the cranes have to do some behaving before they can be identified. The unison call, for example, will always resolve the issue. Males and females not only emit different calls, but each maintains a distinct posture during the call. George was familiar with the unison call of nearly every crane species, and now he shared that knowledge with others.

Though both of the Honolulu cranes were females, George considered that wonderful news. He had already identified the two Red-crowned Cranes at the Southwick Animal Farm in Massachusetts as males. One crane, Justin, belonged to the Southwick Farm, owned by Dan Southwick. The other crane had been sent to Southwick on breeding loan from the Philadelphia Zoo. Until George visited, no one knew both birds were male. Now Throp agreed to loan his two females if ICF could obtain both males and set the four birds up in a breeding situation.

The Red-crowned Crane was George's special passion. Majestic, big (five feet tall), with complex courtship and territorial displays, the bird captured his heart. He couldn't resist making it the symbol of the Crane Foundation. The Red-crowned Crane adorns all official foundation signs, letterhead, patches, and business cards. It's one of the three white cranes, the others being the Whooping and Siberian Cranes. On the Red-crowned, the secondary and tertial wing feathers, the ones closest to its body, are black. When the wings are closed, the tertials lay atop the shorter white tail and give the appearance of a black tail. Except for a black forehead and black feathers on the front of the neck, the rest of the plumage is a blinding pure white topped by the bird's namesake vermilion crown. When a crane is excited, usually during courtship and territorial defense, the crown becomes engorged with blood, brightens, and becomes larger by the action of special contractile muscles.

Beyond its physical beauty is the importance of the Red-crowned Crane in Japanese culture, ancient and modern. Its graceful, sometimes stylized form is on screens, scrolls, prints, ceramics, textiles, and note cards. The crane is prevalent in Japanese literature. It's the symbol of Japan Airlines. Place names on the northern island of Hokkaido, home of Japan's resident Red-crowned Cranes, honor the bird. There is the town of Maizuru, "Dancing Crane," and Tsuruimura, "The Village Where Cranes Are." Tsuruimura was the site of the first feeding station in 1952 during an unusually severe winter that forced the cranes to forage in farmers' fields. Local schoolchildren put out corn, and the birds, wild at first, tamed down and fed on the children's offerings. Now there are a dozen feeding stations on Hokkaido.

In Japanese legends the crane lives a thousand years and is a symbol of longevity to the Japanese people. It's also monogamous and thus a good luck symbol at weddings, a bird of happiness. From the belief in a thousand-year life span came the custom of folding a thousand paper cranes to bring the folder long life and good health. A young girl reached out to the power of that belief not long after the atomic bomb devastated her homeland. Besieged by radiation sickness from the bombs, her strength sapped as she lay in a hospital, she began folding a thousand cranes. After completing only 508, she died. Her friends collected donations from children all over Japan and erected a monument in her honor at the Peace Park in Hiroshima. The statue is of a girl, and in her outstretched hands that reach to the heavens is a folded paper crane.

All four Red-crowned Cranes arrived at ICF in the first part of 1973: Justin, Phil (newly named in honor of the Philadelphia Zoo, who had agreed to the plan), and the two females, whom George christened Hona and Lulu, no explanation needed. So what if Phil had an injured wing that hung down around his hock joint. So what if Hona and Lulu were old birds. Twenty-year-old Lulu was diminutive even for a female crane. Her arthritic hocks were swollen to the size of golf balls, she couldn't straighten her legs completely, and her bent posture made her appear even smaller, like a little old lady. But she was a gentle bird with a kind disposition. The lightest touch of George's hand on her flank, to test her readiness for artificial insemination, brought a contented purring from deep within her snow-white breast.

The males were kept physically but not visually separated from the females for awhile. Cranes can be aggressive and inflict great harm on one another and people if they feel threatened. When George felt that the birds had settled in, he separated them into pairs and allowed them supervised time together. Phil and Lulu were in one pen and Justin and Hona in another. Each pair seemed compatible and soon was allowed to share lodgings on a permanent basis.

Later that spring ICF received permits from the U.S. Fish & Wildlife Service to collect one egg from each of two Greater Sandhill Crane nests in Wisconsin. The eggs were placed in incubators in the old stable tack room. Both hatched and became the first cranes raised at the Crane Foundation. The inaugural aviculture season at ICF was a modest success.

Then came a crushing blow. Justin killed Hona and soon after he died of a liver ailment. No amount of money could compensate for such a loss. Every life is precious. An endangered species is priceless.

George, ever the optimist, had been inviting people to "come by and visit us" even before there was an ICF to visit. Had he known the first person to take him up on his invitation would be one of Japan's most famous ornithologists, he might have added "in a few years." Since he didn't, only a couple of months after the loss of Justin and Hona, George and Ron found themselves hosting Dr. Yoshimaro Yamashina, founder and director of the Yamashina Institute of Ornithology of Japan. It was Dr. Yamashina to whom Ron sent the pictures and plans of ICF the previous fall. At the not-yet-prestigious International Crane Foundation the esteemed scientist met two Greater Sandhill juveniles, two blind White-naped Cranes, and two crippled Red-crowned Cranes. Dr. Yamashina was ICF's first VIP visitor. Miraculously, he was not the last.

After Dr. Yamashina's departure everyone focused their energies on keeping ICF afloat. Ron, George, and Forrest met every Wednesday night to make plans and talk about money they didn't have. Volunteer recruitment for workers and researchers continued and the White House filled up. Lucky guests dined on Ron's latest culinary adventure.

In June, George and Ron got another break. The San Diego Zoo agreed to send two birds on breeding loan to ICF: Casey, a White-naped Crane imported from Japan in 1940; and Dr. Watson, a Wattled Crane wild-caught in Botswana around 1966. The birds were flown to O'Hare International Airport just outside Chicago, a four-hour drive from Baraboo.

George and Ron borrowed a van from Ron's older brother Norm, Jr., and left Baraboo after dinner to pick up the birds in Chicago. Ron drove. They retrieved the birds at O'Hare without incident and were on their way back to Baraboo at about three in the morning.

Ron was exhausted by now, and George convinced Ron to let him drive the rest of the way even though he didn't have a license. His wallet was back in Baraboo. Not that it mattered, because the wallet contained only a Texas license issued to him in 1971 when he was doing fieldwork at the Aransas National Wildlife Refuge. But they were only an hour from home. What could happen? George recalls what happened next.

"I started driving and I was going a little too fast. We got stopped by a Columbia County Sheriff's officer just outside of Portage.

"He said, 'Show me your license.'

" 'I don't have a license.' The cop was seething.

" 'Then pay a hundred-dollar fine right now or go to jail.'

"Neither of us had any money. So Ron took the birds back to Baraboo and the trooper took me to jail in Portage. It had a little cell with a bed and a toilet without a cover. But I took a nap, so it wasn't so bad. Ron had to go home, put the cranes in the barn, and wake up his father and mother and say, 'Can I have a hundred dollars so I can get George out of jail?' "

Picking up birds from the airport was not always so dramatic, but each arrival did generate its own excitement. On February 15, 1974, the Sarus and Brolgas, stuck in Australian zoos for more than a year, arrived in Honolulu and began the requisite thirty-day quarantine. In March, they at last moved in at the International Crane Foundation.

The Australian contingent was quite a load for the plane. Brolga and Sarus Cranes are the tallest of the cranes, standing more than five feet tall. Each is a gray bird with a bare grayish green crown. But the amount of bare red-orange skin on the face and neck differs in the two birds. On the Sarus, it extends down onto the upper neck. And Sarus Cranes have pinkish legs in contrast to the Brolgas grayish black. Both have loud, raucous vocalizations. Ron and George named the foundation's original newsletter the *Brolga Bugle* in honor of the Brolga's ability to get its point across.

When the cranes arrived at ICF, George and Ron let the birds sort themselves out. The Sarus group had five males and only one female. Painless and Gloria went on to produce eleven chicks. Among the Brolgas there were four males and two females. Soon Willie and Olga the Brolga took up residence together in one pen. Willie's name was actually Will-he. He was named after researchers spent hours watching him display with Olga, all of it leading up to the anticipated copulation, when he suddenly seemed indecisive. Everyone always wondered, "Will he or won't he? Will he? Will he?" He did. In 1979, Willie and Olga made avian history when Lindsay hatched on August 30. She was the first Brolga ever hatched in the United States and the first outside of Australia since the 1920s.

Another significant event of 1974 was the importation of six Common Crane eggs from wild nests in Sweden. George and Ron hoped to eventually import Siberian Crane eggs to expedite captive propagation of that highly endangered species. When they had a secure captive population, they wanted to return Siberian Cranes to the wild. But before they could dare ask their Soviet colleagues for the endangered Siberian eggs, they had to prove that carrying crane eggs across an ocean was feasible. They needed a model whose population was secure and whose nests were accessible. The Common Crane in Sweden met their qualifications.

Approximately eleven thousand pairs nested in Sweden, another two thousand in Norway, and perhaps seven or eight thousand in Finland. Though only remnant populations still nested in other parts of Europe, including Turkey, Austria, Estonia, Germany, and Denmark, the Common Crane as a species was secure. Estimates of the Asian population were even more encouraging at sixty thousand to one hundred thousand birds. But politically and geographically those nests were out of reach. Nearly all of the Asian group nested within the USSR.

No one had ever attempted an egg transport of this magnitude. Indeed, the whole science of transferring eggs was fairly new. For several years the Patuxent Wildlife Research Center had been collecting Sandhill and Whooping Crane eggs from a few locations and flying them to the research facility in Maryland. They had more experience than anyone. But crossing state lines is one thing. Crossing an ocean is another. If you break an egg, you can't just pick another one from the next carton.

Eggs must be collected late in the incubation period because young embryos are very susceptible to harm, even death, from the handling that occurs in such an operation. Even so, an egg only a few days away from hatching still needs to be maintained at constant and high temperature and humidity. Artificial incubators have to be set at 99.5°F and 86.6° relative humidity. Could a simple insulated box maintain the necessary environment for nearly twelve hours? What if bad weather prevents the scheduled departure? How will a commercial airline and its staff react to a box on board that won't fit under the seat? How will Ron and George justify the expense if the experiment is a flop? What will happen to their Siberian Crane conservation plans if this mission fails?

In the late afternoon of March 10, 1974, on the estate of Dr. Victor Hasselblad in Sweden, Dr. Olaf Swanberg and Mr. Nils Wellberg quietly removed one of the two eggs in each of six wild Common Crane nests. The male crane incubates the eggs during the day, and the female usually takes over in the afternoon. If the two men approaching the nest frightened the male and caused him to flee the area, the female would still take her turn on the nest for the night. Swanberg and Wellberg took the eggs from the marsh and placed them in incubators at Dr. Hasselblad's home. The next morning they packed the eggs into a custom-designed box sent from Baraboo that had several layers of insulation, a hot-water bottle, and ventilation holes for temperature control. From the estate, the eggs were flown to Stockholm, then Copenhagen, and on to Chicago in a Scandinavian Airlines jet. Airline personnel let the eggs ride in the cockpit.

The box arrived at Chicago's O'Hare Airport at 4:45 P.M. Student researcher John Baldwin met the plane and drove the odd cargo back to Baraboo. George and Ron were with prospective donors in the lounge above the incubation room when John arrived at 9:00 P.M. that night. In the presence of their guests, they opened the box and removed the lid, then a layer of foam rubber, the hot-water bottle, and lastly a form-fitting piece of styrofoam that covered the six eggs. They were all intact—all except one that had a tiny hole from which an incessant peeping could be heard. The egg was pipped. Incredibly, the chick was hatching.

Their excitement was tempered by the realization that the chick's timing, though a great public relations stunt (the guests became major supporters on the spot), was cause for concern. The transport box could only approximate the proper humidity necessary for a successful hatch; if the egg's delicate membranes dried out they would harden and the chick would not be able to break free.

They quickly put the pipped egg into the hatcher and the other five eggs into the incubator. In an incubator the eggs are secured in trays, and an electric timer triggers a revolving mechanism that automatically tilts the trays so the eggs get turned, much as the parents do on the nest. This prevents the developing embryo from getting stuck to the sides of the shell. A couple of days before the chick is due to hatch, however, the egg must no longer be turned.

Thirty-six hours after the pipped egg was placed in the hatcher, an exhausted but healthy chick lay resting in the hatcher. They named it Olaf. A second chick hatched three days later and a third three days after that. Eventually there were six healthy Common Crane chicks, a remarkable success rate. By early August, Olaf and his companions, Nils, Victor, Thor, Droopy, and Inga, were testing their seven-foot wingspans on graceful flights around the foundation.

Five of the birds, including Inga, turned out to be males. Fortunately, the San Diego Wild Animal Park had several females. After the Swedish birds matured a bit, Mrs. Thor, Mrs. Olaf, Mrs. Nils, and Helga (for Victor) arrived from California and moved in with their designated mates, while Mrs. Inga flew in from the Bronx Zoo.

Of the five males, Olaf was the most magnificent. When the cranes matured and were put into breeding situations, Olaf alone was allowed to continue his flights over the Baraboo Hills. When George let him out of his pen for a flight, Olaf strutted slowly in a small circle, the picture of dignity and superiority. If someone was with George that Olaf didn't know, he'd point his bill down and expand his red crown as he walked purposely in a threat display. Then he faced into the wind and leaned forward with his wings open just a bit to await the right moment. A few long high-stepping strides, a few deep pulsating wing beats, and Olaf was aloft. He headed west toward County A Road until he gained altitude. Then he veered north and circled over the neighboring farm and the breeding unit down below. Most flights ended at George's side with a spectacular unison call. It was hard to deny Olaf his moment. Or maybe it was George who would not be denied.

With a growing crane population came more and new responsibilities. George and Ron drifted into niches each felt comfortable in. George devoted most of his time to managing the birds, though he didn't neglect his fund-raising duties. Ron was more at ease keeping tabs on the business end of ICF, that is, when he wasn't at Cornell working on his degree or slogging through a marsh in India.

Sandhill Crane eggs were also brought to ICF. Most were part of student research projects examining crane behavior and physical development. Greater Sandhill Crane eggs were collected from wild nests in Wisconsin and Idaho. A handful of Florida Sandhill eggs were also sent to ICF. The Patuxent Wildlife Research Center contributed eggs of Greaters and Floridas from their captive flocks. In 1976, ICF was set to receive four eggs of the Lesser Sandhill Crane from Cheryl Boise, who was studying them in Alaska, but one chick, whom Cheryl named Al, hatched before the plane left and had to be left behind. Cheryl raised the chick at her base camp. Al was flown to ICF later that summer and subsequently was discovered to be more of an Alice than an Al.

All the Sandhills lived in the nonbreeder field that was fenced in 1975 on the site of the old horse pasture. They brought a special quality to the nonbreeder field, perhaps because of all the species in the field only the Sandhills are native to Wisconsin. The cranes were penned, to be sure, but the vast expanse of the field, as opposed to the breeding facility down below, gave the illusion of freedom. Sometimes when you entered their realm the cranes would ignore you and continue to forage for insects. You could watch and not be an intruder. They were gray forms in the distance moving through the grass, heads down, bills searching. Some mornings you might not even see all of them unless you hiked through the entire field, down the hill, and into the far recesses of the old horse pasture. And it was good that they had their own space. When you were with them, the moment was all the more special.

Most visitors to ICF think that all the Sandhill subspecies look the same. Well, they do. One description suffices for all six subspecies: bare red forehead and crown covered with some black filoplumes; cheeks, chin, and throat pale gray, sometimes a whitish gray; gray neck, tail, and bill. It's a gray bird. But you may see a brown-bodied Sandhill in spring. A glorious warm, toasty brown. Nesting Sandhills paint themselves with local dirt. It probably helps camouflage them on the nest.

Three of the Sandhill subspecies are so plentiful that accurate counts are difficult. A half a million Greaters and Lessers funnel through the Platte River during migration, and that's just one migratory flyway. There may be another twenty thousand Lessers breeding in Siberia. The nonmigratory Florida Sandhill population is estimated at five thousand birds. But biologists work feverishly to keep the fifty or so Mississippi Sandhills from crossing over to the abyss of extinction. A question mark still hangs over the Cuban Sandhill, but reports have trickled out that indicate the population is steady at one to two hundred and hanging on.

The Lesser Sandhill, smallest of the subspecies, is the only one easily distinguished. The Canada Sandhill isn't as small as the Lesser or as big as the Greater. But for the volunteers who raise the cranes, feed them, change their water buckets, and walk with the birds in the fields, the differences between the birds are immense.

Cam was a female Florida Sandhill who arrived in an egg from Patuxent in 1975. By the time she was two years old, her calm demeanor set her apart from most of the other cranes. She spent hours foraging near the edge of the woods down the hill or quietly followed the water truck through the field, keeping a discreet distance from the boisterous mob that pecked at the wheels and looked in the back seat for the bucket of hard corn. "Crane candy," the staff called it, because the birds ate it like it was a rare imported confection. Cam was always easily recognized. She was the one who didn't poke people. Trustworthy Cam became the first crane to visit schools. She rode loose in the back seat of a car. And she danced; sometimes alone, often with me. We bowed and threw sticks in the air and spun around until I was dizzy.

One day we were joined by Pat, another Florida Sandhill only a year old. Pat had the same gentle character as Cam, and he became the second crane member of ICF's public education program. George and I took him on a training ride to the local hamburger drive-in for lunch one afternoon. He rode in the back seat of my subcompact car. But most of Pat's time was spent searching for bugs in the field, sleeping in the sun, preening, and dancing.

I couldn't resist tossing Pat a few extra pieces of corn every day. I always said good morning and asked him how things were going before I entered my blind to carry on dispassionate observations of the Hooded Cranes. Everybody talked to the cranes, but I felt kind of silly anyway, maybe because I knew my comments weren't idle chatter. I really did wonder how he was doing. I never touched him, although at times he stood so close I was I sure that I could. It would have been an invasion of his personal space, tolerated but probably unwanted. Pat spent his days with the other cranes, not with me. What reason did I have to think that I could ever be part of his world or even meet him halfway? In a couple of years he and Cam would probably pair up. That was his future. Though Pat and Cam wouldn't breed for several more years, their dancing was important for the development of a secure pair bond.

One early spring morning I was stunned to find a nest outside my blind. Later, while I was in the blind, I heard a crane vocalizing softly. It was the same low guttural call I'd heard every morning for the past week, but I had no clue as to its source. This time it sounded very close—as close as the brand-new nest beside my blind. I peeked outside and there was Pat. I stepped out of the blind and scanned the field for Cam. She was nearby but apparently not interested in Pat's handiwork. He continued to call (later I learned that it was a special vocalization used only by nesting cranes). After a quick look around to be sure no one was watching, I sat down on the nest. Pat sat down beside me and I gently rested my hand on his silvery-gray back. He didn't seem to mind. We sat together for a while on our nest, in shared silence. The next morning there was a second nest beside my other blind. Pat maintained them for a few days, possibly with the futile hope that his hard work might come to some fruition. Within a week, though, both nests had disintegrated. Only the flattened grass and a memory remained.

But all was not peaceful in the field. Not as long as Rusty and Freaky were around. They were Greater Sandhills hatched from wild eggs in 1974. Freaky was so named because his upper and lower bill crossed at the tips and had to be trimmed back on a regular basis. Rusty and Freaky were pals. No one else seemed to like them because they were aggressive to everyone, birds and people. One morning I was blindsided by Freaky and suffered a bloody nose. In the mid-70s, visitors were routinely taken into the old pasture for a close look at the cranes. Bodyguards came in handy. Needless to say, a walk in the field was soon eliminated from the tour schedule.

Rusty might not have been everyone's ideal captive Sandhill Crane, able to peacefully coexist with tourists and researchers, but he was one heck of a bird. At least, Stella seemed to think so. Stella first visited the International Crane Foundation on March 17, 1975.

Red-crowned Crane chick. *Photo courtesy of International Crane Foundation.*

She stayed long enough to meet most of the cranes in the field and then left. But she came back and stayed a little longer the next time. Her visits became more frequent until finally she spent the night. Stella was a wild Sandhill. She was named after Estella Leopold, Aldo Leopold's widow, who visited ICF when her health allowed.

Rusty was the object of Stella's attention. They often foraged together in the field and unison called. When she first arrived, Stella kept a nervous distance from the staff, often allowing them no closer than fifty yards. A few months later, she walked calmly past people who stood only fifteen feet away. Everyone thought Stella and Rusty would nest, but it didn't happen. Perhaps the human traffic and presence of so many other birds was a little too much for a truly wild crane.

Down below in the breeding unit, though, there was a nest. Lulu and Phil, despite their physical limitations, were showing normal reproductive behaviors two years after their arrival at ICF. George and Ron were convinced that because of his injured wing Phil couldn't jump onto Lulu's back, maintain his balance, and successfully copulate. Even if he was able to mount her, his wing drooped so low that he might trip over it. They had to use artificial insemination. Disappointment and helplessness set in when Phil's semen samples proved to be of very poor quality. There was a low sperm count and poor motility among the few sperm present. Still, George and Ron persisted. They had to.

Twenty-two-year-old Lulu did her part and laid four eggs from May 3 to May 18. (Cranes normally lay two eggs. If the egg is removed, the crane will continue to lay as long as she is in breeding condition.) Phil stood guard at the nest when George collected the eggs. A week later each one proved to be infertile even though it had been "covered" by Phil. During the next ten days, there was no discernible breeding behavior from the birds. But as June approached, Lulu began to spend more time at her nest. The staff collected semen from Phil. Again the quality was inferior. They inseminated Lulu anyway. But George was anxious, almost desperate, to produce chicks at ICF that year. He wanted to show that ICF had a breeding program. So they collected high-quality semen from a White-naped Crane (Casey) and also gave that to Lulu. It was a controversial decision even though hybrids can be used for studying behavior. It had already been done at Patuxent in 1974. A Whooping Crane–Sandhill hybrid was created because of plans to cross-foster Whooping Cranes into Greater Sandhill nests at Grays Lake National Wildlife Refuge in Idaho. Since there was a possibility that the Whoopers might later hybridize with the Sandhills, wildlife biologists wanted to know what a hybrid would look like and how it might behave. But there was no such research plan at ICF.

Lulu laid two more eggs on June 4 and 6. Both were fertile. But what were they? The first one, Tancho, hatched on July 7. Tsuru followed on July 9. But what were they? Closely related crane chicks look pretty much the same; differences are subtle. The staff compared pictures of White-naped and Red-crowned Crane chicks with the two downy apparitions before them. They looked at down color, leg color, and head shape. There were no answers. Only time would tell.

George and a student, Barbara Brownsmith, kept a close watch on the chicks, who had to learn how to feed themselves in their first few days of life. In the wild, a parent crane presents food items, mostly small bugs, to its chick. Though the young bird does forage on its own to some extent, the adults provide a steady meal ticket. But if Tancho and Tsuru ate too much, their rubbery legs might bow out or buckle from the excess weight. Dehydration can also be a problem. On a dehydrated chick, the rubbery skin on its legs hangs in bags down around its feet. Colored marbles in a shallow red water bowl encouraged Tancho and Tsuru to investigate and, ultimately, drink from the bowl. Everything seemed to be progressing smoothly. Then one afternoon when the chicks were about four weeks old, George noticed that the mats in Tancho's little pen were clean. The bird hadn't defecated. Barbara and George alternated watches. Tancho weakened before their eyes. That night he was lethargic, wouldn't eat, didn't eliminate. Next morning the situation was unchanged. The chick had some type of obstruction in his intestine. George called a local vet who assisted at ICF occasionally. Tancho could not have survived a trip to another city in search of a bird specialist. Time was running out. Tancho needed surgery. He might die from the procedure, but he would definitely die without it. The vet discovered that a portion of the chick's lower intestine had telescoped in on itself, preventing the passage of feces. He straightened out the intestine and released the impacted fecal matter. But in the end, the trauma was too much for Tancho's little body.

George and Barbara felt defeated. They didn't want to label this chick as one who simply wouldn't have survived in the wild, a natural mortality. And it was more than the fact that Tancho was one of the first cranes conceived and hatched at ICF, more than his membership in an endangered species. They couldn't deny his scientific value to ICF, but the loss cut deeper. Barbara felt they had "a connection with the spirit of this bird."

That left Tsuru. He was a strong bird, whatever he was. The answer to his identity got closer when he developed pin feathers; the down that had hugged his body now hung in wisps on the ends of the developing feather shafts. Blood and nutrients in the bases of the shafts nourished the growing feathers. When at last Tsuru's plumage broke free and pushed beyond the confining sheaths, everyone was both relieved and amazed. Tsuru's breast feathers were white. His primary and secondary wing feathers were black. Somehow, Phil had done it. Tsuru was a pure Red-crowned Crane.

While the mystery of Lulu's eggs was playing out and Stella was ogling the bachelors in the field, George and Ron continued to ask zoos and private breeders to loan their cranes to ICF. "Shipping season" (spring, summer, early fall) was a busy time at ICF. The San Antonio Zoo sent a female Wattled Crane to keep Dr. Watson company. Upon meeting in adjacent pens, the two birds danced immediately and then quietly stood about three feet apart, the chain-link fence between them. A couple of weeks later, Mrs. Watson moved in with the Doctor.

A new species' arrival always heightened the excitement. And if the birds also presented a management problem, as did the Hooded Cranes who arrived in 1974 and 1975, George eagerly took up the challenge. Wild Hoodeds breed in Siberia, but ICF's birds had been living in California and Florida. Little was known about Hooded Crane breeding biology. Prior to World War II, nearly thirty-five hundred Hooded Cranes wintered in Japan. When the fighting stopped, fewer than four hundred remained. The population was able to recover, however, and in 1975 there were almost three thousand cranes. Japan has protected them since 1955. Another group of two hundred fifty birds winters in Korea. The Hooded Crane was declared a national treasure in South Korea in 1970 and accorded legal protected status. Not until 1974 did a Russian ornithologist discover the first Hooded Crane nest in Siberia.

Though the Hooded Cranes that ICF received were wild-caught years before, they never tamed down. They were "flighty" in the presence of people, difficult to handle without causing extreme stress and risking injury. Therefore, artificial insemination was not in the management plans for these birds, and neither was viewing by visitors. ICF had no zoolike exhibits with expansive spreads between the birds and people. Limited space and funds dictated that the cranes be housed with security, breeding, and access by staff as the primary concerns. All of the Hooded Cranes, four pairs and an extra female, were housed in the main barn, one pair to a stall, each with access to an outdoor yard. If someone peeked into their stall, the birds immediately went outside. The yards extended out into the nonbreeder field and therefore were inaccessible to viewing by the public. A visual barrier about four-and-a-half-feet high along each fence prevented the birds from seeing each other.

These cranes, like most zoo birds ICF received, were pinioned: the primary section of one wing had been surgically removed and they couldn't fly. But the pairs could hear each other, and when one unison called, another voiced its own declaration of territorial rights. What made the Hooded Cranes' ICF living quarters unique were the floodlights installed over each pen that were controlled by an automatic timer in the barn. Every day someone trudged down to the last stall, climbed a ten-foot ladder, and reset the timer to add a few more minutes of light to the cranes' photoperiod, the same one experienced by wild Hooded Cranes at the high latitude of their native Siberian breeding grounds. It was a simple but critical change from the environment they'd experienced during all their previous years of captivity. Each bird now had privacy, a confirmed partner of the opposite sex, and a light cycle that was conducive to breeding. All anyone could do now was wait. They waited for two years. Then, in 1976, the International Crane Foundation recorded the first captive-hatched Hooded Cranes in the world when Pookie hatched on June 4 and Sim followed two days later. Pookie was named for Russian ornithologist Yuri Pukinski, who discovered that first wild Hooded Crane nest.

By the late 1970s ICF no longer went begging for birds. A Blue Crane from the San Diego Wild Animal Park arrived in 1976 to become the twelfth species in the collection. Formerly called the Stanley Crane, it's the national bird of the Republic of South Africa, a bird of the African grassland, and it really is blue—a muted powder blue, close to a bluish-gray. Its beauty doesn't have the dramatic brilliance of the Whoopers or Red-crowneds or quite the exotic quality of the Wattled and Crowned Cranes with whom it shares the eastern part of its range. Elegance. That's the Blue Crane. A dense covering of loosely layered, elongated feathers on the head and upper neck give the bird a distinctive bouffant look. Extremely elongated secondary flight feathers reach to the ground, tips gracefully trailing the bird.

ICF's first Blue Crane was named Killer. To stand and admire his grace and wonder how such a beautiful bird could be so named was to give Killer the opening he needed to answer your question. His pen was his palace. If you employed a stick to hold him at bay, he pecked it, then grabbed the stick with his bill, pushed it down to the ground, and attacked it with his feet. Killer was paired with Priscilla from the National Zoo. He enjoyed her company. Killer and Priscilla produced ICF's first Blue Crane chick in 1980.

Learning about the particular requirements of each species that came to ICF was only half the battle. Adjusting to the idiosyncracies of individual birds, their personalities, likes and dislikes, and the methods they used to communicate those feelings was the other half. And it was often a battle.

Casey, the forty-four-year-old White-naped Crane, developed quite a reputation early on. Part of it was due to his virility. He produced five times more semen than the average male crane, and all of high quality. He also harassed the aviculturists. But Casey got so wrapped up in his threat displays—stamping his feet, throwing his head back, and growling—that they could usually finish their task before he got around to attacking.

Daily routines incurred a new risk when a six-foot-tall Indian Sarus Crane from the nearby Henry Vilas Zoo in Madison was deposited on ICF's doorstep by his keepers. Joe was extremely aggressive toward people and presented an interesting challenge when it was time to clean his pen. The doors that enabled staff to easily lock cranes inside during winter worked just as well when they wanted to lock a bird outside. Volunteer Frank Femali's experiences with Joe were typical.

"I had this broom. Joe hated that broom. I'd lean it against the outside of the fence. Joe would leave his house and go outside to attack it. Then I'd run into the house real fast and shut the door so he couldn't get back in. I'd retrieve the broom and clean up. One day I leaned the broom against the wall next to the window, which was open a few inches. Joe pulled the broom out through the window, into his yard, and destroyed it."

The first Whooping Crane arrived at ICF in April 1976, preceded by her reputation. It was the famous Tex, a ten-year-old imprinted Whooping Crane on loan from the Patuxent Wildlife Research Center. She preferred people to cranes. Specifically, she preferred male people, and George was going to be her mate. After a respectable period of dancing and nest building to bring Tex into breeding condition, George was going to inseminate Tex with semen from George II, a Whooper from the Audubon Park Zoo in New Orleans who arrived a week after Tex. To avoid confusion between Tex's two companions, George II was promptly renamed Tony.

Later that fall two Siberian Cranes took their places in the breeding unit. Wolf Brehm, of the Walsrode Vogelpark in what was then West Germany, had agreed to loan his ancient Siberian Crane to the foundation. The bird had been imported to Europe from India before World War I and was at least sixty years old. The second Siberian Crane came from the Philadelphia Zoo. She had been trapped in India in the 1950s. ICF now had two of the eleven Siberians in captivity in the world. And if their ages weren't enough of a concern, no one knew what their genders were. Luckily, their behavior and unison calls identified them as a pair and they were bestowed with the names Wolf and Phyllis. They proved compatible and soon shared a yard together. ICF was now home to 104 cranes of fourteen species.

In less than a half-dozen years, ICF became known as the place where all the cranes were. The foundation was recognized as a leader in captive crane breeding, with more successes in their short period of existence than most zoos and private breeders had during several decades. From a collection of crippled, barren, and geriatric cranes ICF had coaxed chicks and eggs from five endangered or threatened species: Red-crowned, Hooded, White-naped, Siberian, and Whooping.

So in February 1977 when a Red-crowned Crane was found poisoned in a rice field north of Seoul in South Korea, Professor Won Pyong-oh of the Korean Council for Crane Preservation (KCCP) contacted the International Crane Foundation. The poison was meant for Ring-necked Pheasants, which farmers in the region consider agricultural pests. A flurry of letters and paperwork secured an endangered species import permit in record time. Because this was an emergency, the United States Department of Interior waived the thirty-day public comment period that normally follows each permit request. The Department of Agriculture also expedited their papers. Korean Airlines provided free transportation, and within a month the crane was in Honolulu to begin its thirty-day quarantine. Despite its poor health, the bird survived and was flown to O'Hare International Airport on April 26.

Ron again borrowed the van from his brother's business in Portage, and I accompanied him at four in the morning to pick the bird up at O'Hare. The drive was no problem. What we found waiting for us in the cargo terminal was a different matter. The bird's crate was bigger than the bathroom at the White House. It wouldn't fit in the van. How were we going to get the bird back to Baraboo? Ron turned to me and said, "We could uncrate him and you could hold him while I drive."

"I have a better idea. You hold him and I'll drive."

Holding a five-foot-tall wild crane for four hours didn't have much appeal for either of us, and it really bothered the cargo handlers, who rushed forward with papers for Ron to sign.

"We don't want anything to do with this if you're going to open that box."

Upon further examination, we determined that the crate was not as wide as it was high. If we slowly turned the crate on its side, giving the bird time to walk onto the side panel, which would then become the floor, it would fit into the van. And the crane would still have room to stand up. Now the cargo handlers were more than happy to help—anything to get us far away from them. The ride back was especially peaceful after the anxious moments on the loading dock. When the bird was uncrated in Baraboo, we were all relieved to see that Won, named in honor of the professor who rescued him, had not been damaged in transit.

Won was one of several new Red-crowned Cranes at ICF in 1977. Old and beloved Lulu, the aged Red-crowned Crane, had her best season yet. Seven Red-crowned Crane chicks hatched with the support of artificial insemination and Ueno, a virile male on loan from the Ueno Zoo in Tokyo. Then came what Ron called the "Three Arrivals in White." The first was twenty-year-old Angus, a male Whooping Crane who was to be Tex's sperm donor. Angus was a full brother to Tony (nee George II), whose limited contributions to the cause thus far necessitated the import of an understudy.

Next was Zhurka, a Red-crowned Crane from the Moscow Zoo. No one knew her precise origin, but the Russians said she was a gift from the People's Republic of China to the Soviet Union in the late 1950s. Zhurka's tameness and mellow attitude around people suggested she had been hand-reared. Apparently she was the only Red-crowned Crane in captivity in the Soviet Union and an extremely popular attraction at the zoo. Though she had only ducks for company at the zoo, Zhurka made a nest and laid three eggs in spring 1977. Recognizing that her reproductive potential was wasting away in Moscow, the zoo offered Zhurka to ICF on breeding loan. In her first breeding season at ICF, less than one year after she arrived, Zhurka laid an incredible sixteen eggs, eleven of which were fertile, and four of those fledged.

Finally there was Hirakawa, a Siberian Crane from the Hirakawa Zoo in Kagoshima, Japan. This was the Siberian Crane George had tried to obtain five years before. She had been at the zoo since 1969. In November of that year a high school student found her in Okinawa. The bird's brown head and neck marked her as a juvenile. Siberian Cranes are rarely seen in Japan, and never as far south as Okinawa. She probably became separated from her parents during their migration from Siberia to the wintering grounds in China and, after an exhausting detour over the China Sea, landed in Okinawa. Her fatigue was so great that the student walked right up to her. For eight years she entranced visitors to her namesake zoo with her pink face and delicate voice, so different from the low raucous bugle call of the more familiar Red-crowned Crane. Now she lived at the Crane Foundation next to Wolf and Phyllis.

Phyllis proved to be prolific egg-layer. Unfortunately they were all infertile. Still, her twelve eggs in 1977 were not an insignificant achievement. She was at least twenty-four years old and had never laid an egg before in her life. ICF hoped that the younger Hirakawa might succeed where Phyllis came up short. No one had ever bred Siberian Cranes in captivity.

Phyllis never got another chance at the record books. On January 21, 1978, she was found dead in her pen. Wolf had killed her. Most likely it was misdirected aggression. Hirakawa's presence in the next pen had stirred him up into an agitated state. From Korea George had been monitoring the comings and going of cranes at ICF. A sixth sense told him there might be a problem with the introduction of the new female next to Wolf and Phyllis. George sent a letter with instructions to separate Wolf and Phyllis. It wasn't done. For whatever reason, the people on staff at the time either didn't think Wolf's reaction warranted the move or didn't believe that George could possibly be that attuned to the situation from a distance of thousands of miles. It caused a serious rupture in George's relationship with the staff, not to mention the setback to Siberian Crane captive breeding.

But shortly after Phyllis's death the staff had to pull together and prepare for the arrival of six endangered cranes. George and Ron had received word in 1977 that Hong Kong's Department of Agriculture and Fisheries had confiscated six White-naped Cranes from an animal dealer who didn't have the necessary permits. The Hong Kong Botanical and Zoological Gardens lacked the space to properly care for the cranes, and government authorities contacted ICF for advice on finding a home for the birds. ICF replied calmly that they would be thrilled to accept the cranes. All parties concerned agreed it was the best course of action. Unlike Won, the Red-crowned Crane from Korea, these White-napeds were not in poor health, so rushing the paperwork was not a concern. But just getting permits through normal channels proved to be more difficult than dealing with Won's emergency status, ironically because of regulations that were instituted to protect wildlife.

The United States and many other nations had signed a 1973 document called the Convention on International Trade in Endangered Species of Flora and Fauna (CITES). CITES was intended to restrict trade in endangered species on the international market, and White-naped Cranes were on the endangered list. In order to buy, sell, or trade any endangered plant or animal, the parties involved had to obtain permits from their governments. Before the U.S. government would grant a permit, ICF had to prove that the country of origin had no objection to the exportation. The problem was that Hong Kong was not the country of origin. The birds might have been smuggled out of the People's Republic of China. One bureaucrat in the U.S. Department of Interior suggested that the birds be returned to China and released. However the Chinese would have to admit the birds had been smuggled out of their country, and no one was actually sure the cranes had in fact originated from China. After months of discussions, endless telephone calls, and exhaustive paperwork, the permit was finally issued and the six White-naped Cranes came to ICF in 1978.

Adding birds to a species group increases that group's genetic diversity, an important component of a healthy captive breeding population. Wild cranes are especially significant because they bring a new gene pool to the captive stock. But there was one species for which ICF did not even have its first representative.

Next to a world map in the barn was a drawing that showed all fifteen crane species. Each crane was shown in its unison call posture except one: the Black-necked Crane. No one knew what a Black-necked Crane looked like when it vocalized.

Least known and last discovered of the world's cranes, the Black-necked was as shrouded in mystery as the cloud-covered Himalayan peaks that border most of its range. The Russian naturalist-explorer Nikolai Prezhwalsky was the first to describe the species in 1876 when he saw several pairs near Lake Koko Nor in northeastern Tibet, a country in the clouds.

Tibetan villages sit among mountain peaks at twelve thousand feet above sea level. It's a harsh land, difficult to get to, harder still to live in, with days of scorching heat and nights of bone-chilling cold. One researcher reported that water froze every night in May. Winter wildlife observations are survival tests. Few outsiders ever venture to this part of the world. The route to Mount Everest's crest is a congested freeway compared to the trickle of foreign travelers to the Tibetan Plateau. Even before the Chinese occupied Tibet in 1950, few foreigners were allowed in the region.

Prior to the Chinese occupation, Tibet was a stronghold of Buddhism, and the Buddhists protected the region's wildlife. With the influx of the Chinese and the flight of the Dalai Lama later in 1959, the Buddhist influence declined somewhat. Parts of Tibet now have roads where before there were only paths. Black-necked Crane habitat might have been altered, perhaps destroyed. No one knew for sure.

What little was known about the Black-necked Cranes in the early 1970s had to be pieced together from written accounts by the few people ever to see the bird in the wild. Between Prezhwalsky in 1876 and the last published report in 1948 there wasn't much to go on. The cranes preferred to breed in marshes and bogs and on islands in lakes of the Tibetan steppes. Observers confirmed nesting in Ladakh in northern India at altitudes of thirteen thousand to fifteen thousand feet. Black-necked cranes were observed breeding in southwestern Tibet along the Indus River and southern Tibet near the Brahmaputra River. There were reports of both wintering and nesting Black-neckeds in Szechwan and Yunnan provinces in China to the east and southeast of Tibet. Northern Assam's Apa Tani Valley was home to a small flock of not more than two hundred birds. The pioneering French ornithologist Jean Delacour found a few Black-neckeds in Vietnam near Hanoi in 1931. He and a colleague trapped two and shipped them to Delacour's private collection in France.

The Vietnam birds were considered an unusual occurrence. Black-necked Cranes, unlike most other migratory cranes, engage in regional movements, moving up to high-altitude marshes for nesting and coming down to lower, somewhat warmer areas for the winter. Tens of thousands of Demoiselle and Common Cranes, which breed farther north than the Black-neckeds, cross the Hindu Kush Mountains and the Himalayas on their way to ancestral wintering grounds. But the Black-neckeds never completely leave their mountain homes.

Population estimates for the Black-necked Crane in the early 1970s were an optimistic seven hundred to nine hundred birds. But those numbers were spread over hundreds of miles from Ladakh in northern India, to Tibet along nearly its entire southern border, and into China on the west. A new census was difficult even for the researchers who lived near the lands of the Black-necked Cranes. The physical challenges of the terrain pale next to the political complexities of the region. Jurisdiction over most of the crane's territory is hotly disputed by Pakistan, India, and China. Travel to any of the occupied areas, even by nationals of the occupying country, presents risks. When ICF researchers, including Ron, wanted to join their Indian colleagues on a field expedition in 1976, their request was denied. On that same expedition the research team, which included the revered ornithologist Salim Ali, wanted to explore potential nesting habitat, a group of lakes near the Indus River north of Ladakh. But all they did was look at it from a nearby hill. China and India both claim that land.

In 1978, two more expeditions on the Indian side of Tibet sought out the Black-necked Crane's remote haunts. During January and February, Lavkumar Khacher found the Apa Tani Valley empty of cranes. During the past twenty years the local people had obtained firearms, and hunting probably drove the cranes away. He did find about twenty pairs in Arunachal Pradesh and a small winter population, no more than fifty pairs, wintering in Bhutan. He had information from the International Council for Bird Preservation (ICBP) World Working Group on Cranes, chaired by George, that some marshes north of Tibet harbored large numbers of Black-neckeds, but that area was politically off-limits to him. In India, Prakash Gole continued the search in Ladakh during the breeding season. It was the same area he visited two years before with Salim Ali. In the shadow of a Buddhist monastery on a hill overlooking the plain, Gole observed one nesting pair near the village of Hanle, elevation fifteen thousand feet, from May 5 to May 12. He left the area to search for other cranes, and when he returned the pair was gone. Local people told him the nest had been deserted for at least a week. A second nest, in Chushul, south of Hanle, had two eggs. Then the female disappeared. Left unprotected, the eggs were destroyed, presumably by a predator. ICF had hoped to obtain twelve Black-necked Crane eggs and either transport them to Baraboo or set up a captive breeding situation at Ladakh. But there weren't even twelve individual birds to be seen, much less twelve productive pairs.

What about Black-necked Cranes in China and Tibet? In Chinese zoos? George had been writing letters to Chinese ornithologists for several years seeking historical information about the birds. Did they know where the cranes were now? Was anyone planning to look? For years George received no reply. Cultural and scientific exchange with China was just beginning anew. Some of the ornithologists, shut off from their work since the Cultural Revolution, were only just returning to the field.

In 1973, Shiro Nakagawa, director of the Ueno Zoo in Tokyo, visited China. He saw two Black-necked Cranes at the Beijing Zoo, three at the Shanghai Zoo, and no evidence of breeding. A zoo employee told him that Black-necked Cranes are "not so rare" in the wild. But in 1976, in a long-awaited reply, the Beijing Zoo rejected ICF's request to trade for Black-necked Cranes because "this is a rather rare and precious animal and we are keeping only a very few." Years would pass before the mystery was solved.

Diane Pierce

FOUR

Crane People

W ith each year's passing the International Crane Foundation grew a little bigger, its scope a bit broader. After six years of contending with a dearth of cranes and then struggling to care for more than one hundred cranes, of confronting behavioral and health management problems, and paying creditors just enough to keep them happy, ICF was beginning to hold its own in the wildlife conservation community. But during those lean years ICF was like the prairie compass plant, whose modest twelve-inch-tall stalk after three long years in the soil belies deep labyrinth roots that may stretch twelve feet down into the prairie sod, and whose first flower must wait yet another two growing seasons. ICF had an expansive nurturing lifeline unseen by the casual observer.

Norm Sauey, Jr., made his company van available to ICF whenever Ron and George needed to pick up cranes at the airport. He also let ICF use his office's photocopier. Ron told his brother Don that it would be "appropriate" for Don to have the honor of paying one thousand dollars to own the first "Salute to the Dawn" print. But it took more than money and equipment to develop ICF in the early days. Several years before, Ron's father had hired a local retired farmer to supervise the maintenance of his property. And even though the farm was now the Crane Foundation, Norman still owned it and Howard Ahrensmeyer still looked after it and, by extension, George and Ron.

It was Howard, small of stature but wiry with strong, tough hands from years of farming, who built the crane doors in the horse stalls. He built the feed boxes for the birds. In later years it was Howard who plowed the roads so the water truck could get through to the cranes in winter and Howard who laughed and pulled the truck out when it got stuck because someone ventured where Howard had not plowed. He took pity on a researcher sitting in a plywood blind buffeted by the north wind in January and rigged up a space heater with a one-hundred-foot extension cord. Every day, even after he retired in 1981, Howard took Samantha, the farm's resident black Labrador watchdog, for a long walk. Sam was a total failure as a watchdog but everybody loved her. Especially Howard. And all the college "kids" who flocked to ICF loved Howard. Ron credited Howard's "horse sense" with helping to convert Nodoroma into the Crane Foundation. Looking back, you might say Howard was the first volunteer at the Crane Foundation. He set a standard for generosity of heart and spirit.

When Ron finally returned to Cornell in January 1973, it was George's turn to be alone in Baraboo and keep the foundation afloat. Continued progress on the conversion of the farm into a research institution made it necessary for George to raise funds and possible for him to ask zoos and bird parks to loan cranes to ICF. He contacted zoos that had loaned birds for his Cornell study and many who hadn't. He asked the federal authorities for permission to collect one egg from two-egg Sandhill Crane nests (cranes usually end up rearing only one of the two chicks).

George was a prolific letter writer who bordered on being a workaholic. He continued his correspondence with the Japanese in hopes of securing some Red-crowned Cranes. He wrote to fellow scientists, both friend and stranger, updating them on the progress of ICF and his fieldwork of the past year. If ICF was to be more than just a collection of captive birds, their colleagues had to know about their work with the wild cranes. And the captive cranes had to be studied as well. In 1973, the first graduate student arrived at ICF. Karen Voss from the University of Wisconsin visited the foundation for a tour, talked to George, and came back to study the ontogeny of behavior in Sandhill Cranes for her master's thesis. That scene was repeated many times. A student or potential volunteer came to ICF out of curiosity, met Ron or George, and never left. Word of mouth was often their only recruitment service.

George's ability to talk people into giving up time, money, and labor became legendary. He'd corner students and ask them gently, "Would you mind doing a few things besides your research?" And before they knew it they were cleaning pens, watering birds, pulling weeds, giving tours, and sweeping the barn. The payback was a personal involvement in the building of the International Crane Foundation. Having everyone contribute to all aspects of running ICF, from unloading wood shavings to publishing scientific papers, fostered a camaraderie among the students and volunteers. It gave them a sense of belonging, even a sense of ownership. They doted on "their" birds. And once you volunteered, whether you took care of birds or helped out in the office, you were forever known as an ICFer.

One of the earliest ICFers was Frank Femali, Ron's cousin. Frank was a scrawny fifteen-year-old kid in 1973 when he arrived for his first summer in Baraboo. He couldn't even identify a Sandhill Crane. Even though George asked Frank to help him pull up fence posts, a strenuous task that took weeks in the hot sun, Frank returned to ICF the next three summers and lived in the White House each time.

Frank was the first of many volunteers who were never quite sure what they'd have to do next. Water the cranes? Sure. All you had to do was hitch the flatbed trailer with the water trough to the truck, fill the two-hundred-gallon trough with a half-inch-diameter garden hose, drive to each pen, and dip the bucket in the trough to get clean water. Before they had a truck they put the water trough on a toboggan and slid it down the hill. A bucket of water weighed about thirty pounds. It weighed more when you were chased by an ornery crane like Casey or Joe. Water the plants? Sure. The "plants" were hundreds of trees and shrubs. They were watered in the same arduous manner as the birds. Frank was so moved by his experiences at ICF that he composed a poem that read in part,

> *Though George may run you through a stamina test,*
> *At ICF you cannot rest.*
> *But this year I wasn't slow,*

Because with Casey involved, you never know.
We really did have a good crew,
And our parties were a real "whoop de doo."
I'm sorry when I called you names like toad,
When you told me to clean the road.
When you worked me to the bone all day,
I tried not to groan, even without pay.

One summer day in 1973 when George and Frank were wrestling fence posts, a car pulled into the driveway and a man and a woman got out. They stretched a bit after their drive up from Madison. The man needed to stretch. Herb Malzacher stood six-foot-six. His barrel chest and flaming red hair and beard made him look even bigger. Helen, his wife, had porcelain skin. She was slender and wore her blond hair in a long braid down her back. Herb and Helen walked out into the field to meet George, who always made time to talk to visitors, especially if he picked up the scent of volunteer labor.

Herb was a zookeeper in Madison by way of Oklahoma and Omaha, where he met Helen. He took care of the elephants. Helen's business was computers. She worked for the state of Wisconsin. Before they left that day, Herb yanked a few fence posts out of the ground. They returned two weekends later on Herb's next days off and kept on coming for the next six years. Herb often came alone when he wasn't working during the week. He was delighted to work with the cranes and help out doing anything that was asked of him. Helen, by her own admission, was "more comfortable pushing a pencil than a wheelbarrow." But George asked her to help plant and water the hundreds of trees and shrubs, and Helen did it. Only later did George discover that she was better suited to files than flora. After Herb and Helen met Ron, they joined him and George and Frank at the White House. Ron permanently reserved the first-floor bedroom for Herb and Helen.

There were volunteers for all sorts of tasks. Robin Squier from Milwaukee, fresh out of college in 1974, visited ICF with a tour group. "I remember getting off the bus and being greeted by Common Crane chicks. I met George and it was, 'Oh, you finished college and you don't have a job lined up? Then you have to come back and work here.' " Robin helped transcribe behavioral data from films and assisted Dr. Marie Oesting, the wife of a local university professor, with administrative duties for a couple of years. Marie also translated German papers. Dorothy Mudd came up from town to type letters. Retired schoolteacher and Baraboo native Lucille Thompson was probably one of the easiest recruits. On a visit in 1972 to Owen Gromme's trout pond with Gerald Scott's adult biology class, Lucille found herself walking between the artist and her old teaching companion. "Scott," Gromme said, "those two boys have some idea that they're going to have something to do with cranes, and you and I must do everything possible that we can to help them." That was all Lucille needed to hear. She typed, answered the phone, gave tours, and took pictures. After a few photography courses at the University of Wisconsin's extension in Baraboo, Lucille set up her own darkroom and began photographing cranes and people at ICF. The first picture of the first Hooded Crane ever hatched in captivity in the world was taken not by *Life* or *National Geographic* but by Lucille Thompson.

The human resources for ICF to draw on were boundless. Harold Bessac in Dalton, Wisconsin, made plastic identification signs for the crane pens and leg bands for the birds. Elizabeth Anderson, a graduate student at Cornell, translated Russian papers. An electrician, Ben Peterson of Peterson Electric, once billed ICF for only part of his time. The sixth-grade class at East Elementary School collected Christmas trees for windbreaks in the crane pens.

The first foundation-wide health checkup for the birds took place at 8 A.M. on November 3, 1975, and was done by volunteers from the United States Departments of Agriculture and Interior, the Wisconsin Department of Natural Resources, and Marquette University. Volunteers who raised the chicks were called Chick Mamas and Chick Papas.

In 1976, Candice Ruppelt and Linda Aanonsen, biology students at Edgewood College in Madison, raised the ninety-two dollars they needed to build an 8' × 12' wooden world map in the main barn. A color photo of each crane species with an inset map showing its range in detail was placed in the proper world region. Their map became the starting point for all the tours.

Also in 1976, members received the first "Crane of the Year" 8" × 10" color photo courtesy of Danny Weaver and his staff at

Agri-graphics, Ltd., in Cary, Illinois. Agri-graphics specialized in livestock photography, but Danny met George in the mid-1970s, got interested in cranes, and the next thing ICF knew, it had a premium to offer the regular members. Danny went on to produce prints for exhibits in Moscow and at India's Keoladeo National Park.

The Crane Foundation didn't only take contributions of labor, talent, intellect, and money. Occasionally someone showed up because of what ICF had to offer and then ended up donating their services. A case in pont was an unsuspecting, soft-spoken, thirtyish artist working on a commissioned painting in Michigan who needed a live Sandhill Crane model. On a sticky summer day in 1976 the artist drove her old pickup truck across Michigan, north through Chicago, and on to Wisconsin. She had decided to visit ICF on the advice of Lawrence Walkinshaw, author of the landmark *Cranes of the World*. After a long day's drive the artist arrived in Baraboo, headed straight for the foundation, and asked to see whoever was in charge. It wasn't the first time Diane Pierce had met George Archibald.

Nearly eight years before, Diane had been at Cornell for a small show of her work. A couple of friends in the graduate school gave her a tour of the laboratory of ornithology and then insisted she meet their friend George and see his cranes.

"So we walked down to the cranium, or whatever it was called, and there was George up on the roof issuing forth crane calls. I enjoyed this tremendously. It was obviously a behavioral approach that was innovative."

Now, eight years later, George emerged from the foundation's nonbreeder field to greet Diane. He led her through the steel gate and into the pasture, showed her a good place to sit, and left. The cranes promptly untied Diane's shoelaces and stole her pencils. When George saw her sketches, he suggested they visit the incubator room.

"George thought maybe I could paint the youngsters when they had dried off and got a little firmness in their rubbery legs at about four days of age. His idea was that I would paint them at four days, four months, and four years and create a book. Owen would also contribute paintings.

"I'd put the chicks in a little terrarium with a heat lamp, a water bowl, and a red dowel. Often I'd be laying on the floor to get down to the level of the chicks, trying to capture them exactly. It was arduous."

For the next five years Diane visited ICF regularly to work on her watercolors of the young chicks. Some of her pencil illustrations adorned stationery that ICF sold to raise money.

Almost everything that needed to be done during the first six years was accomplished by volunteers, most of whom, it seemed, stayed in the White House. Motels were not a realistic option. Students were the bulk of the transient volunteer work force, and many came and went throughout the year. Ron didn't live in Baraboo full-time yet, so it was no problem to let his home be a staging area for crane people. Diane relied on the White House for lodging, and that's how she met Ron.

"He loved cooking. He liked to bring everyone together and a meal was one way to do it. There were quite a few wonderful meals around the dining-room table. I'll never forget one pie with vanilla wafers all around the edge and this beautiful creamy filling. He liked being a good host."

Helen Malzacher also has good memories of Ron's hospitality and recalls, "Ron would always say that he never knew when he woke up on Saturday or Sunday morning how many people would come down for breakfast." Once there were nearly thirty people in the house. Mealtime was a real challenge. Helen often brought food to last a week, but it never made it past Friday night's supper. The deal when Ron cooked, using just about every pot and utensil available, was that his customers had to clean up. So many people did dishes at the White House that he had to label the cabinets so everything could be found again.

George often showed his slides after dinner, much to the chagrin of regular White House visitors. He usually showed too many, and it was always the same show (he hadn't been that many places yet). With so many people coming and going throughout the year at the White House and the lights always dimmed for the show, George probably thought he had a new audience each time.

George's slide shows aside, the White House was a stimulating environment. People were often returning from or heading off to some exotic corner of the world. Students were full of hope and excitement, brimming with ideas. In the guest book that Ron set out are the words of friends from around the world and just down the road.

Owen Gromme with Tex. *Photo courtesy of International Crane Foundation.*

"It was interesting" is Diane's understated summation of that era. "You never knew who might come walking in but you'd get acquainted. Ron always made it feel like home. There was even a piano to play."

You didn't have to be a crane person to work at ICF or live in the White House. An open mind and a willing spirit were the only requirements. Kiogi Emali could attest to that. He was a gardener from Japan who wanted to visit the United States and test the market for his specialty in bonsai and miniature gardens. He obtained a visa contingent upon employment, which he found at a dairy farm. Ron learned about Kiogi, discovered he was pretty miserable with the cows, and convinced the farmer to let Kiogi come to ICF. Kiogi lived in the White House, helped take care of the cranes, and Ron taught him English.

ICF was a great equalizer. Everyone came with one purpose, to help the cranes. No one shied from the hard work, though you might not know that if you witnessed a dozen able-bodied people about to embark on a day of physical labor begging rides to the foundation a few hundred feet away.

Perhaps George's best-known rallying cry was, "Sure, why not?" It was his response to any suggestion, idea, or plan that had even the remotest possibility of succeeding. Since some of the schemes actually worked, who could argue? After all, there was an International Crane Foundation, wasn't there?

One plan that George hatched seemed as futuristic in the early 1970s as the Crane Foundation itself. He wanted to make a prairie on the Sauey farm in the ten-acre cornfield on the hillside. It was Ron's turn to say, "Sure, why not?" At that time only biologists talked about habitats and ecosystems. Ecology was a brand-new science. It had been only a few years since the first Earth Day. And George and Ron wanted not just a prairie but also a forest and marsh area for the interpretive program. They wanted "the ICF visitor to end his tour by understanding that for the survival of the world's cranes, large expanses of open habitats are required—not chain-link [fence] and turkey pellets."

Allan Anderson, a graduate student in landscape architecture from the University of Wisconsin, became the first prairie person at the Crane Foundation. In September 1973, Allan began analyzing the site, collecting seeds from prairie plants, and planning the restoration. The prairie project brought a whole new group of people into ICF's sphere: the garden clubs. Plant people learned about cranes while bird people learned the difference between forbs and grasses. The second prairie person was Charlie Luthin. In 1977, he and other volunteers planted the first one-quarter acre with seeds they collected from eight grass species and thirty-eight forbs, or prairie flowers.

But there were still some tasks for which people actually had to be hired and compensated. The building of the breeding unit was one. The second big job was erecting a ten-foot steel-mesh fence around the eight-acre horse pasture to provide an area for immature and unmated cranes. Norman Sauey wasn't going to pay for this. Ron and George had to raise the money themselves. The cost: $32,725.00. It was their first big fund-raising effort. They approached various foundations through the administrators that represented them. Sometimes they received an introduction through a mutual friend. Sometimes it was a cold call. Each time they patiently explained who they were, what they were doing, and why the cranes of the world needed help.

The first letters went out in 1974 just as spring came to the bluffs. By July, George had secured a pledge of ten thousand dollars contingent upon ICF raising the rest of the money. So they planted a hedge (courtesy of the Jung Seed Company, which had already donated hundreds of trees and shrubs) to hide the fence they knew they were going to build. But months later, with the trees ablaze in fall colors, George out of the country doing fieldwork, and the rest of the money nowhere in sight, Ron inquired if perhaps, just maybe, they could use the ten thousand dollars for an education center? Finally, when the snow slowed down everything in Wisconsin except Ron's letter-writing campaign, the remaining funds were secured. The fence went up in spring 1975.

The effort and persistence George and Ron needed to raise the thirty-two thousand dollars was trivial, however, compared to the planning, precision timing, and Herculean effort needed to pull off the Great Lasagna Luncheon.

The search for corporate funding had been relentless. Finally some people actually accepted an invitation to visit the Crane Foundation—sixty people. Naturally Ron and George, being gracious hosts, decided to offer them lunch following their tour. Then they broke the news to their unflappable volunteers. Lunch for sixty when ICF didn't even have a picnic table for the volunteers!

One month before "The Day," the work crew gathered at Herb and Helen's house in Madison. They decided it wouldn't rain that day and they could set up the tables outside. The vote for a simple menu featuring lasagna was unanimous. During the next several hours they made gallons of tomato sauce and cooked several pounds of noodles. Everything was put in the freezer until The Day, when Herb and Helen transferred the entire operation to Claire Sauey's kitchen.

While Ron and George showed off their modest Crane Foundation, the kitchen crew began assembling the lasagna and put the first pans in the ovens. Spotters monitoring the tour's progress ran back to the house saying, "They're coming up to the corner." The cooks groaned and assembled more lasagna. "They're going around the corner." Lasagna was flying in and out of the two struggling ovens. "They're at the top of the hill." In a panic and powered by a surge of adrenalin, the crew readied the next pans. "They're here!" Claire sprung into action as only a mother can. She opened the trunk of her Cadillac, loaded all the lasagna, and sped off (carefully) to the foundation next door.

The Day probably wasn't the fund-raising presentation the executives expected, but it was pure ICF. And it was a success. The Crane Foundation is still receiving support from guests of The Day.

Every dollar that came in was of vital importance, and sometimes a dollar is all that came in. Four membership categories were offered beginning in 1974: Life, $1,000; Supporter, $500; Associate, $100; Friend, $10; Student, $1. A few newspaper and magazine articles quietly spread the word of the crane place on the hill above Baraboo. Individual memberships began to trickle in. Donations also came from a sixth-grade class at a Racine, Wisconsin, elementary school. A junior high school in Hillside, Illinois, collected enough money for a print of "Sacred Cranes over Hokkaido." The Washington high school in Germantown, Wisconsin, raised $1,000 for its own life membership.

Ron and George continued their solicitation of corporate support. On a typical day letters were sent to an executive of Wisconsin Power and Light, the owner of a furniture store in Baraboo, and the chairman of the board of a steel-casting company in Milwaukee.

Every donation, be it $5 or $500, received a thank-you letter from George or Ron. They weren't identical "thank you for your tax-deductible donation" letters. They were informal, chatty, newsy letters that talked about everything from how the weather affected the birds to the latest research plans. And if Ron or George wasn't around, whoever was running the office kept up the tradition.

Though tours of the foundation were offered by appointment, frequently people drove up the hill just out of curiosity. If someone had time (and someone always made time) the visitors received a tour. Every tour finished in the lounge, where Owen Gromme's huge canvas "Salute to the Dawn" graced the fireplace. No one got out of that lounge without a membership form. Many people who joined ICF those first few years became sort of "off-grounds" volunteers. They returned home and told their friends and organizations about ICF, arranged for George and Ron to give slide presentations, and encouraged others to support the Crane Foundation.

These people provided more than a financial network. Friendships were forged that would last a lifetime. Peg (Loomis) Ridgely from the Madison Audubon Society drove up one day with a friend, and George spent the afternoon showing them around. From then on Madison Audubon was another source for public programs and volunteers. And Peg found a birding companion in Ron. Herb and Helen's home usually had an ICFer or two staying over, and they made a lot of runs to the airport to pick people up or see them off. Gladys and Gerald Scott brought their friends and family to ICF. Gerald even gave tours. Gladys always had room at her dinner table for hungry volunteers and guests. Owen and Anne Gromme provided a much-needed haven for Ron and George, who went to their home for a square meal, encouragement, and advice. The Gromme's told their friends about ICF. They introduced Ron and George to many of their associates. Two of them were John and Mary Wickem, who later served on the board of directors. Twenty years later Mary is still board president. The Wickems provided solid administrative and financial advice. They became close to ICF and Ron and George yet remained objective and able to make the hard decisions often necessary to keep a nonprofit organization from going under.

Ron and George were consumed with construction, obtaining cranes, and raising money. In addition, Ron still had his graduate studies and fieldwork in India and George was planning a trip to South Korea. Even so, there was another Crane Foundation project that had to be developed. They needed a newsletter that would keep the members informed about ICF events such as hatchings of rare cranes and crane conservation around the world.

A four-page quarterly, *The Brolga Bugle*, debuted in the fall of 1974. Ron was the editor. His assistant on that premier issue was John Seaberg, a Baraboo high school student. The original *Bugle* had five sections. "Making Tracks" was a progress report on ICF's development. "Milestones" was a breeding report for ICF and zoos and collections around the world. Because Ron wanted to educate as well as report, "Cranes in Review" listed books and articles about crane research and wetland conservation. The "Feature" was an article about anything pertaining to cranes. It might be George or Ron telling about their work with the wild cranes or Ron's piece about cranes in art. Last, but most certainly not least, "Contributions" listed people, companies, and foundations that had donated money, labor, and materials during the previous three months.

For the first six years Ron received editorial assistance from Katherine "Tockie" Green, a friend of the Grommes from nearby Briggsville. Tockie began her volunteer service with ICF in 1973, when she was seventy-one years old. Visiting Tockie for a proof-reading session was a treat. Her rural home was a wildlife refuge officially recognized by all the animals in the area. Sandhill Cranes nested on a small marsh behind her barn.

The Brolga Bugle was printed in town. Even Ron joked later about the tiny print size, which he claimed some members dubbed "Excedrin Headache #234." That was changed in 1985 when a grant from Clairson International (headquartered in Florida, the world's largest manufacturer of vinyl-coated steel-rod storage products, and a Sauey family company) enabled ICF to use color and expand the newsletter to eight pages. In that inaugural color issue, Ron recalled the newsletter's name change in 1982 from *The Brolga Bugle* to *The ICF Bugle*. The change was prompted when he was "told of a college journalism instructor who used the name of our humble newsletter as a classic example of what NOT to name a newsletter. 'Unfamiliar name,' the august professor said. 'No indication of the newsletter's subject . . . too vague, too foreign, too forgettable.' "

But the young *Bugle* served its purpose admirably. It was a window through which the members watched the International Crane Foundation grow. They were told when cranes arrived at ICF, where they were going to live, and who would be their mate or next-door neighbor. They learned the "house name" of each bird (those weren't White-naped Cranes in pen J-3, they were Casey and Granny). The breeding history of every crane and whether the females had ever laid eggs was passed on to the members as it would be to a gathering of scientists.

Members were the first to learn of rare hatchings. Most had their first introduction to Siberian, Red-crowned, Blue, Wattled, and the rest of the world's cranes through *The Bugle*. Readers learned of dreams and hopes for the foundation. They met the board members who would help shape ICF's future. And they were invited to contribute in some very unusual ways.

The "Wish List" appeared on the back page of *The Bugle* for a number of years. It was an unabashed plea to members for items ranging from the mundane to the bizarre that were essential for the daily activities of the ICF staff. For the birds they asked for beak clippers, water buckets, calipers to measure eggs, a dehumidifier for the incubator room, and surgical scissors. In the office they asked for file cabinets, a typing table, and a paper cutter. The prairie people needed canvas seed-collecting bags and trays for growing prairie plant seedlings. That meant the education department needed magnifying glasses and hand lenses so visitors could look at the prairie flowers and binoculars so they could birdwatch on their tour. They even asked for a world atlas and dictionaries: German-English, Japanese-English, and Russian-English. The aviculture staff requested a washer and dryer to launder their work clothes on the property and semen extender (for the cranes). They also needed a phase-contrast microscope for studying crane semen. It cost $2,500. ICF received $1,500 from World Wildlife Fund–U.S. toward its purchase and appealed to the members for the rest. They didn't ask for the remaining $1,000. They asked for $10, $20, $50, or whatever a member was able to donate. Anybody who made a contribution was promised a look at crane semen magnified two thousand times.

George, Barbara Brownsmith, and Tsuru. *Photo courtesy of International Crane Foundation.*

Undoubtedly, premiums like an intimate view of crane semen did much to increase the membership. In 1975, at the end of their first membership year, ICF boasted 406 of the faithful: 279 from Wisconsin, 28 from Illinois (but that included most of Ron's relatives on his mother's side), 17 from Japan, and the rest from other states, provinces, and foreign countries. Six years later there were more than 1,500 members.

On the outside everything seemed to be proceeding as well as could be expected. By 1976 the International Crane Foundation had the most complete collection of cranes in the world. An average of two hundred people joined the foundation each year. A few corporations became interested in ICF and supplied much-needed financial transfusions when the picture got bleak. But for the people on the inside there was no time to relax. For everyone involved it was the first time they had created and administered a nonprofit organization. Since ICF was the only place in the world just for cranes and was attempting research, breeding, and conservation on a scale never before seen, they could look to other institutions for advice only on a limited basis.

Perhaps ICF's greatest good fortune was the quality of the people who volunteered in the early years. ICF's very existence depended on these people. All the money in the world to buy crane food and water buckets doesn't do any good if there is no one to feed and water the birds, clean their pens, do artificial insemination, collect the eggs, and raise the chicks. Students worked on their research without the benefit of stipends. Their published papers and graduate degrees helped establish ICF's reputation as a research facility. When Ron and George were busy with overseas projects, Forrest Hartmann remained behind to keep an eye on the budget (such as it was) and Milly Zantow, a volunteer administrator who arrived in 1975, had to contend with all the office work and sometimes even take care of the cranes.

Milly met George in 1973 when she called ICF and asked if someone would give a program to the Federated Women's Club, of which she was program chair. Ron had returned to Cornell but George said, "Sure." When Milly mentioned that dinner was included he assured her he wouldn't miss it for anything. All during dinner George questioned Milly about volunteering at ICF. She said thanks but no. She had a young son, she lived on a farm, her husband preferred that she not get a job, and it just wouldn't work out.

But Milly did agree to type George's dissertation, a service she provided to graduate students when she lived near the University of California. By the time George brought his thesis out to her farm, Milly and her husband, Woody, had bought a house in Sauk City. "I'm too busy moving. I can't do it now." Later George showed up at her new home and said, "You didn't think you'd get away just by moving, did you?" It was spring 1974. One year later Milly finished typing. George had written extensive sections in longhand. There were notes in the margins and arrows leading everywhere. Shortly after that, Milly agreed to serve as volunteer administrator. She had to learn which crane was which and how to feed it, organize the books to keep better records of donations, correspond with government agencies and learn to swim through the red tape in search of endangered species permits, and decide how much to pay each creditor every month on bills they couldn't pay in full.

Milly's gentle voice and soft brown curls that framed her face gave no hint of the steel will and determination that lay within. But she came by it naturally. Her father homesteaded in Oklahoma when the federal government opened up Cherokee lands to white settlers and served on the constitution committee when Oklahoma became a state. Milly lived there for the first eighteen years of her life, until 1941, when she went to Virginia to care for an ailing sister. Her family learned to make ends meet because they had to.

Milly drew on everything in her background to get her through her three-year tenure at ICF. Her Oklahoma farm days taught her to tough things out and how to work around animals. Her work in a military hospital gave her a heightened awareness about sanitation and transmission of disease. Most of all, her family supported her through the twelve-hour days and the seven-day weeks. *Bugles* were often strewn across her living-room floor while her family helped sort them by zip code. Forrest recalls Milly as a woman "who wasn't afraid to get her hands dirty; who added maturity to the organization and probably wasn't always appreciated." Milly could pick up the slack and patch up a hole. If she saw something that had to be done, she simply did it and went on. Perhaps that's why her contributions weren't always noticed.

Although Forrest was only a phone call away if Milly needed him, Howard Ahrensmeyer was always on site. "If anything was wrong or out of place, he'd come in and we'd talk about it. He could fix anything. If it hadn't been for him, it would have been a much harder job for me." And, with Ron and George gone so much of the time, much lonelier.

During the winter of 1974–75, Ron conducted his first observations of the Siberian Crane in India accompanied by Paul Spitzer, also from Cornell. At the Keoladeo Ghana Wildlife Sanctuary near Bharatpur in northern India, they found the entire winter population of Siberian Cranes in India—sixty-four birds. Ron knew from communications with Dr. Vladimir Flint of the Soviet Union that a second flock of about three hundred cranes nested on the tundra marshes of Yakutia in northeastern Siberia. But where did the India birds breed each summer? Where did the Yakutia birds flock in winter? China, most likely, but no one knew where. How much longer could the Keoladeo birds survive their treacherous migration route through Iran and Afghanistan?

Meanwhile, George joined South Korean ornithologist Dr. Kim Hom Kyu at the Han River just south of its confluence with the Imjim on the northwest coast, near the Demilitarized Zone (DMZ) between North and South Korea. In 1973, ICF had helped Dr. Kim secure funds from the New York Zoological Society for a survey of wintering cranes. He determined that the Han River was a major winter roost and feeding area for fifteen hundred White-naped Cranes that nested in China and the Soviet Union and wintered in Japan and Korea. The area was going to be altered by agricultural development. George, Dr. Kim, and Dr. Won Pyong-oh, with the help of a media blitz on radio and television, persuaded the South Korean government to set aside a ten-kilometer stretch of the Han River as a natural monument, protected from industrial and agricultural development.

George's next stop was the DMZ. Just before he arrived, the South Koreans discovered a tunnel from the north, and the region was under even more tension than usual. Armed with his United Nations permit, George was able to enter the DMZ, where he confirmed the presence of several Red-crowned Cranes at the Bridge of No Return. The idea of a feeding station began to take shape in George's mind, and one morning he scattered one hundred pounds of rice on a field south of the bridge. Two cranes flew in to feed. The next day there were eight, and thirty-five came on the third day.

Diplomats at the UN were seeking a way to diffuse the latest tensions between North and South Korea, and George found himself in the right place at the right time. At a meeting at Panmunjom, representatives from North and South Korea agreed to participate in a cooperative feeding station for the Red-crowned Cranes. The North Koreans even sent photographers to take pictures of the birds.

While Ron and George were overseas that season, graduate student John Baldwin from the University of Wisconsin took care of the birds. Forrest had to contend with ICF's bills by himself. Ron and George came home in the spring, but as the winter of 1975–76 approached, they again prepared for their field seasons. With Milly now in the office, the Crane Foundation would be run by four people from three corners of the world. George's first base of operations that winter was Iran. Assisted by the Iranians, George planned to trap, wing-tag, and release Common Cranes. The birds would then be tracked during migration and located on their breeding grounds in Siberia. The idea was to identify successful breeding pairs and use them to cross-foster Siberian Cranes much like the plan about to get under way for the Whooping Crane in the United States. George also planned to visit the Keoladeo Ghana Sanctuary in India and check out Siberian Crane migration roosts in Afghanistan.

Ron was unable to secure a visa and didn't go back to India until late winter of 1976. That winter Eddie Soloway and Jim Bruskewitz took care of the birds. George remained a presence at ICF despite being halfway around the world. He showed up several times a week in the mailbox with a new list of questions, orders, and concerns. From Iran he sent reminders to Milly to include membership-renewal envelopes in the next *Bugle* and worried about whether any money was coming in. He asked if the visual barriers were installed yet in the Hooded Crane pens. With his mind in overdrive he sent instructions for shifting cranes to different pens and modifying latches on doors. He became frustrated when he received a letter indicating that something contrary to his instructions had been done. Then he remembered that mail took a whole month to reach him. Sometimes it was just a case of letters crossing somewhere over the oceans of the world. It was also a bit difficult for George to accept that with a board of directors in place, even if it was only Ron, Forrest, and himself, there were now certain administrative protocols that had to be respected.

It was just as frustrating for the people in Baraboo. Finances were still a persistent worry. Milly often used her own money to pay bills and wasn't always able to reimburse herself. She figured that was easier than contacting her two fund-raisers in India and Iran. Jim and Eddie kept a close watch on the birds, but then Jim had to leave. Eddie was great when he was there, but Eddie was a bookworm— when he ran out of books he was compelled to go to the Madison library for a couple days and lay in a new supply, and then Milly had to feed and water the birds. Despite the inconvenience, Milly enjoyed Eddie's company and was delighted when he was around.

From his remote outposts, George thrived on news from Baraboo. While it took a month for letters to reach him, phone calls were even more of an ordeal. In Iran he had to make a line reservation four days in advance and still wait several hours for his call to go through. When

Milly wrote that ICF had received a major donation, George jokingly wrote back, "Why don't you give yourself a better salary? Say, $3.00 an hour. Can the budget take it?" (When she finally did get a paycheck, she used it to buy a freezer for the foundation.)

George's letters weren't always full of directives. He also wrote about his field experiences. Much of the work was physically taxing. Some of his field assistants in Iran had no experience and little enthusiasm. Lack of experience never bothered George; a dearth of enthusiasm drove him nuts. But there were respites from the work. On November 21 he wrote from Iran of leaving the "crowds and pollution of Tehran behind to spend two wonderful days in Kavir National Park, a desert preserve." He told about his camp at a 350-year-old brick fortress once used by camel trains and described the peace of the desert, songbirds migrating from northern Asia, desert sheep, and sand grouse. Then he added, "I'm worrying that you may be having problems and I am selfishly escaping to this paradise." In that same letter he wrote, "Please remind Eddie and Jim to water and turn my plants every second day."

The atmosphere at the Crane Foundation during this period was not something Ron was completely comfortable with. After several years, the hand-to-mouth existence was beginning to wear on him. He liked organization and order in his life. At times ICF seemed anything but organized and orderly. With Milly in the office and Jim and Eddy managing the birds, Ron scheduled some traveling in the United States. When he was in Baraboo, he often did his paperwork at home. George's visit to India in February 1976, while Ron was still without a visa, was not the happiest circumstance.

Until Ron could get back into the field, though, the "International" part of the Crane Foundation was pursued by George. After India, he embarked on a flurry of travel that took him to Afghanistan for 2 weeks; Moscow for a few days, where he met with Dr. Flint and made plans to collect wild Siberian Crane eggs and take them back to Baraboo (Ron had initiated the correspondence with Flint); then back to Afghanistan before returning to Iran in April.

During his travels, George sent two important communications to ICF. On March 23, he sent Milly a telegram with an urgent request that she get a new visa approved for him and send it to the American embassy in London. George, a Canadian citizen, had let his papers expire, and he couldn't get back into the United States.

Seven days later the United States Department of State sent a telegram to the London embassy confirming George's visa had been approved. The approving government official was Secretary of State Henry Kissinger. The second piece of correspondence was a letter dated April 18:

"I planted 12 tulips in the begonia bed under the eaves of the lounge. Are they up?"

Eventually, George returned to Baraboo. The Wednesday night board meetings started up again. Some observers of ICF saw that Ron and George had very different personalities. Ron was methodical, quiet, and not interested in the limelight. He sought stability. Ron dealt with the media, but he didn't seek it out. George was, by all accounts, more flamboyant. There was no end to his ideas and plans. He wouldn't let the political climate deter him from encouraging cooperation among North and South Korea, China, Japan, the USSR, India, and a host of other countries. He was a salesman, and he sold ICF to prospective financial supporters. Ron and George's different styles didn't cancel each other, they balanced each other. ICF needed a dreamer. And it also needed stability.

Each of them not only recognized how he was different from the other but was also aware of how he related to ICF and how he affected the people around him. From the field George took a break from his spate of directions and admonishments and wrote to Milly, "I am an extremely independent-minded person, even as a child. And now at ICF I find it very difficult to accept constraints although I know I must. I know that the diversity of characters at ICF leads in the long run to stability although it practically kills us in the process, trying to accommodate each other and coming through as friends."

In the fall of 1976, it was Ron's turn to escape into the field, and he returned to Keoladeo. When he wasn't collecting data he was giving slide programs, birding with members of the Bombay Natural History Society, joining the maharajah for tea at Bharatpur, and improving his Indian cooking. After running into some acquaintances from Milwaukee, he declared that "either it's a small world or a large International Crane Foundation."

While Ron waited patiently for the wintering Siberian Cranes to arrive, he watched "flock after flock of Greylag Geese winging their way here" and realized it meant the cranes weren't far behind. In the meantime there were the wild Sarus Cranes and their young. He noted the adults had "a head as bright as a ruby and legs a brilliant vivacious pink, not like captive specimens." He kept Milly up-to-date on his field notes. Four Siberians on November 15. Nineteen the next day.

Ron, too, sent Milly a letter from the field that sought to explain how he felt about his role at ICF:

"Continual change and constant uncertainty cause bewilderment and unhappiness. That's why I don't stay around the barns at ICF. I'd go mad. When I think of how I so often left you alone there and sneaked back to the peace and tranquility of my numerous hideaways, I wonder how it is you still call me a friend."

But friends they remained. Even in a financially secure, well-established company there are going to be a few rough spots, and ICF was brand-new, with a shoestring budget. Everyone had to grow into their roles. They had to learn both to assume and delegate responsibility.

As ICF matured, the need for formal public programs became evident. So did the need for a permanent staff. Volunteers couldn't run the foundation forever. Captive management of cranes was becoming more sophisticated. Media requests for information increased with the successes of each breeding season and each researcher's tantalizing tales of adventures in foreign lands. Volunteers would always have a place at ICF because there wasn't enough money to hire a staff large enough to do all the work. But by the late 1970s it was time to begin the transition from a volunteer work force to a paid staff assisted by volunteers. ICF entered a new phase in its development.

The growth pattern that the Crane Foundation experienced is common to all nonprofit institutions. Many organizations collapse after the first five years. Changing financial needs and evolving personnel responsibilities can overwhelm the small group of friends who established the organization with nothing more than dedication to a cause. People who ably fill certain niches in the beginning, who willingly do whatever tasks are asked of them and even ones that aren't, who do the work of three because they are the only person in the office or on the water truck when there should be three, can find it difficult to accept a new role when the grass-roots backyard project becomes a business. As more people get involved in day-to-day operations, these individuals have fewer responsibilities. Sometimes it's tough to let go. And sometimes the people in charge, Ron and George in this case, have to make tough decisions. The transition was as difficult for them as it was for the people who were part of the process.

Since George was responsible for taking care of the cranes, it fell to him to hire the first full-time aviculturists. He needed two. He went through several. The passage of time has given him perspective on that troubled era:

"In the early days, when anyone showed up and was willing to work and willing to help us, I was willing to work with them, no matter who they were or what their background. I always seemed to be able to find something for them to do. I developed a philosophy that everything will work out and that everyone has something to contribute. When it came time to hire people for positions at the Crane Foundation, I had the same philosophy. Very naive. So when we advertised for the jobs, I thought everyone who interviewed would work out, and I never thought very carefully about who I hired. That was a big mistake. I should have been much more selective and had job definitions developed better. Because things weren't clear, there were a lot of misunderstandings.

"I came to realize that as an administrator, one of the most important things you do is hire people. I learned to hire people that are smarter than me but that I can trust. I think the most important characteristic in any person is their integrity. I [now] try to figure out who I can work with before I hire them rather than being casual about it, thinking that magically everything is going to work out.

"So it was my fault that we had those problems during the late 1970s. I felt very badly. It was one of the hardest things I did, letting some of those people go. Of course, the relationships have never been reestablished."

Eventually the aviculturist situation settled down. Slowly the other departments—administration, education, and field ecology—moved into the new era as well.

Joan Fordham became the new administrator in 1979. A Baraboo resident, Joan worked in the office with Milly for several months prior to Milly's resignation, so she was well prepared for her new assignment. Milly saw the new direction that ICF was taking and realized her time had ended. She had given as much as she could. It was time to move on. Joan helped guide ICF for the next ten years through a radical period of growth and increasing stature and sophistication.

DiANE Pierce

FIVE

No Business like the Crane Business

One of the earliest crane management lessons learned at the Crane Foundation is that in winter you must attach the water heater to a brick before placing it in the bucket or else the crane will spend the afternoon tossing it around his or her stall. A crane's natural curiosity makes it pretty adept at identifying a situation ripe for mischief. If there's a loose screw one minute, there won't be any screw the next. Also, keep an eye on snowdrifts. After one particularly heavy snowfall, gusty winds built drifts nearly ten feet high against the perimeter fence of the nonbreeder field. Timely intervention by the staff prevented an international parade of Gruidae from escaping to the Wisconsin Dells.

Animals in captivity often present behavioral displays no field biologist could ever imagine. Sometimes the action is an extension of the animal's natural behavior—cranes toss sticks in the air when they dance, so why shouldn't they throw an expensive water heater into the stratosphere? Artificial living arrangements may dramatically exaggerate one particular component of an animal's behavioral repertoire. Wild cranes vigorously defend vast territories, sometimes several square miles, in which they nest and rear their young. Putting a crane or pair of cranes into a thirty-six-hundred-square-foot pen just makes it easier for them to patrol the borders. Neighboring cranes and often people are met with a clamorous unison call. If that doesn't make you back off, if you insist on giving the bird fresh food and water, expect a series of threat postures including ruffle-preen, drop-wing, and (your final warning) the crouch threat, in which the crane drops to the ground in front of you before springing up into an all-out charge. Human caretakers are only exposed to this aggressiveness for one or two brief periods each day. But cranes in adjoining pens must contend with their neighbors constantly because, naturally, cranes don't make their point in fifteen minutes and give it a rest. As long as the stimulus remains, that being the next-door neighbor, the aggressive displays continue.

Canvas stretched across each fence seemed an easy, economical way to provide visual barriers between the cranes. But they could still hear each other, and every tiny gap of exposed fence revealed the feet or eyeballs of a pacing crane. The more determined of the birds continued their backyard disputes. In no time the canvas was ripped and frayed from jabbing bills and kicks from sharp-clawed feet. So ICF collected used Christmas trees from the townspeople and local schools. The trees were wired securely to the fences on both sides. The cranes still paced and vociferously defended their territories, but the impenetrable "forest" held strong.

Beyond the challenge of keeping the cranes comfortable in their enclosures and safe from themselves was the difficulty of breeding them. The work of pioneer crane researchers provided a foundation that ICF built upon. One of the earliest captive breeding programs was initiated after World War II by Dr. Tadamichi Koga, then director of Tokyo's Ueno Zoo. His motivations were practical as well scientific: the endangered Red-crowned and White-naped Cranes could no longer be imported from mainland Asia due to the political climate. If the Ueno Zoo wished to continue to display the species, the captive birds currently in the collection would have to reproduce. Dr. Koga and his colleagues observed that both wild and captive cranes will lay a second clutch of eggs if the first one is destroyed or fails to hatch. They also learned that a female crane will continue to lay as long as she is in breeding condition if the eggs are removed from the nest. Neither of these actions was unheard of in birds. Ducks and chickens are well known as indeterminate layers. Many passerine birds such as robins, cardinals, sparrows, jays, and the like, produce two clutches a season when weather and food conditions are favorable or if their first clutch fails. But now this behavior was confirmed in cranes. By increasing egg production among their captive cranes, Dr. Koga and his staff could work on improving artificial incubation techniques and refine the process of hand-rearing the chicks.

In the United States in the early 1960s, a group of people at the Patuxent Wildlife Research Center led by Dr. Ray Erickson was studying captive breeding of Greater Sandhill Cranes. The plan was to use that knowledge in a program for endangered Mississippi Sandhills and Whooping Cranes and ultimately return the offspring of those rare species to the wild. After examining the population dynamics of the endangered Whooping Crane, which had been studied intensely since conservation efforts began on its behalf in the early 1940s, Erickson concluded that taking one egg from a two-egg nest would cause little, if any, adverse effect on the Whooping Crane flock's reproductive success—cranes rarely raise two chicks to fledging. A cooperative agreement between the United States Fish & Wildlife Service and the Canadian Wildlife Service (the birds nest in Canada) allowed Erickson to test his theory, which subsequently proved correct. For five years the Patuxent crew studied egg removal from nests, transport of eggs, artificial incubation, hatching, egg disinfection, and handling methods.

In 1965, Congress passed legislation establishing the Endangered Species Wildlife Research Program at Patuxent. With the additional funding the biologists were able to develop increasingly sophisticated protocols for managing captive cranes. Dr. George Gee of Patuxent performed the first studies on cryogenic preservation of crane semen. Frozen semen had been used for years in the cattle industry, but crane semen was much more delicate. Freezing it and preserving it with liquid nitrogen might someday enable several institutions to establish a cooperative captive breeding program without subjecting their cranes to the stress of shipping crates and cross-country airplane rides.

Another member of the Patuxent team was ethologist Dr. Cameron (Cam) Kepler. He studied Whooping Cranes that hatched from wild eggs collected in Canada. When Cam first arrived at Patuxent, all of the Whoopers were living in one large enclosure. Cam observed the birds and noticed that they seemed to sort themselves out in a hierarchy. Based on their behavior, Cam guessed who was male and who was female and put each pair into its own pen. He also used a vocalization to ferret out the sexual identity of each bird. It was a technique he learned from a young Ph.D. student from Cornell who was studying Patuxent's cranes. That the unison call is a sexually specific vocalization was not yet widely accepted by the scientific community, but an enthusiastic George Archibald had confidence in his data. So did Cam Kepler. Cam used the unison call to back up his behavioral analysis. He and George were vindicated whenever a suspected female laid an egg. If the egg was fertile or copulation was observed, all doubt was removed as to the other bird's identity.

That artificial insemination (AI) would be included in any captive management plans at ICF was assumed from the start because just having male and female cranes doesn't guarantee reproductive success. The Crane Foundation's AI program was based on George Gee's work at Patuxent. He was the first to successfully artificially inseminate cranes. Just how, you may ask, does one retrieve the semen from Bird A and get it to its proper destination in Bird B? George explained the process in a 1974 article for *International Zoo Yearbook* that bears some resemblance to how it was explained to me when I was drafted onto the AI team.

First you have to catch the crane. Understandably, most birds object. Very few are willing volunteers like Lulu and Tex. It is desirable that the crane become accustomed to being handled so that it will relax, not feel too threatened, and be able to perform the necessary function. Protocol called for the birds to be put through the paces of AI at least one month before any eggs could be realistically expected. This means that when we got to Killer's pen, we sent George in first. After things quieted down, we opened the door and hoped it was man that had subdued bird.

In his article George states that the apprehended bird "should be held in a standing position between the collector's legs, bird facing into the corner, collector facing the opposite direction." That was my job. He didn't call me a collector. I was the stroker because my task was to "gently but firmly stroke the thighs with a milking action until Response A is observed." You need good hands for this. Response A occurs when the bird relaxes, raises his tail, and stops kicking the stroker.

Now comes the tricky part. An assistant, which we called the tickler, "massages the cloacal area until Response B—slight protrusion of the upper cloacal lip with simultaneous ejaculation of one or two drops of thick milky semen." The alert assistant collects the semen in a shot glass and transfers the fluid to a small needleless syringe. The male crane's participation in the operation is now over. At this point I always handed Killer back to George and left the pen.

Next comes the *really* tricky part. The stroker handles the female in the same manner as the male. The shooter, with help from a third person, will inject the semen directly into the oviduct to ensure the greatest chance for fertilization. A female crane has only a left oviduct as do all female birds. It's a weight-saving evolutionary adaptation for flight. In some cranes the stroking action produces a response that reveals the oviduct. In others the cloacal opening is gently manipulated until the oviduct is visible. It takes at least four hands to do this quickly and with minimal disturbance to the crane. At Patuxent, George Gee determined that maximum fertility occurs when AI is performed every three days during the breeding season.

There are many reasons why AI is necessary: there may be only a few birds of a particular species in captivity and they don't like each other; maybe they like each other but one or both is physically impaired (Lulu and Phil); maybe just being pinioned causes clumsy attempts at natural copulation (more likely to happen with the larger cranes); staff may want to breed specific genetic lines; or you may have a bird that is never going to look twice at anything wearing feathers (Tex, the imprinted Whooping Crane).

And then there is the explanation offered by Dr. Burton A. Russman, father of Shirley Russman, an ICF intern who joined the aviculture staff in 1981 and 1982.

A.I.—Why?

Progeny may come and go
Starting merely with "hello."
The male and female think it's great
To simply, slyly, propagate.

The natural way, we all agree,
Is fun, and more, it's all for free.
To us it's only common sense
To think in terms of future tense.

But cattle, sheep, and avian friends
Sometimes won't go to "bitter ends."
They don't agree that it's a treat.
Perhaps, to them, it's indiscrete!

But Man just can't respect their wishes.
He probes inside their secret fissures.
It seems he cannot tolerate
Just leaving each to his own fate.

So, join the crowd—syringe in hand.
We'll fertilize throughout this land.
And after them—well, wait and see.
You may be next—or even me!

Artificial insemination is not without some risks. After one AI session during which I was the stroker and we inseminated old Granny, a White-naped Crane, George was all the way out of the pen before he realized that I wasn't behind him. As I had started to massage her flanks, Granny stamped her feet repeatedly until she settled down. When she finished, she had a leg down each of my rubber boots. I was stuck. George had to lift her out so I could walk again.

·Artificial insemination does have benefits in addition to helping a sperm complete its assigned mission. Examine the ejaculate under a microscope and you'll know the current breeding condition of the male. Check the width of the opening between the female's pelvic bones and you'll know how close she is to laying the egg. This information can be the difference between life and death for a developing embryo. Lulu became so arthritic she couldn't sit down and incubate. An egg laid on a chilly morning could be quickly rescued by a waiting aviculturist. (Considering Lulu couldn't sit down to lay eggs either, it's amazing she never broke one. Credit the staff members who built up her nest with straw to minimize the drop.)

Artificial insemination played a vital role in ICF's early breeding successes. The first White-naped Crane chicks were products of AI, as were Red-crowned Crane chicks Tancho and Tsuru. But the Hooded Cranes that reproduced in 1976 were left alone to copulate naturally. Their extreme fear at being handled coupled with their diminutive size, about three feet tall, dictated a hands-off policy. However, in this situation, George also looked to Gee and the work at Patuxent to end the nonreproductive status of Hooded Cranes in captivity.

It was Gee who explained to George that breeding pairs of Sandhills at Patuxent responded to an increased day length commencing in February. Since Hooded Cranes breed in extreme northern latitudes, George guessed that they, too, would react positively to such an environmental manipulation. In 1975, George had floodlights installed over the Hooded Crane pens, and the extended photoperiod schedule began on March 1. There were no nests and no eggs during the first year of the experiment. Put in perspective, however, that wasn't surprising. The cranes had only been at ICF for one year, and birds often need a few breeding seasons to adjust to new surroundings. Also, it had been many years since the birds had been exposed to a biologically correct photoperiod. Physiologically, they probably needed more time to get back on track. ICF repeated the experiment in 1976 with the now famous results: Pookie and Sim hatched out in June. The following year, two pairs produced three fertile eggs. Also in 1977, the Bronx Zoo tried the technique on two Hooded Crane pairs and one of them produced fertile eggs.

Other species presented different challenges. What do you do with a crane whose breeding cycle is linked to a rainy season in its native habitat? Such was the case with the Black and Grey Crowned Cranes and the Brolga Cranes. Complicating the situation was the fact that in their homelands their breeding seasons coincide with the United States' winter months. ICF couldn't reverse the seasons in Baraboo, but they could make a rainy season.

Garden hoses and lawn sprinklers do not a monsoon make, but it was enough. The hose and sprinkler system also met two vital criteria: it was inexpensive and easily installed by amateur plumbers Nina Petrovich and Charlie Jahn, the two students working with the Crowned Cranes. Every other day from June through August two pairs of Crowned Cranes were showered for one hour in the early morning, at noon, and in late afternoon. Nina and Charlie observed the birds for one hour after each shower and at the same times on "dry days." Sure enough, courtship and breeding activity increased on rainy days. One pair produced four chicks.

Flushed with the success of the Crowned Crane study, George decided to try "raining" on the Brolgas. Willie and Olga had been paired since 1974, and researchers observed breeding behavior each summer, but nothing ever came of it. The sprinklers were installed in 1977 and initially the birds had the same shower schedule as the Crowned Cranes. Whether it was the cumulative effect of three rainy seasons or the modifications in the shower schedule in 1979 no one will ever know for sure, but that summer Willie and Olga finally produced a chick. Lindsay, their offspring, was named after the student who studied them in 1979.

A bird's behavior and health is influenced not only by external factors such as temperature, photoperiod, humidity, and housing, but also by internal factors, primarily diet. There were plenty of commercial bird feeds for George to choose from, and most would be fine for immature and nonbreeding cranes. But adults that lay eggs require a unique combination of nutrients and a high level of protein to produce strong eggshells and to compensate for the physical stress a bird is subjected to during the breeding season. Egg production is a tremendous strain on a bird's energy resources.

George decided to try the same diet that Kerry Muller, then of the National Zoo in Washington, D.C., had put together for his birds. It was a combination of a commercially produced poultry supplement and "Turkey Chick Starter." Muller gave the grain mix to cranes that had no breeding history, including Blue, Crowned, Sarus, and Hooded Cranes. Each pair laid eggs and most were fertile. That was good enough for George. Many of ICF's adult cranes matched the description of Muller's birds, nonproducing but potential breeders.

Young chicks, however, don't require all that extra protein. Their nutritional needs are different, and often the amount of food they consume must be regulated. In captivity chicks don't get the long hours of strenuous exercise that come with foraging all day in a marsh. So from the moment they hatch the little ones are weighed every day and carefully observed for the debilitating, sometimes fatal effects of overeating: weak legs and deformed joints.

The facilities and equipment used for raising chicks at ICF throughout the 1970s were hardly high-tech. Ron's old pheasant coop was the extent of luxury living for the little pioneers of captive breeding. Newly hatched chicks spent their first couple of weeks on the floor of the incubator room. A long rectangular pen was subdivided into smaller compartments, each with its own suspended heat lamp and furnished with a red water bowl and a red dowel dangling above a red food dish. The concrete floor in each pen was covered by carpet swatches in a riot of oranges, reds, purples, and greens. Paisley was a popular pattern. During the first several days of each chick's life, volunteers sat on bruised kneecaps beside the little pens dipping the red dowel into the water to encourage the chick to drink and then coating it with crushed pellet food and waving it in front of the baby in a pathetic imitation of a parent's bill holding a delectable grasshopper. This continued until the chick showed steady, substantial weight gains, indicating it was eating on its own. Chicks in the incubator room were weighed on a laboratory gram balance scale. Once moved to the Chick House, they were loaded onto an old grocer's scale that measured in pounds and ounces—not very good lab technique, but cheap and available. Over the years ICF staff, students, and volunteers collected data that created an accurate picture of a chick's growth stages in spite of less than ideal conditions and practically no pre-existing data with which to make comparative studies. They learned what a healthy chick of a particular species should weigh upon hatching and how many grams it should lose during the first twenty-four hours as it absorbs its yolk sac. They charted the average daily weight gain of a healthy chick and how many inches the bird grew each week (some species are five feet tall after only four months).

All the chicks needed more exercise than the Chick House pens afforded, so they were taken on walks, runs, and gambols across the expansive lawn. An occasional side trip through the parking lot was usually a group decision by the chicks. The Chick Mamas and Chick Papas (the job titles were George's idea; they exist to this day) mixed generous doses of tender loving care with rigorous adherence to diet and exercise regimens. Much of the data collected appeared in research papers and master's theses authored by students. On site, the information was passed along season by season to each new volunteer. Off site, it traveled a lot farther.

In June 1981, a letter written in Italian arrived from Signor Franco Monaci of Pisa, Italy. Among the collection of exotic birds on his estate was the only pair of Sarus Cranes in Italy. Each year he obtained fertile eggs, the chicks hatched, then developed leg problems and died. Could ICF help him and his birds? Development Coordinator Alice D'Alessio became the coordinator of the rescue effort. The problem seemed to be the chick's diet. Alice and the aviculture staff sent articles containing instructions for hatching and rearing cranes to Signor Monaci. In October ICF received another letter from Italy. Signor Monaci proudly informed ICF of Pippola's hatching that summer, and he added, "she is truly beautiful, and has already reached 60 centimeters." Enclosed was a picture of Pippola with Signor Monaci's caption: "Pippola, little female Sarus Crane, born in Pisa, Italy, with the assistance of Signor Franco Monaci during the month of July, 1981, and following the instructions of ICF. Grateful thanks to Signor Putnam [Mike, head aviculturist] for his learned experience, and to Signora D'Alessio for her courteous interest."

George and Ron determined early on that captive breeding would be just one aspect of the Crane Foundation, but for a while it seemed that nearly all of their limited resources, money, energy, and time were devoted to taking care of the birds. Public programs developed slowly. Volunteer tour guides presented basic information about crane biology and conservation, but beyond that each tour was a little different. Everybody pretty much made up their own script. Anecdotal stories about the birds accounted for much of the material, and the tours had a style unique to those early years—spontaneous, intimate, and casual. When you visited the nonbreeder field you found out who was bullying who. Right after your tour guide explained about crane aggression came the line about the birds' attraction to shiny objects—like your eyeballs. And so many species in one place! Nowhere else in the world could you see the sight now before you. A tour was like a visit to a crane convention where each bird's name tag listed a different hometown and you just couldn't keep up with the introductions.

But by the late 1970s Ron and George were giving increased consideration to the need for public education. They couldn't increase the membership roster without it, and ICF relied almost entirely on membership donations at that time. In 1977 Baraboo native Terry Quale, a former student researcher, was hired to be a public information officer. Of course, she also had to function as secretary, tour guide, aviculturist, driver, "gofer," and good sport. Terry put together a slide show for schoolchildren who couldn't visit the foundation. When possible, a friendly Florida Sandhill, Cam or Pat, accompanied Terry. On-site tours began to follow a basic agenda but were still subject to the whimsy of the tour guide. Not until 1978 did ICF hire a full-time education director, John Weissinger, a graduate of Cornell University.

Fresh from his master's in environmental education, John approached ICF about developing their education programs. He had known about ICF since a chance meeting with Ron a few years before at the Cornell Laboratory of Ornithology. One short visit to Baraboo left a positive impression, and John became an ICFer.

"I realized [the facility] was small, but I also realized it was growing. I thought it had lots of possibilities not only for education, the foundation, and for conservation, but also for me. So I was very excited."

The foundation didn't have any money for John's salary, so as soon as he arrived in February 1978 he began applying for grants. The Kohler and the Patrick and Anna M. Cudahy Foundations responded favorably, but the funds didn't arrive until summer's end. Even with the grants John earned only around $8,500 annually. His wife taught science at the local junior high school and did freelance writing to supplement their income.

A self-taught artist with a love of science, John felt wildlife art was "a perfect marriage of the two" and used his talents to augment his education materials. He wrote and illustrated a twenty-page booklet, *CRANES, CRANES, CRANES*, that ICF sold for one dollar. He encouraged teachers to bring their students for tours and took his programs to the schools. On site he began to bring order to the friendly chaos of the tour program.

"We organized a slide introduction [to the tour]. People would come in and I'd give them a short slide program so they'd get a feel for what the whole place was about. We showed it in the little lounge area at first, and then eventually we fixed up a barn and had exhibits in there. Then we had the regimen of walking around the property to various stations. It evolved over time."

But a little more than a year later changes in ICF's infrastructure caused John to reconsider his future at ICF. Milly had resigned and George hired a new administrator and the two new aviculturists. (It wasn't until Milly's ill-fated replacement departed several months later that Joan Fordham was given the administrator's position.)

Then George left the country for fieldwork. In his absence some of the new staff engaged in power plays that clouded the focus on what should have been everyone's goal: the birds, the foundation, and getting the word out about cranes and conservation. Several months later John, feeling his position had been eroded, decided it was time to move on. Looking back he sums up his ICF experience as exceeding some and falling short of other expectations:

"The birds were wonderful. I found that very exciting. I was not expecting the worldwide contacts that George and Ron had. I didn't expect the enthusiasm that everyone affiliated with the place had. I enjoyed the people I met and worked with very much for the most part."

For John, what fell short was some of the organizational aspects: "[They] weren't as good as I would have liked. Who was in charge? Who was my boss? What was I expected to do? A lot of what I did was on my own. Granted, I was breaking new ground. I was learning and they were learning at the same time. [But] I was incredibly frustrated at times."

Time has given John perspective on those years, and he bears no grudges. He was simply caught in ICF's growing pains as the foundation crept away from the all-volunteer era into a new age of multitiered employees with prescribed levels of authority, responsibility, and accountability.

It was not an easy environment to settle into. Employment at ICF was not for the timid. Salaries (when they existed) weren't competitive, and benefits were almost nonexistent. ICF attracted young, enthusiastic people, pioneers of a sort, who could afford to take a financial risk and work for the Crane Foundation. They were free to express their talents in innovative ways. There had never been a crane foundation before, so who was to say whether there was a right or wrong way to solve a problem? The freedom was glorious, but the stress sometimes took its toll.

John's replacement arrived on New Year's Day 1980, but no one, including the replacement, knew it. On that day a recent graduate of Carlton College in Northfield, Minnesota, coaxed his ancient pickup truck along the interstate to Baraboo. Scott Freeman had a thousand dollars in the bank and was about to begin a nine-month stint as a full-time ICF volunteer. He found himself in this predicament because of his good friend Konrad Liegel, whom he'd known since their undergraduate days. Konrad found out about ICF when he received a fellowship to the Leopold Reserve the previous year and met another "fellow," Charlie Luthin. Charlie recruited Konrad to continue the prairie work, and Konrad talked Scott into helping him. They both worked part-time at the Leopold Reserve and lived with George in his one-room cabin in the woods a few miles north of ICF.

By summer's end Scott, out of money, informed George that he'd be moving on. At the same time, however, ICF received new funds to support the education coordinator's position, vacant since John Weissinger had left. (An education intern, Marge Winski, ran the tour program for the 1980 season.) The job was offered to Scott. At the interview George told him, "Scott, you're going to go out and educate the world."

That sounded okay to Scott. "I was twenty-five and willing to do it. But Joan Fordham sat down and prepared a fairly detailed job description so I knew more or less what I was getting into. Of course, it had the famous No. 11, which was 'and other duties which may be assigned.' "

Many more people were now visiting ICF than when John first established his tour procedures.

"You had to have one body for every twelve to fifteen people, and the body had to be highly trained," Scott continues. "It was killing everybody to try and give tours. When I came they were giving two tours a day, seven days a week, during the tour season. And that was for about eight to ten thousand people a year. If everybody has to be led on a guided tour, it's very expensive in terms of efficiency. And as an educator, I don't like the guided tour at all. It makes the audience passive.

"We developed a lot of curriculum materials for school groups to use, large detailed packages to be used at different grade levels. The teachers and students could use the materials and didn't have to be led around."

But George felt strongly that personal contact with visitors was vital to spreading enthusiasm about the cranes and communicating the need for a worldwide effort to save the birds and their habitats. So the education programs, both for schools and tourists, offered the options of guided or do-it-yourself tours.

For families with children Scott invented Ichabod Crane. Actually, Ichabod existed only on a cassette tape. Slip him into a hand-held player and he narrates your walk around the foundation. In his old squeaky voice Ichabod told the children (and, rumor has it, more than a few adults) about marshes and what ICF was doing to improve habitat for cranes.

It wasn't just the professional educator in Scott that led him to use humor in his programs. "One of the lovely things about the Crane Foundation was George and Ron's beautiful sense of humor. That's the way people got excited about supporting the Crane Foundation. It gave a real human touch to the conservation staff."

Another of Scott's innovations was the two-projector slide show with taped narration that opens each tour and is still being used today, although the script has been revised several times in the intervening years. The "theater" was the same barn at the southeast corner of the property that had been swept out and made somewhat fit for human habitation during John Weissinger's tenure.

Enlightening visitors about wild crane populations, ecosystem restoration, and captive crane management was only part of ICF's educational effort. Opening its doors to tomorrow's scientists, giving students a chance to go beyond their textbooks into the field and contribute to the worldwide effort to save cranes also became a mission of the Crane Foundation. But just as public tours of the grounds were not in George and Ron's original blueprint for ICF, graduate research was not something they thought ICF could initially support. They were preoccupied with getting the place built and finding money to pay the utilities and feed the birds. In the beginning, they were also just trying to get some birds. How could ICF support graduate students? Where would they live? What financial resources would they expect the Crane Foundation to provide? With George gone half the year on fieldwork and Ron either at Cornell or in India, who would supervise the research? So in spring 1973, George had to carefully assess the situation when University of Wisconsin at Madison graduate student Karen Voss asked if she could study the cranes for her master's thesis.

Her first visit to ICF only a few months before had ended her search for a thesis, at least in her mind.

"I had seen cranes once, a couple of years prior to that visit, as part of an animal behavior class, but I had never seen a crane up close until the day we took the ornithology class up to the Crane Foundation.

"It was a revelation. I was absolutely enthralled by the birds. I couldn't believe these birds were here, so close to Madison. I left there knowing that I wanted to study those birds."

One of the best things George ever did for ICF was take a chance on Karen. When she wasn't pulling twenty-four-hour shifts studying the development of behavior in Sandhill Crane chicks at the foundation or sitting in a cramped blind observing a wild pair raise their youngsters, Karen did her share of feeding, watering, and cleaning. Her husband, Marty, in medical school at the time, got drafted onto the work crew.

Ron and Karen had met briefly as undergraduates at the University of Wisconsin. Renewing their acquaintance, Karen was surprised to learn that the Ron who once disdained rugged, uncomfortable field trips was planning a study of Siberian Cranes in India that would surely be lacking in creature comforts. Karen remembers one expedition in Wisconsin that tested everyone's mettle.

"George would often go out with me to find cranes nesting around the Baraboo area. We found a pair with two chicks. George was very interested in coaxing them within camera range for some photography.

"We went out quite late one night (it wasn't planned to be a midnight excursion, but it just got later and later) and built a blind on the edge of the field where George expected the birds would come to feed the next day. Marty and Ron came with us. It was hot, hot, hot and mosquitoes to the nth degree.

"We built a blind of damp green branches and laid down in our sleeping bags. All I had was a down bag, but it was either sweat or be eaten alive by mosquitoes. We took along a half-grown Sandhill chick who walked all over us all night long. I woke up at dawn and looked over and there was George, no sleeping bag, a midriff exposed about eight inches, absolutely covered with mosquitoes and sleeping right through the whole thing. The cranes never came but it was a memorable night."

In the end all of George's concerns about whether ICF could support graduate students, financially and academically, dissipated. In the end, it was the students who supported ICF.

Besides the cranes, the only thing ICF provided the students was free publicity in the *Bugle*. There was no money for housing, but there was the White House. Stipends were nonexistent, seven-day work weeks common. Before, after, and in between their observations, everyone fed and watered the birds, cleaned pens, exercised chicks, gave tours, and joined the AI crew. A sense of community, almost a subculture, developed during those years that persists to this day.

Looking back years later George freely admits, "We never would have survived without the students." They were young people who asked for nothing and gave so much. Out of their enthusiasm the Crane Foundation emerged.

Although Ron and George established the foundation as a center for crane research and breeding, today it is almost as well known for its ecosystem restoration work. ICF's early prairie restoration had stalled briefly when Allan Anderson left.

Then in late autumn 1976, Charlie Luthin from Freeport, Illinois, accompanied a local biology club on a camping trip to Devil's Lake State Park. Charlie had visited ICF briefly during the previous two winters when his friend Eddie Soloway was taking care of the cranes. Now he put a tour of the Crane Foundation on the club's agenda. During the tour Charlie drifted away from the group and ran into George, whom he had heard about from Eddie. They talked away the afternoon. Charlie returned to the foundation after dinner, and as they sat on the hill overlooking the breeding unit George looked out over the cornfield on the hillside and said, "We want to restore all of this into native prairie."

The idea intrigued Charlie. He'd already been involved in a prairie restoration in his hometown a couple of years ago and was studying botany at the University of Wisconsin at Stevens Point. He visited ICF once more in early 1977.

"George asked me what I was doing after I finished school. I said I'm not doing anything. He said, 'Why don't you come here and do the prairie?' I said fine, I'll do it. All of a sudden I had a reason to graduate."

Charlie began his prairie work in spring 1977. He scouted out prairie remnants in the area for seed collecting. Until he obtained a car late in the summer, he did all his traveling by bicycle. The rest of his work was preparing the site for the first planting. He wouldn't use chemicals, so all the weeds were pulled by hand—his hand. Charlie worked alone the first year. He had no money for equipment or even his own housing. For a while, along with another student, he lived with the parents of Bea Wenban, Ron's old high school friend.

"I tried various schemes to raise money," Charlie recalls, "most of which failed." He did receive a CETA (Comprehensive Employment Training Act) grant the second year, which allowed him to hire an assistant but did not provide a salary for Charlie. Then in 1978 he became one of the first Leopold Fellows at the Aldo Leopold Memorial Reserve. The modest income paid for food and he lived on the reserve, commuting to ICF and dividing his time between the reserve and the Crane Foundation. Additional expenses that year were covered by a small grant from the Wisconsin Garden Club. Besides starting the restoration, Charlie planted a prairie nursery. During the long winters he weighed, packed, and stored seeds for future springs.

George and Ron were delighted with Charlie's progress. Ron was a knowledgeable prairie enthusiast and often went with Charlie on seed-hunting expeditions. But Forrest Hartmann was not so pleased. He was concerned that the prairie would drain resources from the birds. Since ICF was still scraping for money and developing its captive management plans, his feelings were not entirely unjustified. But Charlie's prairie wasn't siphoning any funds from the birds; he supported himself, and the project was important to George and Ron. The prairie stayed. Charlie, however, left in 1979.

"Half the education of being at the Crane Foundation was meeting the people that went through there," Charlie recalls. "I'd sit around at the White House and Leopold's Shack and hear about people's wild adventures in India and Africa and other far-off places. I grew up in the Midwest and always figured I'd spend my days in Wisconsin. They opened my eyes to a bigger and greater world out there. It was time to move on."

But for every old ICFer that moved on, several wide-eyed newcomers moved in. Volunteers who worked through the grassroots era still lament the passing of the old ways even though at the time they appreciated that daily operations had to change for the benefit of the birds, ICF, and even the people who were going a little nuts trying to do it all.

In 1980, ICF began advertising their new paid internship program for college students and recent graduates. Participants stayed at least three months and completed a special project under the supervision of the department head. Yes, ICF now had bona fide departments with assigned staff. Under the new system a student could work in aviculture and assist with crane care. Education interns gave tours and did a project in museum design, audiovisual production, curriculum development, or public affairs. Those in field ecology assisted with plant-community restorations and landscaping. The specialization only served to strengthen the Crane Foundation. It attracted a greater diversity of students, each of whom had a part to play in bringing together people and cranes. It was this program that brought Shirley Russman to ICF when she was an undergraduate at Lake Forest College in northern Illinois. She went on to do her masters at the University of Wisconsin-Madison on crane sperm morphology, after which she was hired as an aviculturist at ICF. Once on staff, Shirley applied for a grant and began studying cryogenic preservation of crane semen (freezing it for extended periods of time). When she entered veterinary school she passed her work on to a friend who expanded it for his masters.

Word of mouth was still an important recruiting tool. If Lisa Hartman's friend, ICF's brand-new education director, Scott Freeman, hadn't told her about an opening she might not have applied for an aviculture position. Lisa joined the staff in 1981 and stayed six years. With increased management stability and decreased staff turnover ICF's collective energy wasn't drained by the mere act of survival. They could afford to venture out into nontraditional avenues to involve people with crane conservation. But sometimes things got a little extreme.

On April 12, 1991, central Wisconsin was hit by a spring blizzard. Roads were a mess and some schools had to close. The temperature dropped steadily until it felt like the middle of winter instead of the third week of spring. The next morning 2,611 people in sixty Wisconsin counties across the state arose before dawn, pulled on their long underwear, resurrected their down parkas, stumbled to their cars, and somehow found their way along various unlit country roads to 1,578 rural wetland sites by 5:30 A.M. Once at their designated area, each group turned off their car's engine (and with it the heater) and got out to stand in the freezing darkness. They were listening for Greater Sandhill Cranes. It was the 17th Annual Wisconsin Sandhill Crane Count. Two hours later 8,382 cranes had been either seen or heard.

It all began in 1975 when Steve Schmidt, a teacher at Middleton High School forty miles south of Baraboo, visited ICF. With George and Ron's encouragement, Steve decided to have his class count Sandhill Cranes in their home county of Columbia. The cranes they counted didn't establish the Greater Sandhill Crane's status in Wisconsin for 1975—Wisconsin has seventy-one counties, and they only partly covered one. But on that morning there was a connection between the land, a bird of the ages, and a group of young people who would someday play a role in preserving open lands. Steve decided to count again the following year. And the year after that. A high school class project became the Wisconsin Sandhill Crane Count.

From 1975 through 1981, the Wisconsin Wetlands Association sponsored the count assisted in various years by the Citizens Natural Resources Council, the John Muir Chapter of the Sierra Club, the Audubon Societies of Madison, Milwaukee, Winnebago, Lakeland, and Wisconsin Metro, and the Wisconsin Society for Ornithology. It was a fairly local event in the beginning that involved only the counties immediately surrounding the Crane Foundation. By 1980 about 200 people observed 178 survey sites in eight counties. Counting methods were standardized the next year and the numbers jumped to 760 people at 490 sites in thirty-two counties, and it's been growing ever since.

The Crane Foundation completely took over the organizational responsibilities for the count in 1982. Though the information collected (especially in the last ten years) gives a general picture of Wisconsin's Sandhill population, the data must be interpreted cautiously. One has to take into account the increased number of counties and observers each year, which leads to an "increased" crane population. Also, the same sites were not always surveyed each year, and that makes for inconsistencies in distribution figures. If the data don't stand up to the most stringent scientific scrutiny, why spend so much time and energy on the count? Because it gives three thousand people the opportunity to spend a few moments with the wild cranes, to experience a bird that's been gliding out of the skies and onto the marshes for eons. The Wisconsin Sandhill Crane Count lets participants know what it sounds and feels like to have wild cranes and wild wetlands. These are the people who will ultimately protect the marshes in Wisconsin. The intimacy of the count, with observers assigned to a single quadrant in a county, allows an up-to-the-minute accounting of the health of various wetlands. Are they shrinking due to agricultural drainage or encroachment by woody plants? Has a new house chased away cranes that used the marsh in the past? Any change, no matter how subtle, is sure to be noticed by the counters, who come out each year to check on "their" marsh.

Every year more people volunteer. Some folks only do it once, while others are setting longevity records for participation. There are avid die-hard birders who simply can't help themselves and devoted crane people and their curious companions who can't believe their friends really get up at four in the morning, drive to a lonely road, and stand around in the dark.

Bad weather causes a certain amount of attrition and leads to a depressed count. In 1990 a claustrophobic fog was so thick that observers couldn't see the edge of a field only thirty feet from their car. The only way to count was to listen for calls, and four thousand fewer birds were recorded. The next year saw the blizzard and plummeting temperatures the day before the count. About three hundred counters decided to sleep in that icy morning, but that still left nearly three thousand undaunted souls, and the count went on.

On another crane count that ICF sponsored, snow was the last hardship anyone had to think about. In 1988, Marion Hill, on staff in the education department since 1984 after five years of volunteer service, went to Kenya and Uganda to help organize Crowned Crane counts.

In Kenya, Marion met up with Joseph Rugut, who had previously studied at ICF for one month. They traveled throughout the country visiting schools and talking to teachers and students. Marion found her audiences well aware of the problems facing wetlands and of the burden overpopulation places on the land. But with minimal resources, economic and social, solutions were difficult to implement. A crane count was an indispensable education tool and an excuse for the local people to get out and experience the African countryside, not unlike their counterparts in Wisconsin. Marion had to arrange the count around the schools' vacation schedules. No one had cars, and that restricted the number of survey sites. Most of the participants were students, as were the first Sandhill counters in Wisconsin more than ten years before. It will take time before enough data is collected that can be analyzed and used in formulating conservation programs in Kenya. But it only took one season to bridge the gap between the cranes and the people who must protect them.

Marion also had a week of meetings with wildlife clubs and teachers in Uganda in an effort to initiate crane counting in that country. The people were still reeling from the deposed regimes of Idi Amin and Milton Obote, and the country was politically unstable. Marion called the U.S. embassy in Nairobi and asked if she could get into Uganda. The embassy responded, "You can get in but we can't guarantee you can get out." Marion went in.

"I had to," she says. "Paul had everything set up for me and he was waiting." Paul Mafabi had also been an intern at ICF. And so Marion began one of the most wonderful and most trying weeks of her life.

"It was very difficult to work in Uganda. There was very little electricity or running water or any of the basic supplies and here I was trying to save the wildlife. I held a workshop for teachers. For three or four days, we talked about wetlands and general conservation problems, not only cranes but most of their wildlife. There weren't that many people left in the schools. Many of the educated people left when Amin came in. I was working with the secondary-school teachers. Marvelous people. To me they were the heroes because they stayed."

Marion and Paul were assisted by the minister of the environment, who loaned them a land rover. Included in their group were six Ugandan bodyguards. Getting through the roadblocks they ran into would have been impossible without those men. Years later Marion is still overwhelmed with gratitude for their protection and companionship. She did her best to hide her uneasiness with the guns that were everywhere. Her bodyguards had guns, as did the soldiers at roadblocks. Even thirteen-year-old boys were heavily armed. It was only the day before she left Uganda that Marion learned there was intense civil unrest and the current president was struggling to retain power.

When her week came to an end, Marion's ordeal to leave Uganda began. Now she had to get through roadblocks set up every five miles on the way to the airport. Once there, she found chaos at the ticket counter and no planes. Knowing she had to be on a television program in Nairobi that afternoon, Marion joined the pushing and shoving, managed to get an official to take her ticket, watched as her luggage was searched, and tried to stay composed when they searched her next. Finally a plane appeared and they boarded, all except the Ugandans, who were detained even if they had tickets. The passengers waited four tense hours in the sweltering plane before they were allowed to fly to Kenya.

Marion returned to Kenya in 1989 but was unable to continue her work in Uganda or see her friends again. Her memories are of a "beautiful country and people who were the most wonderful, most gentle, most protective, and most astute people that I have met in a long time. They knew what had to be done to protect the wildlife. They had no resources, no funds. The work that needs to be done there is overwhelming."

The Crowned Crane counts in Africa were another demonstration of ICF's desire to work with people and cranes on a local level and the Crane Foundation's willingness to confront conservation problems in the face of an array of intimidating obstacles: politics, geography, logistics, and the competition between people and wildlife for a chance at a decent life. Marion Hill's leadership under trying circumstances was a proud achievement for ICF. But as much as Marion gave to the project and the Crane Foundation—her energy, time, and adrenalin—she gained as much from ICF.

"I was fifty-one when I started at ICF. I have a degree in criminology but I married immediately after graduation and had three daughters. After my children grew up I realized my real love, which I didn't pursue when I was younger because I didn't think I could make a living at it, was environmental studies. My work here has been one of the highlights of my life. I have grown more, I think, working here than in the fifty years before I started. I extended myself to do things that I never believed I could do. I am comfortable speaking in front of groups, which I never was before. The travel to Africa was a real revelation to me because I went alone and I discovered that I can do these things alone."

Marion resigned her staff position in 1989 but continues to volunteer at ICF. Her professional and personal ties to the foundation remain strong. She still feels "one of the best things about ICF is all the people that pass through."

ICF's goal to advance education about all the issues affecting wild and captive cranes worldwide did not stop with schoolchildren, tourists, and local villagers. Professional ornithologists and scientists needed to exchange information, bounce ideas off one another, and, in some cases, simply meet the faces behind the reports.

In 1975, the first International Crane Workshop afforded that opportunity. Together with Dr. James Lewis, a biologist with the United States Fish & Wildlife Service and chairman of the North American Sandhill Crane Committee, Ron and George organized the first meeting ever for crane researchers. On September 2, colleagues from Canada, Japan, and all over the United States arrived in the Baraboo. Throughout the day ICF staff, volunteers, and students shuttled the guests from airports and bus stations to the Devi-Bara Resort near Devil's Lake State Park, where the conference was held. Dr. Ray Erickson, in charge of the Whooping Crane program at Patuxent, was there along with George's old friend Cam Kepler. David Blankenship of the National Audubon Society reported on Whoopers wintering at Aransas National Wildlife Refuge in Texas. Lorne Scott came from Saskatchewan to tell about the Whooping Crane Conservation Association. Cranes on the Platte River in Nebraska had their advocates, as did the Florida and Mississippi Sandhills. From Japan came Dr. Hiroyuki Masatomi, an authority on Red-crowned Cranes, and Dr. Tadamichi Koga, former director of the Ueno Zoo. Lawrence Walkinshaw, the dentist who parlayed his interest in cranes into a worldwide trek in search of all the species and became one the first authorities on crane behavior, also took part in the four-day workshop.

When they weren't listening to papers about breeding biology, habitat management, migration, and radio telemetry, the participants visited Necedah National Wildlife Refuge, birded the vast Horicon Marsh, and paid their respects at the Aldo Leopold Memorial Reserve. At the banquet on the final night, Dr. Walkinshaw showed slides of his expeditions to meet the cranes of the world. Then a group of local schoolchildren under the guidance of teacher and ICF volunteer Rochelle Robkin performed a crane dance to wrap up the evening. The scientists left Baraboo with an agreement to meet again in 1978.

Though the 1975 meeting was billed as an international conference, only four of forty papers presented dealt with species not native to North America. But the Crane Foundation was only two years old, and the only foreign studies it was involved in were Ron's Siberian Crane project in India, which he began only a year earlier, and George's work in Japan and Korea. The December 1978 meeting in Rockport, Texas, cochaired by Ron and Jim Lewis, was advertised simply as a "crane workshop." Still, it had an international flavor. There were two papers on the Siberian Crane, one on the Hooded, and another on the Common Crane.

George wrote eight resolutions that the participants signed, including a plea to the India government to protect Black-necked Crane habitat; acknowledgment of Red-crowned and White-naped Crane habitat protection by the Korean Council for Bird Preservation; a congratulatory statement to the Soviet Ministry of Agriculture and the Iran Department of Environment for their joint efforts on behalf of the Siberian Crane; and a request that the Cuban government allow research on the endangered Cuban Sandhill Crane. Four additional resolutions concerned Sandhills and Whooping Cranes in North America.

The featured field trip of the conference was a boat trip down the intercoastal canal that cuts through the Aransas National Wildlife Refuge to view wintering Whoopers. Captain Brownie Brown didn't let a deck full of ornithologists intimidate him. He pointed out every avian specimen lest the jabbering scientists miss a species. And when he cut the engine and drifted in for a closer look at a Whooping Crane pair with a chick, everyone rushed to the port side of the deck to gaze out at the white birds. The juvenile wore colored leg bands that Canadian wildlife biologists placed on him twenty-four hundred miles ago in Canada's Wood Buffalo National Park. You can never see too many cranes, even if you look at them for a living.

More crane workshops followed, at Grand Teton National Park in Wyoming in August 1981 and in March 1985 at Grand Island, Nebraska. A gathering of crane biologists was no longer a novelty. On October 24, 1981, ICF held its own first annual research meeting on captive cranes in Baraboo. Crane people found a voice and spoke to a multiplicity of issues that concerned cranes.

With the Crane Foundation's continued help, scientists had a mainstream forum to exchange and disseminate information. The resolutions they signed spoke to the worldwide conservation community, and ICF's participation in international conservation activities steadily grew. In 1980, ICF, along with the International Council for Bird Preservation, the International Waterfowl

Research Bureau, and the Wild Bird Society of Japan, cosponsored an International Crane Symposium in Sapporo, Japan.

After working for decades in isolation, crane biologists were ready to soak up every opportunity to share their experiences. George and Ron saw a great need for a truly international meeting that would transcend all political borders and ideologies. The meeting site had to be reasonably accessible to most of the world's crane biologists, which dictated that it be held somewhere on the Asian continent. And it had to be in a country that symbolized both the dangers and hopes for wild cranes. They decided to convene the 1983 International Crane Workshop in India, home to five crane species.

Geography wasn't the only reason for choosing India. The late prime minister Indira Gandhi was an enthusiastic supporter of wildlife conservation, and there were practical considerations as well. The rupees that the U.S. government receives for the grain it sells there can only be spent in India. These funds were made available to ICF through the involvement and support of the United States Fish & Wildlife Service and enabled ICF to pay most of the costs of the workshop. Besides ICF and the USFWS, a consortium of more than a dozen individuals, governments, and private organizations cosponsored the meeting and gave financial and logistical support. The workshop was held at Keoladeo National Park, where the Siberian Cranes wintered.

It was a historic meeting. For many participants it was the first time they met other scientists studying not only the same species of crane but the same population. One session brought together all the Asian delegates: Indian, Chinese, Russian, Bhutanese, Korean, Iranian, and Japanese. Biologists from the USSR, China, and Japan planned a cooperative nest survey of Red-crowned Cranes in their native countries and conducted the survey the following year. The Working Group on European Cranes and the Working Group on African Cranes were formed at the India conference. All told there were 187 participants from twenty-four nations.

The conference solidified ICF's role as mediator and initiator of cooperative international environmental projects. Though George's work in Japan and Korea and Ron's studies in India laid the groundwork, it was a daring venture that covered ten thousand miles from the Siberian tundra to a high-tech lab in Wisconsin in 1977 that put ICF on the map of international conservation.

SIX

Siberian Express

More than a century ago you could have seen Siberian Cranes in India, China, and Iran during winter, Pakistan and Afghanistan in spring and fall, and Siberia in summer. A few observers from that era reported them as abundant in India and China. But biologists in the twentieth century were having a tough time finding the birds.

Not since 1891 had Siberian Cranes been observed wintering on the vast wetlands of the lower Yangtze River in southeastern China. Those birds, according to the literature, were supposed to nest in eastern Siberia. In May 1961, a Russian ornithologist did find a nest in Yakutia in extreme northeastern Siberia. It was the first confirmed nesting. In September the cranes headed south. To China? Probably. But where did their journey end?

At the Keoladeo Ghana Sanctuary in north central India, ninety-two Siberian Cranes spent the winter of 1973–74 feeding on sedge tubers in jheels, the shallow lakes and ponds that form during the monsoons of July and August. In early March, they began a northward migration of more than three thousand miles that took them over the Hindu Kush Mountains. Then they disappeared. Biologists assumed the birds landed somewhere in western Siberia. Exactly where, no one knew.

No one saw any Siberian Cranes in Iran that winter nor had the birds been seen since the mid-1800s, when it was assumed that population went extinct.

In middle to late March 1974, thirteen Siberian Cranes showed up at the Astrakhan Nature Reserve on the north end of the Caspian Sea in the Soviet Union. Where did they come from? Would the India flock veer that far west, more than one thousand miles, on their way north? Not likely. And where were these thirteen birds headed? Where did they nest?

What about the Siberian Cranes found hanging dead in outdoor markets in Pakistan? Were they from the Keoladeo flock in India? How many Siberian Cranes had succumbed to the hunters? And what about rumors that Lake Ab-i-Estada in Afghanistan harbored Siberian Cranes in late March? Where had these birds wintered and where were they going?

The only thing everyone knew for certain was that habitat loss, the draining of marshes for agriculture in the Siberian Crane's historically important winter ranges, was a disaster for the species. This complicated and discouraging situation prompted George and Ron to declare the Siberian Crane ICF's "target species" in the fall 1975 *Bugle*. They had what appeared to be a straightforward two-part plan to help the birds.

First, Ron would return to India to continue research on the Siberian Cranes' winter ecology at the Keoladeo Ghana Sanctuary. What he learned would be imparted to the Indian government so that the remnant wintering areas could be preserved. Second, ICF and the government of Iran had agreed to a cooperative venture to re-establish Iran's winter flock of Siberian Cranes. This was the plan to catch and mark some of Iran's wintering Common Cranes, find them at their nests in Siberia, give them Siberian Crane eggs to hatch, and wait for the Common Cranes to lead their foster chicks back to Iran for the winter. After weeks of failed attempts during the winter of 1975–76, George and colleagues from Iran's Department of the Environment did catch and attach colored streamers to the wings of seventy-seven Common Cranes. Now the operation moved to the Soviet Union.

Ron had been corresponding with Dr. Vladimir E. Flint of the Central Laboratory for Nature Conservation in Moscow ever since he tackled the Siberian Crane study. Flint was recognized as an authority on the Siberians. When the tagged Common Cranes left Iran in early spring of 1976, George alerted Flint. Later that summer, Flint informed ICF that five marked Commons had been sighted on the breeding grounds. It was a start. Better than not finding any birds at all the first year. Considering that there were seventy-seven cranes spread out across thousands of square miles of remote wilderness with no roads and that the nesting area of the Iranian Common Cranes had never been determined, five is a pretty darned good start. Besides, they had time to find more birds. ICF didn't have any Siberian Crane eggs for the cross-fostering part of the plan. Taking eggs from wild nests in eastern Siberia was a logistical nightmare—Commons and Siberians don't nest at exactly the same time. So the scheme called for using eggs from captive cranes who could be induced to lay earlier by manipulating their photoperiod with floodlights. There was just one small problem: Siberian Cranes had never bred in captivity.

In 1976, there were only eleven captive Siberian Cranes in the entire world. Two of those birds, the aged Wolf from Germany and the barren Phyllis from Philadelphia, were scheduled to arrive at the Crane Foundation that fall. The eastern flock would have to play a role in saving their western counterparts. Eggs from the Yakutia nesting grounds would be collected and flown to ICF to be hatched and become the nucleus of a captive stock that would eventually number fifteen pairs. Eggs from the ICF cranes could then be used in the cross-fostering project.

This project involving American and Soviet scientists would not have been possible before 1972. In that year President Richard Nixon signed off on the U.S.–USSR Environmental Agreement. The Crane Foundation's work fell under the jurisdiction of the Office of International Affairs (OIA) of the United States Fish & Wildlife Service. Raisa Scriabne and her supervisor, Earl Baysinger, had the task of making sure all the red tape was stuck on all the right papers. But first George had to take time out from his fieldwork to visit Moscow and persuade the Soviets that transporting eggs of an endangered crane species ten thousand miles made perfect sense and wouldn't be all that difficult.

On the evening of March 25, George was met at the Moscow airport by a young American woman, an ICF volunteer of sorts fluent in Russian, who was assisting with the project (which didn't quite exist yet) as part of her Cornell University master's thesis, "Four Case Studies in U.S.–USSR Wildlife Conservation Cooperation." Elizabeth (Libby) Anderson had visited ICF while an undergraduate at the University of Wisconsin at Madison. A Russian major, she was also interested in biology and the environment. After listening to George rattle off all the foreign lands ICF hoped to work in, including the Soviet Union, Libby offered her services as translator, thus becoming one of the few volunteers to recruit herself before George uttered his famous "What are you doing this summer?" line.

Back at the hotel, George telephoned Flint. It was the first time they spoke. George's first impression was of a friendly man. At eleven o'clock he and Libby had a snack of bread and caviar and then took a quiet walk around Red Square, just across from their hotel. The next morning Flint met them and all three walked to the zoological museum. Vladimir Flint was a tall man, just over six feet, with a full beard, glasses, and a ready smile. His voice was thick from too many years of Russian cigarettes. His English was slow and deliberate, the words carefully measured. He functioned well within the bureaucracy but loved being in the field. They talked all morning. Flint was ready for ICF.

Several years before, Flint was looking through mail from abroad when he realized that one letter was not addressed to him personally but to the zoological museum. As he put it back in the envelope his eyes caught the words *Siberian Cranes*. He thought, "It will not be a crime if I read it." It was from George. Flint saw that George's letter ended up with the proper administrator, and then he wrote back. By the time George arrived in Moscow, Flint knew all about ICF and the plan to transport eggs to Baraboo.

Flint could not collect the eggs that year (ICF had optimistically sent an insulated transport box before George's visit), but he agreed to do it in 1977. Flint, however, did not have authority to approve the project. Vasilii V. Krinitskii, head of the Department of Nature Reserves in the Ministry of Agriculture, did. At three o'clock that afternoon, Krinitskii joined the meeting. For the next two hours he grilled George. "Why do you want to do this? Why do you need eggs from our wild cranes? Who will pay for this? Will the eggs survive the journey? How long will it take? Can the Crane Foundation, a mere three years old, handle an undertaking of this magnitude?" And then, "You don't even know where the nests are!"

Flint was acutely aware of the difficult task before them. In 1965 it had taken him all summer just to find one nest. But he sat back in his chair, calmly blew out a puff of cigarette smoke, and said quietly, "I know where they are." Krinitskii was convinced and vowed to do all he could to help. A transcript of the meeting was sent to Earl Baysinger in the OIA. He would meet with Soviet officials later to finalize the details.

On November 19, 1976, an agreement was signed by officials from the United States Department of the Interior (which has responsibility for the Fish & Wildlife Service) and the Soviet Ministry of Agriculture "whereby the International Crane Foundation and Soviet specialists may cooperatively work on the study and preservation of cranes in the United States and Russia." They agreed that in June 1977, six Siberian Crane eggs would be collected from the Yakutia nesting grounds and flown to ICF. Additionally, two Soviet scientists would be allowed to visit ICF and other centers involved in crane conservation.

When Ron arrived in India in autumn 1974 to begin his research, the flock of ninety-two Siberian Cranes that wintered in India the previous year had decreased by nearly 30 percent to sixty-three birds. In 1976, when George visited Keoladeo prior to his Moscow meetings, there were only sixty-one. In autumn 1976, Ron returned to India. Every day he rode his bicycle to the marsh. There he waited for the birds to arrive from their mysterious northern breeding territories. When they did, he counted fifty-seven.

There were reports of Siberians from other parts of north central India, so Ron surveyed the birds' historical range. Most of the wetland areas were gone or altered so drastically as to be unrecognizable as crane habitat. The sad reality emerged that the only birds wintering in India were at the sanctuary. It had once been a private hunting reserve for the former ruler of Bharatpur state, H. H. Col. Sawai Brigendra Singh, the maharajah of Bharatpur. After India's independence in 1947 Bharatpur state became part of Rajasthan, and in 1953 the area became the Keoladeo Ghana Sanctuary, a state park administered by the government of Rajasthan. But the sanctuary's status as a state park did not provide much security for the birds. There were heavily traveled roads running through the mosaic of jheels, and local people grazed their livestock, sometimes as many as ten thousand cattle and domestic water buffalo. The sanctuary was only three miles from Bharatpur, a city of fifty thousand people. More than one million people lived within a two-hour drive in the cities of Jaipur and Agra, the latter the home of the Taj Mahal. Seven villages surrounded the sanctuary.

Through the 1976–77 winter Ron monitored human-crane interactions, cattle-crane interactions, and motor vehicle–crane interactions (not many, the birds avoided feeding near the roads during periods of heavy traffic). He determined that they eat sedge tubers almost exclusively. He studied the plumage of the seven juveniles he saw, noting the cinnamon brown feathers that had not yet been molted and replaced by the gleaming white of adulthood. As spring approached and the birds readied themselves for another treacherous migration across mountains and deserts, Ron prepared for his own journey to Lake Ab-i-Estada in east central Afghanistan, seven hundred miles north of the Keoladeo Ghana Sanctuary.

If the huge saline lake was a staging area for the India flock as some theorized, he expected to see approximately the same number of birds as had wintered at Keoladeo. Finding those birds at the lake would solve another piece in the migration route puzzle. Just as important, if there were Siberian Cranes wintering at other India locations that no one had located, they, too, would probably stop at the lake. In that case Ron might see more than fifty-seven birds.

On March 17, Ron and six others, including the U.S. ambassador, set out from Kabul in three jeeps with enough food and water for two days. Some of the roads were paved, but others were deeply rutted dirt paths. The heat was oppressive. Seven dusty, bone-rattling hours later they were within sight of the lake. The jeeps rested. Under a relentless sun Ron peered through his spotting scope. White birds. Big white birds. "Could be just egrets," he told himself, careful not to rush to any conclusion. Shimmering waves of superheated air distorted the view. They piled back in the jeeps and drove closer. Ron got out again and set up his scope. They were egrets all right. But there was something else, too. Cranes. Siberian Cranes. With miles of shoreline to explore, they had the good fortune to find the birds almost immediately.

But were these the India birds? Ron and his companions slowly counted. Fifty-six. One was missing. Ron recognized several individual birds from his winter study group because of plumage patterns in the juveniles and, in one case, a physical deformity in an adult male. Moreover, Ron saw seven chicks in India and there were also seven here at Lake Ab-i-Estada. He was confident he was watching the same flock.

The party camped the night and returned to Kabul the next day. Gear packed, Ron turned to the lake once more.

"I looked back at the tiny band of white cranes standing at the water's edge, totally dwarfed by the immensity of the lake and the distant mountains. Never before had the plight and tragedy of the Siberian Crane struck me with such force; never had these birds looked so fragile, their hold on existence so tenuous."

June 1, 1977. At Vladimir Flint's direction, filmmaker Edward Nazarov flies to the Indigirka River region in Yakutia in eastern Siberia. He searches a territory where he has previously photographed a crane pair. His job is to determine when the cranes begin laying their eggs. Flint must collect the six eggs about one week before they hatch. Watching from his blind, Nazarov concludes that egglaying commenced around June 8 and radios the information back to Flint in Moscow. They have no choice but to assume the population will be fairly homogeneous with respect to egg-laying dates. The terrain (an immense marsh with barely a square foot of solid ground to step on), the distances involved, and the expense of the expedition make it impossible to canvas the entire area and know exactly what is going on where. Flint decides to collect the eggs on June 29–30.

On June 12, Flint and a colleague fly out to the Indigirka River, and on June 15 they begin an aerial survey. Over the next five days they locate forty nesting pairs. Flint plans to send trackers to check the nests before he chooses which eggs to collect. In case that isn't possible, he picks five nests with dry hummocks nearby to serve as landing pads for the helicopter. Six more people join the team on June 21 and spend the following week observing wildlife in the area. Nazarov returns to his blind for more photography.

June 27. Thick fog blankets the tundra. Rain pelts the base camp. The helicopter is grounded.

June 29. It's time to collect the eggs but the fog has not lifted. It shows no sign of breaking. Flint wonders if the expedition has any chance left of success.

Night of June 30. The moisture-laden shroud over the marsh blows away in the darkness.

George and Ron with Aeroflot. *Photo courtesy of International Crane Foundation.*

July 1. Sunshine. The helicopter takes off immediately with everyone on board. First they stop to pick up Nazarov, who has bad news. The chicks in the nest he was filming hatched on June 29. The estimated hatching dates were incorrect. There is no time to carefully check and pick over more than three dozen nests. Flint decides to head for the five nests he marked for just such an emergency, but things get worse. At each nest the chicks have hatched. They find one four-day-old chick. All the others have moved into the marsh with their parents. Flint would say later that these were some of the worst moments of his life.

In desperation they fly over the entire nest area and discover that in low parts of the tundra the nests still contain eggs. Two are collected and a couple hours later they find another two-egg nest and take those as well. It is now July 2. Fuel is running low. They will not be able to search for more eggs. They must return to Moscow.

The intense vibrations from the helicopter will harm the developing chicks, so the biologists suspend the egg box with springs and elastic bands. To monitor the situation they place a glass of water atop the box. There is not even one ripple on the way back to Moscow, a twenty-five-hour journey.

On the same day that the fog grounded operations on the tundra, Libby Anderson left Dulles International Airport in Washington, D.C., for London. A connecting flight landed her in Moscow on the afternoon of June 28. She was met by Alexander Nikolaevski from the Ministry of Agriculture and Tanya Shkuratova, a research biologist from the Central Laboratory for Nature Conservation (CLNC) who was Libby's liaison. While Flint and his team were anxiously waiting out the fog, Libby spent those three days touring the CLNC and Moscow Zoo and enjoying a dinner party at the home of a CLNC staff member. She knew there wouldn't be much warning of Flint's arrival with the eggs, so each day she reserved a seat on a flight out of Moscow. Then on July 1 Libby received word that Flint was scheduled to arrive in Moscow at 2:00 A.M. on July 2. Though Flint left Yakutia on July 2, and the flight to Moscow would take more than twenty-four hours, his arrival date was still July 2 because he was traveling east for such a great distance.

At midnight on July 1, Libby left the dinner party and returned to her hotel to pack. By 4:00 A.M. Flint had not arrived so she went to bed. Two and a half hours later Nikolaevski called: "Flint is here." By 6:45 Libby and Tanya were in a taxi speeding down the highway to the Moscow airport. En route they overtook another taxi. Libby looked over at its passengers, wondering who else would be on this road at this hour of the morning. She remarked to Tanya on how much the man in the other taxi looked like Vladimir Flint. Then she looked again. It was Flint, still in his tundra field clothes, making his own dash to the airport.

They narrowly missed the next flight out, so Libby booked a seat on an Aeroflot to London. When it was time to board, airline personnel almost didn't allow Libby to bring the egg box on board. "Too big," they said. Flint explained the situation and they relented. Libby took her seat. The box rode with the pilots in the cockpit. Flint's work was done. Libby was on her own when the same protests were raised by British Airways in London and Northwest Airlines in Chicago. Each time the airlines bent their rules for the special cargo, but in one instance not before Libby threatened to stick the eggs down her blouse to keep them warm if she wasn't allowed to bring her box on board.

In Chicago an inspector from the Agriculture Department's Animal and Plant Health Inspection Service (APHIS) examined each egg and sealed the box with two numbered metal strips. Then came a final, short plane ride to Madison, where a joyous ICF greeting party awaited Libby and the eggs. Another APHIS inspector accompanied the entourage to the Biotron at the University of Wisconsin. There the inspector cut the metal strips and placed the eggs in an incubator. Because Libby had traveled east to an earlier time zone, it was still July 2. For the eggs, it had been a forty-six-hour journey from the Siberian tundra to a high-tech incubator room ten thousand miles away.

At nine o'clock the next morning George and his assistant, ICF volunteer Bill Gause, checked the eggs for fertility. Instead of using a high-intensity light to view the contents, a technique called candling, they placed each egg in a bowl of warm water and watched for movement. An egg with an advanced embryo floats high in the water with the narrow end pointed down. Sometimes it moves as the embryo shifts within. Infertile eggs or those with dead embryos float low in the water. It was time to find out if there was life in the eggs and whether the forty-six-hour journey had been too stressful.

The two medium-sized eggs were placed in the bowl. They rested high in the water and then started bouncing around. George and Bill could barely contain their excitement. The other two eggs were much larger and darker. They rode low in the water, motionless. George gently shook the eggs and felt the contents splash around like water in a bottle. Either the embryos had died a long time ago or the eggs were never fertile. But they still had two good eggs. Considering what Flint went through to get any eggs at all, no one was complaining. Like two tightly wrapped gifts waiting for their special day, the eggs went back into the incubator until it was time for them to open.

The Biotron has an aura of science fiction about it. Within its walls researchers conduct biological experiments under rigidly controlled conditions. One room is surrounded by cast iron for high-pressure experiments. Another is built on springs to minimize vibrations. The Crane Foundation's room was kept at 98.75°F in case the incubator, set at 99.75°F, broke down. Both the room and incubator's temperature and humidity were monitored by a computer. Should either vary by even one-fourth of a degree, the computer would alert an engineer. But while George didn't have to worry about the eggs' environment, he and Bill did have to turn the eggs several times a day as do the adult birds at the nest because the Biotron's incubator was a stationary rectangular box.

After five days of vigilance, turning the eggs day and night, George and Bill were rewarded when they heard one chick scratching the inside of its shell. It had broken through the air cell at the top of the egg and was struggling to make a pip hole. George put the egg in a hatcher, where the temperature is lower and the humidity higher than in the incubator. On July 10, Vladimir, named in honor of Dr. Flint, emerged tired and wet. Two days later he was joined by Kyta. On August 2, having met the requirements of their USDA-imposed quarantine and tested negative for Newcastle's disease, Vladimir and Kyta headed for home in the Baraboo Hills.

ICF's tiny parking lot was jammed for the next several days as locals and tourists, having read newspaper accounts of the chicks' incredible journey, flooded the staff and volunteers with requests for tours and a glimpse of the tiny cranes. A sign out front said "Tours by Appointment," but no one was turned away. The students working at ICF that summer did their best to accommodate the crowds. Newspapers in Wisconsin had been following the story since the eggs arrived in Madison. Vladimir and Kyta became a national media event. More than anything ICF had done in the past four years, this venture commanded the public's attention and imagination.

Vladimir and Kyta didn't disappoint. Though most crane chicks look similar, the first things everyone noticed about these two rare birds was their down and their eyes. Their down was thicker than any other species, perhaps to help protect them from cool Siberian nights. It was darker, too. Not quite the golden toast brown of other cranes but more of a smoky brown. And their eyes were baby blue. As adults they'd have yellow eyes, but for now they were a beautiful clear blue. When they peeped, their voices were even higher pitched than the high-pitched sound that all crane chicks emit, a portent of their adult soprano calls.

With one egg run under their belts, everyone decided to do it again in 1978. Certainly it would go even better this time now that everyone had some experience. It was highly unlikely that Flint would have another near disaster on the tundra. Flint wanted to use another egg carrier, one not quite so bulky as ICF's box, which would eliminate problems with the airline personnel. In fact, the jet legs of the trip would be the easiest part. This time Ron would bring the eggs back.

The paperwork wasn't any easier the second time around. Knowing who had what authority and which permits were needed had no effect on the intricate paper trail. But by summer 1978, the red tape was once again stuck in all the right places, and Ron flew to Moscow.

June 30, 2:30 A.M. Ron is awakened in his hotel room by Sasha Nikolaevski, his liaison. "Are you ready?" Within minutes he joins Sasha and others from the CLNC in a taxi and heads to Domoyevedo Airport to meet Flint. When they arrive at 3:30, Flint is already waiting. He has seven eggs. Already things are going well. During the one-hour taxi ride to the international airport Flint fills Ron in on the egg pickup and the long flight back to Moscow:

"We didn't have too much petrol after we collected the last of the seven eggs. In fact, in Russian helicopters there are three warning signs that the aircraft is about to run out of fuel. The last one, a loud buzzing, occurs just before the helicopter drops out of the air. We landed at the airport just as the buzzer went off!"

Just before they reach the airport the taxi pulls over and they get out to take some pictures in the serene dawn light. When Ron opens the modified suitcase, they hear a peep.

"It's hatching!"

"No," says Flint with a wishful tone in his voice, "it's just talking to us from inside the egg."

But when Flint turns the suspect egg over, there is a pip hole. He carefully closes the suitcase. There are twenty hours left to go before this chick will be anywhere near a hatcher.

Six hours later Ron is on an Aeroflot flight to New York. The cabin is quiet except for the low murmurings of his fellow passengers and the incredibly loud peeps emanating from Ron's carry-on baggage. He explains to his fellow passengers about the endangered Siberian Cranes and the Crane Foundation's goal of a captive breeding stock from which the wild population will be augmented. Throughout the thirteen-hour flight Ron listens to his suitcase. He opens it only when necessary to turn the eggs so that precious heat and even more vital humidity will not be lost. If the delicate membranes within the hatching chick's egg, now exposed to the air through the pip hole, dry out, they will harden and the chick will not be able to complete the hatching process.

New York, at last. During the APHIS inspection Ron notices the chick has made considerable progress toward its goal. Being in the suitcase doesn't seem to have hindered its instinctual drive to break free of the egg. The inspector completes his work at 6:50 P.M. Ron has to catch a seven o'clock United Airlines flight at the opposite end of Kennedy International Airport. An Agriculture Department agent tells him to forget about it, that there's no way he'll make it. But Ron is determined: "I have to."

The agent runs after Ron, grabs him, takes him through a locked door to get out of the terminal quickly, and ushers him to a car. They speed along the perimeters of several runways, past taxiing jets, and pull up at another locked door, where Ron and his eggs are disgorged. On the other side of the door Ron finds himself behind the security checkpoint. He runs for the plane, carrying the suitcase in his "outstretched arms like some sacrificial offering," leaving the Agriculture Department agent to argue with the security guard.

When Ron opens the suitcase again to check on the eggs, a Siberian Crane chick, minutes old, looks back at him. A woman on the plane offers her cashmere sweater to help insulate the wet chick, which Ron gratefully accepts. In Madison, George and several ICF supporters including Libby welcome Ron home. When the suitcase is opened at the final APHIS inspection, Aeroflot, still damp and none the worse for his adventures, makes his official debut for the cameras.

Of the remaining six eggs, four hatched, but one died a few days later. Under George's paternal care and with Libby's help, Aeroflot and his companions—Eduard, Bazov, and Tanya—soon joined Vladimir and Kyta in Baraboo.

When Ron and George decided to focus ICF's conservation efforts on the Siberian Crane they became a central clearinghouse through which ornithologists studying the birds in isolated pockets of the world in politically disparate countries could funnel their data. Often the biologists couldn't talk to each other so they called, wrote, and sent telegrams to ICF. In tantalizing bits and pieces, a more complete picture of the Siberian Crane emerged.

On March 15, 1977, two days before Ron and his companions saw the fifty-six Siberians at Lake Ab-i-Estada in Afghanistan, Soviet biologist V. V. Vinogradov at the Astrakhan Wildlife Reserve just north of the Caspian Sea saw three Siberian Cranes fly over. The news reached Baraboo later that summer. Where did these cranes come from? Were they India birds who then rejoined their flock at Ab-i-Estada by flying from Astrakhan to Afghanistan, a distance of more than one thousand miles, in only two days? Not likely. A population of Siberian Cranes once wintered on the south shore of the Caspian Sea in northern Iran, but the only confirmed record of those birds that Ron found in a literature review was from 1773. That another flock of Siberian Cranes had somehow eluded searchers and was the source of the three Astrakhan birds was easier to believe than the scenario of three India birds logging extra flight miles at a time when they needed to build up their energy reserves for a long migration.

Then, one year later, Ali Ashtiani of Iran's Department of the Environment reported to ICF that he found nine Siberian Cranes wintering over near the town of Feredunkenar on the south shore of the Caspian Sea. Local people said the cranes came every winter, had for years, to feed in the fields. The flock was never extinct, just never found. The cranes that Vinogradov saw at Astrakhan were undoubtedly migrants from this flock.

George visited Feredunkenar before the birds headed north. But his elation over their existence was tempered by their choice of winter habitat: right next to a huge waterfowl trap (for ducks) built by the villagers. The cranes' wary nature probably kept them away from the traps, but George heard reports that as the ducks begin migrating to northern nesting grounds, guns become the weapon of choice in a final slaughter. Another concern was whether such a small flock of cranes could sustain itself, whether it retained enough genetic variability to maintain a healthy population. But at least there was hope.

Everyone agreed that the Iran flock's nesting grounds were in the same area (the Siberian tundra is so expansive that "within a few hundred miles" qualifies as being in the same area) as the India population, wherever that was. But that mystery, too, was beginning to unfold.

In the summer of 1978, a group of Soviet campers boating down the Ob River in western Siberia came upon a tall, long-legged bird wading on a sandbar. They easily caught the bird, a chick unable to fly, and turned it over to a local resident at the next village. That winter the bird shared a crawl space under the villager's house and competed with his sled dogs for scraps of fish.

By the following autumn word reached Vladimir Flint that a bird that just might be a crane was found near the Ob River. He immediately gave a directive to biologist Alexander (Sasha) Sorokin: go get the bird. Sasha flew north by plane to the town of Salekhard on the Ob River, twelve hundred miles from Moscow, then south by helicopter for another one hundred miles along the Ob to Gorki. He was met at the airstrip by a villager on a motorcycle who had the bird stuffed beneath his jacket. As Sasha went to greet the man, out popped the head of one smelly Siberian Crane. Sasha couldn't believe it. All those years of wondering where the western flock nested may have come down to one odiferous juvenile crane being handed to him on a rural tarmac.

The bird's trials weren't over. He had three baths in Flint's Moscow apartment to eliminate the offensive fish odor. When he was fit the young crane was transferred to the Oka State Reserve's Rare Crane Breeding Center. And he was given a name, Sauey.

Dushenka, the first captive-hatched Siberian Crane, holds her press conference. *Photo by Kent Taylor, courtesy of International Crane Foundation.*

Sasha returned to the northern wilderness again in summer 1981 to conduct a full aerial survey and confirm the nesting grounds of the western Siberian flock. Flint wrote a letter to ICF in September:

"We have good news! Sasha Sorokin found Siberians in Lower Ob region. He discovered 8 breeding pairs on the river Kunovat, the right tributary of the Ob river, not far to the place where our Sauey was taken."

Finally, a long-missing piece of the puzzle, the western flock's nesting grounds, was in place. And the eastern population's winter range? The Chinese were working on that.

Throughout the winters of 1977–78, 1978–79, and 1979–80, ornithologists Fu-chang Chou and Ding Wenning of the Institute of Zoology in Beijing explored the Yangtze River basin for the cranes. Nearly one hundred years had passed since the last confirmed sighting in that area. Fortunately Chou and Wenning didn't give up easily. Their persistence paid off in 1980 with the discovery of 100

Siberian Cranes on the western shore of Lake Poyang, south of the Yangtze River in southeastern China. They continued their search. If it had taken this long to find 100 big white birds, might there be others? In 1983, they counted 230 in that same area. Then they found 800 Siberian Cranes the next winter in an area just west of Lake Poyang. The world population of Siberian Cranes seemed to be growing exponentially.

Plenty of problems lay ahead, to be certain, but the 1980s ushered in an era of cautious optimism. Besides discoveries of hitherto unknown nesting and wintering territories, the Iran flock was "rediscovered" for a second time. Shortly after George visited Feredunkenar in 1978, the political climate in Iran changed radically. The Ayatollah Khomeini came to power and in late 1979 American hostages began what would be a year of captivity at the hands of Iranian extremists. Concern over the fate of the Siberian Cranes was suddenly seen from a new perspective. George's letters to his colleague Mohammed Reza Vazarie in the Department of the Environment were returned unopened. Everyone—George, Ron, and their Soviet colleagues—could only hope the birds were all right.

One afternoon three years after George visited Feredunkenar and several weeks after the hostages were released, the phone rang in the ICF offices. It was Vazarie. He found sixteen Siberian Cranes wintering in Iran, even more than in 1978. The news couldn't have come at a better time. The India flock was down to thirty-three birds.

Despite the joint effort of ICF and Indian ornithologists, notably the esteemed Salim Ali, to protect the Siberian Crane, each winter's count offered less and less encouragement. Certainly some birds were lost during the twice-yearly migration and others might have been hunters' victims, but the Keoladeo Ghana Sanctuary was still under assault by cattle, cars, agriculture, and too many people. Volumes of research data alone weren't going to save the cranes. People had to become involved. Farmers, hunters, tourists, businesspeople, and government officials all had to be made aware of the dwindling population and the need to save habitat, which would in the long run save an important piece of India's biodiversity.

Seeking help for this problem prompted Ron to leave Baraboo in November 1980 and pay a visit to Diane Pierce on Sanibel Island off the west coast of Florida. Diane was living in a small rented cottage where she spent her days painting on the screened-in porch. She was in the middle of a two-year commission for Don Sauey's Clairson International headquarters, creating what would become a collection of oil paintings depicting Florida bird species. Ron just wanted to see how things were progressing. While admiring her current work, a Louisiana Heron (or Tri-colored Heron), Ron inquired if Diane would be interested in taking "a little time to do an extra project."

Diane knew something was up. "I looked at him and thought, 'Here we go.' He described how they wanted a poster of Siberian Cranes to distribute throughout India."

All Diane had to do was the original oil painting from which the poster would be printed. Her sketches and photographs of ICF's Siberians were her reference materials for the birds.

"But [painting] India was going to be harder. Ron described a lot of the details, the retention ponds, the dikes, little hillocks out in the water with little acacia trees planted on them. I thought I could pull it together. So I worked on the painting that winter. It was a vertical with two adults and a nearly grown chick between them to show the differences in plumage between the adults and the juvenile."

No one paid for the painting. Diane did it for the birds. She and her husband, Skip, ordered a golden frame from New York, one befitting a majestic bird like the Siberian Crane. The Office of International Affairs of the USFWS arranged the painting's shipment to India prior to the CITES convention in New Delhi. With Skip's encouragement Diane decided to fly to India, mostly at her own expense, and personally present the painting during the CITES convention to Prime Minister Indira Gandhi. In keeping with the tradition of shipping Siberian Cranes across an ocean, there was, of course, a problem. The frame was damaged in transit.

Diane, unaware of the situation, arrived in New Delhi at three in the morning after a thirty-six-hour-journey. Politely waiting to go through customs delayed her further. "Everyone kept stepping in front of me. I ended up at the end of the line."

A wild cab ride through the streets of New Delhi followed. "The streets were clogged with ox carts, motorcycles, individual people on foot, every vehicle of every description you could think of. Somehow I ended up alive at the hotel."

Diane barely had time to clean up before presenting herself at the embassy to inspect the painting. The canvas was intact, but there were big gashes in one side of the gold frame. Embassy officials transported the painting to Diane's hotel room so she could supervise the repairs. The local art museum supplied an employee with a little jar of gold paint, who arrived at 5:00 P.M. to fix the damage. He dabbed some paint on the gashes and turned to leave. Diane made the poor man do it again under her watchful eye.

She thought the unveiling was going to be in a small room before a private audience. Instead she found herself standing before all four hundred CITES delegates in a conference center resembling the United Nations, with interpreters wearing headphones sitting in glass booths translating speeches for the attendees. Sir Peter Scott introduced Diane and the painting and spoke of Mrs. Gandhi's interest in wildlife issues. The prime minister had not been told about the painting or that it was a gift to her. She responded with a spontaneous narrative of her lifelong interest in nature. Diane found out later that the painting graced Mrs. Gandhi's bedroom.

Less than two months later ICF received word from Mr. Samar Singh, Joint Secretary of India's Ministry of Agriculture, that the sanctuary's status would be upgraded to national park. In 1982, the government made it official and Keoladeo National Park was born. Private citizens, with the support and leadership of conservationist Harsh Vardhan, then began putting pressure on the government to curtail illicit cattle grazing and gathering of firewood within the park's boundaries.

With the successful discovery of a long-lost flock, elimination of question marks on the Siberian Crane's range map, increased habitat protection, and attempts to regulate hunting along the migration route grabbing all the headlines on the international scene, what was the next move for the people and cranes back home in Baraboo? Captive breeding. There would be no replenishing of the wild flocks without it.

As demanding as the Siberian Crane field expeditions were, the captive breeding scene at ICF was equally trying. After Phyllis's tragic death late in 1977 (killed by her mate, Wolf), hopes for

Siberian Crane chicks rested with the aged Wolf and ten-year-old Hirakawa, who arrived the year before from the zoo in Kagoshima, Japan. Through the fence that separated them, Hirakawa and Wolf communicated with displays and unison calls and appeared to be forming a strong pair bond. As the 1978 breeding season drew near, ICF readied the floodlights that would illuminate their pens and bring a bit of Siberian spring to Baraboo. Wolf built nests along the fence that year and the next. The staff faithfully performed artificial insemination. Hirakawa laid eggs, but all of them were infertile.

As George kindly put it, "Despite his interest in breeding, Wolf's ancient gonads just would not produce enough sperm to fertilize Hirakawa's eggs."

Enter Tilliman on December 17, 1979, another male Siberian Crane loaned by ICF supporter Wolf Brehm of Vogelpark Walsrode in West Germany. Tilliman's exact age was unknown, but he was thought to be at least a few decades old. Not wanting to disturb the pair bond between Wolf and Hirakawa, so important to bringing her into breeding condition, George put Tilliman next to the former Vladimir, now known to be a "Vladimiria." Tilliman delivered to the best of his ability and produced fairly decent semen samples every now and then. In 1980, four of Hirakawa's ten eggs were fertile. None hatched. The exact cause of death of the embryos was not determined. But George knew there was something they could do the next year to improve their chances of success: natural incubation, no machines. Nature does it better than mechanical imitations.

George had already seen the results of natural incubation at the Patuxent Wildlife Research Center, where Whooping Crane eggs incubated under Sandhill Cranes produced healthier chicks. Chicks from the same Whoopers hatched under artificial conditions were not as strong. To meet ICF's pressing concerns, Patuxent and the National Zoo responded with overwhelming generosity and shipped four pairs of breeding Florida Sandhill Cranes to ICF in the fall of 1980. ICF added a reliable pair of White-naped Cranes to the maternity ward.

Everything looked positive for 1981 except Tilliman's semen samples. They were even worse than in 1980. But somehow, three of Hirakawa's ten eggs were fertile. The Sandhills and White-napeds went to work. The staff could only wait. The first embryo died early in its development. The third one hatched but did not live beyond a few hours. It was egg number seven, lucky seven perhaps, that shattered the world record for lack of procreation among captive Siberian Cranes. Dushenka hatched on June 4, 1981. Not until he fledged in late August did ICF confidently proclaim him the first Siberian Crane bred in captivity. Still, even his hatching was international news. ICF supporters across the country mailed clippings from their local papers. The *China Daily* carried the story on page one. In India, Harsh Vardhan and the Tourism and Wildlife Society of India organized a celebration of the event. Dushenka gave the Soviets welcome encouragement for their own breeding program at the Oka State Reserve. George proclaimed Dushenka's emergence a "hatch heard around the world."

The first Siberian Crane bred in captivity was a significant scientific achievement. Dushenka was an addition to the family of Siberian Cranes unwittingly taking part in a massive effort to save their species and to the family of ornithologists around the world linked by hope and determination.

It takes governments, heads of state, and cabinet-level officials to create national parks, approve projects of international cooperation, and (often) provide funds to transform ideas into working programs. But it is individuals, field biologists, amateur scientists, and concerned local citizens who must get those politically cautious and lobbyist-weary officials to even consider drastic and expensive conservation measures. And the success or failure of many programs ultimately rests with the men and women whose passion for the wildlife led them to confront the seemingly unsurmountable obstacles in the first place. They have only themselves for support when logistical and natural disasters threaten to destroy their years of work and preparation or when they are exhausted and fed up with being in the middle of a constant swarm of mosquitoes for months at a time while sharing their study subject's habitat. And it does no good for governments of polarized or outright hostile countries to sign cooperative agreements if the field people can't work together, if they don't trust each other, and if their friendships can't sustain the stress of chasing a dream to save a species. The Siberian Crane project, though still in its embryonic stages, had proved all these points, never more so than during Vladimir Flint's visit to ICF three years before Dushenka's historic hatch.

In May 1978, when Flint and a colleague, Alexander Blistanov, met one-year-old Vladimir and Kyta for the first time, their satisfaction over the chicks' survival of their transatlantic ordeal and the anticipation of that year's egg-collecting expedition was tempered by George's sobering report of the past few months at ICF. The Crane Foundation had just survived a massive viral epidemic that killed twenty birds in the nonbreeder flock.

Federal biologists were investigating the cause. George assured Flint that the disease had not infiltrated the breeding unit down the hill where Vladimiria and Kyta lived and where the 1978 chicks would reside as well. He asked Flint if the project could proceed as planned. Flint took a long, deep breath. Presidents, prime ministers, cabinet secretaries, wildlife agencies, all were of no importance at that moment. It came down to two men standing on a hill, searching each other's eyes, who found the trust and strength to persevere.

Siberian Crane at Bharatpur National Park. *Photo courtesy of International Crane Foundation*

© Diane Pierce

SEVEN

Dark Days

When Joe, the ornery Sarus Crane, was found dead near the water trough in the nonbreeder field on January 11, 1978, the staff was surprised and saddened but not unduly alarmed. Joe had gone to the feed box that morning along with the other cranes, and several hours later he was dead. Usually some discomfort or illness is evident before a bird dies. However, Joe was not a young bird and perhaps old age had claimed the six-footer who made a career of harassing students and aviculturists. In accordance with standard procedures Joe's body was sent to the National Wildlife Health Research Center in Madison (NWHRC) for a necropsy. His weight was below normal. The blood smear was "not remarkable" and "no viruses were isolated from a cloacal swab." The laboratory diagnostician concluded his report with, "At this time we do not know the cause of death of this crane." Not a satisfying conclusion but also not an uncommon one for captive exotic species.

ICF's new aviculturist that year was John Taapken, whom George had hired just before he left for Korea in autumn 1977. That fall was unusually cold and rainy and led into early winter snows that never seemed to end. Daily maintenance chores turned into strength-sapping and time-consuming ordeals. Fresh snowfalls continually obliterated the plowed lanes for the water truck. The foundation's begged and borrowed equipment couldn't handle the

139

season's accumulation of snow. When the truck got stuck John spent hours digging it out. Finally he resorted to hand-carrying buckets to the breeders down the hill and transporting water on a toboggan to the nonbreeders in the field. For the most part John worked alone to maintain the buildings and crane pens. Howard Ahrensmyer, the Sauey handyman, helped wherever possible, and during the most difficult stretches Milly and secretary Elaine Gasser took turns lugging water buckets. Ron also helped take care of the birds that winter. While the weather pushed the staff to their limit over the winter of 1977–78, Joe died and Phyllis was killed by Wolf. The season then passed rather quietly.

George returned from Korea on March 15, 1978. Early that morning John had found a dead Blue Crane near the barn in the nonbreeder field. One foot was caught in a piece of heavy wire. The conclusion was death due to stress and trauma from a freak injury. Later that day George ambled out into the nonbreeder field and stood dumbfounded as another Blue Crane teetered up to him and dropped dead at his feet. How could a bird just drop dead? This one was only two years old. Didn't anyone notice it was sick? Then further out in the field George saw still another Blue Crane wobbling about. He quickly retrieved the sick bird and isolated it in the empty Chick House. Maybe the first dead Blue Crane had also been sick and not fatally injured as originally thought. No one could escape the upsetting thought that there might be a contagious disease in the field.

Another Blue Crane in the nonbreeder field died the next day. Now no one doubted that something was happening to the birds. But no one could guess the magnitude of the crisis that was about to unfold. On March 18, three days after the first deaths, a Red-crowned Crane chick from 1977, one of Lulu and Ueno's offspring, succumbed to the mysterious illness. The next day a dead Sandhill was found in the field, the first of nine Sandhills that would eventually die. More than a dozen birds became ill in the next two weeks. The Chick House was converted into a hospital.

The mood at ICF was close to panic. Virologists, microbiologists, veterinarians, epidemiologists, and other disease specialists from the NWHRC came to Baraboo to take blood samples and cloacal swabs from the birds. Unable to stand by and do nothing, George contacted two local veterinarians, Drs. Martin Westerfeldt and

Marge Losch, and asked the impossible of them, to treat an unknown illness and save the cranes. They responded as best they could under the circumstances and suggested administering a range of antibiotics and other medications to the birds. ICF's entire staff, from aviculture to education to administration with a few volunteers mixed in, was mobilized to treat the cranes around the clock. The medications were adjusted with each new piece of information from the NWHRC. Initial reports indicated perhaps a parasite problem or maybe a bacterial infection. The cranes continued to die—three on March 20, five more on March 22, and then scattered deaths until April 1. The final tally from that outbreak was twenty cranes, all of them from the nonbreeder field. In addition to the nine Sandhill and four Blue Cranes, five Red-crowned Cranes, including four of the seven chicks from 1977, and two Hooded Cranes perished. One of the Hoodeds was Sim, who made history in 1976 by being one of the first Hooded Cranes in the world to hatch in captivity. Only four of twenty-four birds that became ill survived. The Chick House, a place of beginnings, became a house of death.

The atmosphere at ICF was a sickening mixture of tension and fear. Although no one yet knew what the disease was, everyone wondered if it was preventable. George began to second-guess his decision to spend the winter in Korea. He questioned what had transpired over the winter at ICF in his absence. That no one had any answers or theories regarding the cause of the die-off only aggravated the strained relationships among the staff. Some saw no sense in subjecting the birds to medications when the disease hadn't been identified. George couldn't stand by and not try something. He was afraid to leave the birds.

"I slept in the lounge and went back to my cabin to shower and change my clothes in the morning," he recalls. "I was continually washing clothes and going back and forth. Night and day. Week after week."

Caught in what he terms an "inferno of tension," John was still able to understand that more was at stake than the immediate deaths of twenty cranes. "For George, it was the destruction of a dream, unraveling in front of his eyes."

One Sunday morning George went over to the White House to water and feed Ichabod (Icky) and Abby, two Sarus Cranes who lived in the pasture beside the house. Icky and Abby were fixtures at the White House. What people driving by on City View Road must have thought when they saw two six-foot birds instead of horses or cows one can only imagine. Icky's arthritis hadn't slowed him down much. Every morning (4:00 A.M. in the summer) they shattered the peace with their megadecibel unison call. Ron's next-door neighbors, bless them, never complained. The pasture, like the breeding unit, was physically separate from the nonbreeder field and was a "clean" zone. Icky and Abby were considered safe from the disease.

George approached the fence that day and felt his stomach twist into a knot.

"They were out in the field. Icky was standing slouched with his head under his wing, a posture typical of cranes that had the disease. He stretched his neck up, flapped his wings, and fell over on his back. I thought, 'The disease has finally spread out of the nonbreeder field.' I thought the whole foundation was doomed. When Icky got up and walked normally I realized he was just clumsy because of his arthritis."

Too exhausted to laugh, even in relief, George returned to the lounge to lie down.

"I was paralyzed by the whole thing. Very discouraged."

Back in Madison at the NWHRC a pattern was becoming evident in the necropsies. The substantial amount of subcutaneous fat on the cranes indicated they were eating up to the time of death. And everyone reported that behaviorally the cranes were normal nearly up to the moment they became seriously ill. The birds had enlarged livers and spleens that contained tiny, pinpoint-sized lesions, yellow-white in color. The thymus gland and intestines were also affected. The lesions, or inclusion bodies, in the liver cells provided the first important clue to the disease's identity: it was probably a virus.

Nearly a month after the first deaths researchers at the NWHRC identified the killer as a herpesvirus. There were other known avian herpesviruses but this one had never been identified before. They called it Inclusion Body Disease of Cranes (IBDC).

With the virus now isolated, the NWHRC ran tests on the blood samples taken from eleven cranes in March and discovered some dramatic information. Nine of the birds had substantial levels of antibodies in their systems. They had been exposed to a virus but did not get sick and die. But when were they exposed? What was the exact nature of this potentially deadly virus? A blood sample was then collected from every bird at the foundation. Only the cranes in the field, in the pens along the south side of the field, and in the main barn next to the field had been exposed to the virus. All of the breeding birds were "clean." Six months later the seropositive birds still had antibodies in their systems. The presence of antibodies indicated merely that the crane had been exposed to the disease. But was a seropositive crane, though a carrier of the virus, also actively shedding the virus?

Since IBDC could not be isolated easily from blood or fecal samples of live birds that were antibody positive, it was difficult to detect shedding. Perhaps it was only rarely shed. Just how was the virus transmitted? It was like watching someone invade your home and knowing you were in danger but being powerless to do anything about it.

ICF continued to work closely with the National Wildlife Health Research Center, and all parties agreed to quarantine the Crane Foundation. No birds could leave, none could come in. The U.S. Fish & Wildlife Service only had jurisdiction over ICF's native North American cranes and endangered species, which require permits for transfer to other institutions. But much research needed to be done, and ICF did not want to jeopardize the health of other captive crane populations.

Thus far the cranes in ICF's breeding unit down below had been spared, and to help keep it that way the staff restricted their movements between the unit and the nonbreeder field. No one went down below after being in the field. Everyone had to wear different sets of clothes and boots to work in the two areas and pass through disinfectant footbaths on their way in and out of each area and each individual pen. Since fecal matter is a common vehicle for spreading disease, although it had not been proven to be a factor in this virus, all excrement from each enclosure was placed in its own plastic bag for disposal. Would these measures prevent another outbreak? No one knew for sure.

By summer, when the situation had quieted down substantially, George and Ron were still concerned about ICF's survival. They were still under self-imposed quarantine, and there was the question of what negative publicity would do to ICF's reputation. From the beginning there was never any consideration given to sweeping the bad news under the rug. The membership was informed of the epidemic in the spring 1978 *Bugle*. ICF followed breeding-loan protocol and sent letters to loaning zoos and private aviculturists whose birds had died. In one instance they had to cancel the planned shipment of a Red-crowned Crane to Japan because of the quarantine. Always they stated that there had been an outbreak of a deadly virus.

The NWHRC's disease specialists also evaluated the Crane Foundation's cleaning, feeding, and housing situations and worked with the staff to modify the "danger zones." Early conclusions were that the nonbreeder flock contained too many birds in a restricted area. The birds congregated around the only two feeding and watering stations. But breaking up the flock and eliminating those trouble spots didn't address another major concern. If seropositive adults produce seropositive chicks by transmitting the virus through the eggs, and/or if it somehow spread to the breeding unit, was there any future at all for the Crane Foundation?

Until this question could be answered, eggs from positive birds were to be left with the parents for incubation and rearing of the chicks. Only eggs from negative breeders were placed in the incubator. But the dispiriting spring was followed by a dismal breeding season that the aviculturists termed "generally undistinguished" with "low egg production, infertility, egg mortality, and weak chicks" (seventeen chicks hatched from fifty-two eggs and less than a dozen survived). There were no chicks from the antibody-positive birds. The following year a Hooded Crane pair in the main barn did produce two eggs and one hatched. They raised their chick with help from the staff, who supplemented the adults' pellet food with worms and the commercial diet normally fed to hand-raised chicks. Not only was this an opportunity to observe a parent-raised bird, but to everyone's unabashed delight, the chick was negative for the viral antibodies.

If additional testing suggested that positive birds do not pass the virus to their chicks, a process known as vertical transmission, then it might be possible to manage IBDC-positive birds in captivity and not lose their contribution to the gene pool, an especially important consideration in the case of endangered species. But exactly how positive birds would be managed, if indeed they could be maintained without risk to other birds, depended on further research.

Grey Crowned Crane. *Photo by Lawrence Walkinshaw*

Black Crowned Crane. *Photo by George Archibald*

Blue Cranes. *Photo by Sture Karlsson*

Wattled Crane. *Photo by Sture Karlsson*

Demoiselle Crane. *Photo by George Archibald*

Black-necked Cranes. *Photo by George Archibald*

Sarus Cranes. *Photo by Sture Karlsson*

Hooded Cranes (adult with chick). *Photo courtesy of International Crane Foundation*

Eurasian Crane (threat posture). *Photo by Gordon Dietzman*

Siberian Crane (unison call). *Photo by Ron Sauey*

Red-crowned Cranes. *Photo courtesy of International Crane Foundation*

White-naped Cranes (unison call). *Photo by Sture Karlsson*

Whooping Cranes. *Photo by George Archibald*

Sandhill Crane. *Photo courtesy of International Crane Foundation*

Brolgas (with chick at nest). *Photo by George Archibald*

Red-crowned Crane chick. *Photo by William C. Gause*

Tests of stored serum from ICF cranes revealed the virus was present as early as 1975. It probably took the right combination of environmental and physical stresses for the virus to become active in 1978: a long hard winter and overcrowding in the nonbreeder field. Ironically, Joe's death, once thought to have been a harbinger of the epidemic, was eventually attributed to enteritis, inflammation of the intestine. Birds and other animals can be carriers of numerous viruses and bacterial organisms that remain dormant in their bodies until their systems are stressed, often by factors unrelated to the disease. The initial factor in a bird's illness might be inclement weather or a physical injury that weakens its resistance.

By the early 1980s there was still no test to determine whether a bird was actually harboring the virus. Since the antibody test was specific for the herpesvirus, ICF and the NWHRC took the conservative route and considered every antibody-positive bird to be a potential transmitter. But the lack of a definitive shedder test and some rather alarming proposals from a few individuals at the regulatory level concerning positive birds already in zoos and those that might be imported hindered initial attempts to collect data and expand the research.

The U.S. Fish & Wildlife Service wanted to require testing for IBDC as a condition for an importation permit and release from the subsequent quarantine that all imported animals must undergo upon entering the United States. There was hesitancy by some zoos to go along with this. First, the test could not be performed at federal quarantine stations and would have required a longer quarantine than the standard thirty days. This increases the stress for the birds. Many quarantine stations are spartan and basic, little more than concrete-floored, wired pens that are easy to clean but offer the animals few comforts. Second, there was the matter of what to do with cranes that tested positive for the virus. The zoos were given three options: return the crane to its country of origin, euthanize the bird, or keep the bird isolated not only from other cranes but in a situation that prevented contact with wild birds. And one of the proposals concerning management of antibody-positive captive flocks already in the United States was "kill the flock."

Killing birds with serious contagious diseases has always been an option exercised by regulatory agencies such as the United States

Department of Agriculture. It is, as one biologist with the NWHRC says, "the most cost effective and biologically effective way of controlling the disease. It's very easy to do when you have domestic species or individuals that are not worth very much or there is no significance attached to them. So it's not wrong to say that. But there are situations where that may not be something you want to consider." The cranes presented one of those situations.

Since nearly half of the crane species are endangered and additional importations of those species has become increasingly difficult in recent years with the establishment of the Convention on International Trade in Endangered Species, each endangered crane in captivity represents an irreplaceable component of the captive gene pool. Genetic variability is imperative for the health of any breeding population of animals, be it cranes, gorillas, or fish. Under the auspices of the American Association of Zoological Parks and Aquaria (AAZPA), the Species Survival Plan (SSP) seeks to ensure the continued health and survival of captive endangered species by regulating the exchange of breeding animals between member zoos in order to maintain the greatest genetic diversity within the captive population. Additional bloodlines must be imported for some species, and to ban entry into the United States of cranes that are antibody positive could eliminate a portion of the already small gene pool. Likewise, to isolate a bird and not breed it diminishes the variability of the population.

But given that more than a half-dozen years after the outbreak at ICF biologists still didn't know precisely how the virus was transmitted between adult cranes, were the proposed guidelines really too severe? Perhaps. In a study involving about seventy eggs collected from positive birds, vertical transmission was not detected; none of the chicks were antibody positive. Therefore, even positive cranes could be used for breeding purposes as long as the eggs were removed, disinfected, and the chicks hand-reared.

Was it possible to safely manage cranes that were antibody positive? The 1975 serum samples and a few others collected from zoos in the United States and abroad indicated both the presence of the virus at ICF long before the die-off and at other institutions where there had never been an outbreak of the disease. There was agreement among ICF staff, NWHRC disease specialists, and others familiar with the situation that it took the right combination of environmental and physical stress factors to weaken the birds' resistance to the herpesvirus. Careful management with an eye toward avoiding those factors that stimulated the ICF epidemic should prevent any future outbreaks. The only other known deaths from a herpesvirus in cranes occurred in 1973–74 in Vienna, Austria, and recently in Russia and China, but no one could say with certainty if it was the same virus.

So, if the virus was already present in captive U.S. populations, and there seemed to be no vertical transmission, why not allow the exchange of antibody-positive birds? Because there always remains some danger. As the NWHRC biologist puts it, "You have to decide what degree of risk you are willing to accept."

Where cranes are being managed solely for captivity, that decision may be best left to the individual zoo. But where the birds contribute to a release program, even a planned release program ten years down the road, the facilities involved have a greater responsibility. Thus far the virus has not been detected in wild North American crane populations. Ninety-five wild Greater Sandhill Crane serum samples collected in 1976 and 1977 were antibody negative. A larger sample size would, of course, be desirable. In 1993, ICF and the NWHRC will collaborate with the Russians on an investigation into the presence of IBDC in wild Common Cranes. But certainly, no one wants to put a known pathogen into a wild population.

The Crane Foundation decided to put the risk factor for their own birds and future release programs as close to zero as possible by keeping their resident flock as completely free of IBDC as current testing technology will allow. In the early 1980s all antibody positive cranes were transferred to private breeders on the condition that they keep the birds isolated from all other cranes and never ship them to another institution. In the intervening years not one ICF bird that was negative for IBDC (and each crane is tested at least once a year) has later tested positive. All loan agreements for birds shipped to ICF state that the crane will be quarantined for thirty days and tested twice and that a positive bird will be returned to the loaning institution or placed at a third facility designated by the loaning institution. When possible, ICF has an incoming crane tested even before it arrives at the foundation.

Zoos test their cranes on a voluntary basis, but breeding centers managing cranes for release programs follow stringent testing protocols to maintain IBDC-free flocks. In the United States and Canada, the institutions affected the most by these procedures are ICF, Patuxent, and the Calgary Zoo Devonian Conservation and Research Center, all of whom are involved in Whooping Crane propagation and release. As some of the management questions have been answered over the years, what once threatened to be a divisive issue between zoological institutions and various regulatory agencies has instead become a rallying point for cooperation born of a desire to increase everyone's knowledge about the deadly virus. In 1989, the NWHRC began an investigation, led by Animal Welfare Officer Dr. F. Joshua Dein and with the cooperation of the International Species Inventory System (ISIS; it maintains records of all captive zoo animals), into the prevalence of IBDC in captive cranes in the United States. Blood samples from responding zoos revealed that antibody-positive birds were present in several other collections.

More than a dozen years after the die-off at the Crane Foundation, the two biggest questions are still how is the virus transmitted horizontally (between adult birds) and how can a carrier bird, one that is harboring the virus and can shed it, be identified? Lack of financial support has been an obstacle to research efforts, and there have been few thorough clinical studies of the virus.

In 1983, Jo Ann Schuh of the University of Wisconsin at Madison's School of Veterinary Science studied IBDC for her master's degree. Among her goals was the development of a diagnostic test to identify IBDC carriers. As she soon learned, "A major problem associated with IBDC [is] the difficulty in isolating the virus from samples." It proved to be much more difficult than for other avian herpesviruses.

And why wasn't it enough just to assume that all antibody-positive cranes who could be identified were potential transmitters of the virus? Because biologists know that other animals with herpesviruses may appear healthy and test antibody negative although they are infected and shedding the virus. There was no compelling reason to assume that IBDC did not behave in a similar manner. Thus, a crane that tests antibody negative may in fact be a carrier and potential shedder.

Nearly ten years after Schuh's study, a research proposal has been put forth by the NWHRC to develop a DNA probe that will detect the virus. Financial support for the research is being provided by the NWHRC, the federal government's Whooping Crane Recovery Team, and a longtime ICF backer who has supported a wide variety of projects almost since ICF's inception.

To determine whether a crane is actually harboring the virus, the probe will search the virus's "hiding place," the bird's cellular DNA. The viral DNA will react differently to the probe than will the DNA that is part of a crane's normal genetic code. The experimental design calls for examining biopsies of various tissues where the virus is most likely to reside in a clinically normal carrier bird (i.e., apparently healthy but antibody positive), but the ultimate goal is to be able to test blood samples or fecal matter.

Even if IBDC carriers are conclusively identified in the future and they prove to include birds that test antibody negative, it is unlikely that management protocols at the Crane Foundation concerning probe-negative/antibody-positive cranes, those who have been exposed to the virus but do not appear to present an immediate transmission threat, will be relaxed. The 1978 epidemic threatened to crush ICF, but instead it forced the foundation to strive for a new level of sophistication in its aviculture practices.

Changing the way the cranes were housed and cared for cost ICF thousands of dollars for additional equipment and supplies. Increased vigilance over the cranes' health made it necessary to hire additional staff. They learned that it was not always possible to wait for donations. They would now have to identify their needs, figure out the costs, and then actively seek the financial backing to keep the budget in the black. ICF entered a new era that could have overwhelmed the small group of people that had presided over the foundation for the first five years. George saw that the responsibilities were becoming too much for him and Ron to handle alone.

The epidemic, the discouraging breeding season that year, the increasing financial concerns, all were constantly in George's thoughts as he cared for the Siberian Crane chicks at the Biotron in June 1978. He called longtime friend and advisor Dr. S. Dillon Ripley for suggestions. Ripley recommended that ICF expand its board of directors, bring in people with financial and management expertise to help guide ICF. Ron and George agreed, and they issued invitations to supporters they thought might be interested in becoming board members. Everyone met at the Biotron in Madison, and except for two people who felt their advanced years might preclude their active participation in the new board, every single attendee signed up on the spot. There were fourteen members of the new board, including George, Ron, Norman Sauey, Owen Gromme, and Mary and John Wickem. George asked Mary to chair the meeting and she's been the driving force of the board ever since. Today there are twenty-two trustees, including Chappie Fox, the circus man who long ago exchanged birding notes with an enthusiastic teenager who roamed his property. Three other current trustees, Charles Nelson, Fred Ott, and Norman Sauey, were members of the original board.

The new organization meant the end of some working relationships and the initiation of new ones. It was in summer 1978 that Milly Zantow realized that her contribution to ICF had run its course. It was time for new people and new ideas. Forrest Hartmann decided to phase out his involvement and devote more time to other interests. It was going to take fourteen people to replace him! John Taapken, having weathered one of the worst winters in recent Wisconsin history and the worst crisis that would ever befall ICF, decided it was time to move on. The epidemic had put a strain on his and George's relationship. But the parting was amiable. In fact, John left well after the crisis had passed.

The silent threat of disease remains very much a guiding force behind ICF's aviculture procedures even today. ICF continues the practice, started before the 1978 die-off, of giving each crane a health checkup once a year. Blood samples are collected from every bird and analyzed by the NWHRC for IBDC. ICF and other labs screen the samples for other diseases. A disinfectant footbath is kept outside each enclosure even in the absence of known pathogens. Cranes are no longer housed in multispecies groups, and rarely are more than two birds in one pen. Each crane enclosure now has two outdoor yards that are used in alternate years to prevent buildup of fecal matter.

Throughout the depressing weeks of the epidemic it was impossible for George to "shut down"; such behavior has never been part of his psychological makeup. There were the demands of the sick birds and the Siberian Crane chicks at the Biotron. And there was a crane down below in the breeding unit that offered some hope and a promise for a bright future. She monopolized what was left of George's energy. Despite his fatigue he had to visit her every day for several hours. Each morning after another night at the foundation, after he drove to his cabin to get clean clothes and returned to ICF, George walked down the hill to see her. Invariably she was waiting and not too pleased at the delay. But by now each was used to the other's minor imperfections. And George was all she had. His commitment to this crane, a crane unlike any other in the world, began two years before in the early hours of a quiet spring morning.

Diane Pierce ©

EIGHT

Tex

I t was still dark when Ron and ICF researcher John Baldwin left Baraboo at 5:00 A.M. in a borrowed white van. They were on their way to Chicago's O'Hare International Airport. Another crane was arriving that day, April 15, 1976.

But this crane was special. She was a Whooping Crane, one of the rarest birds in the world, and she would be the first Whooping Crane to live at the International Crane Foundation. It was eight years since George first met her at the Patuxent Wildlife Research Center in Laurel, Maryland, and one year since he first requested she come to live at ICF. Now, in the chill of an early spring morning, the moment had arrived. Ron and John would spend only minutes at the airport, then turn around and drive straight back to Baraboo. There was sure to be quite a reception when they returned: newspaper reporters, a television crew, ICF staff, and enthusiastic friends.

Because even as Whooping Cranes go, this was no ordinary endangered bird. This was Tex. Nine years old. Never laid an egg. Thought she was human. Nothing sent her into a frenzy of vocalizing and dancing like the sight of a dark-haired man. And George was going to be her mate (with the help of artificial insemination).

It was imperative that Tex produce offspring. The turbulent thirty-six-year history of Whooping Cranes in captivity had made

Tex an important player in a genetic drama. The plot was the rescue of Whooping Cranes from the threat of extinction.

Tex's story began in 1940 in southwestern Louisiana when a fierce August storm drove thirteen tall white birds inland from the privacy of their coastal marshes. When the storm abated only six birds returned. The fate of the other seven remained a mystery, except for one. Fifteen months later a federal game management agent identified a large white bird with an injured wing as a Whooping Crane. It had been cared for since the storm by a well-meaning gentleman who didn't know what it was. The bird was sent to the Audubon Park Zoo in New Orleans, where it was named Josephine. She lived alone in a pen for the next seven years.

Whooping Cranes were probably never as numerous as their abundant relative the Sandhill Crane, but their numbers were never lower than in the late 1930s. Fourteen birds were counted at the Texas wintering grounds in 1938. Before the population plummeted, Whooping Cranes nested in Illinois, Iowa, Minnesota, and North Dakota. There were even Whoopers at Cape May, New Jersey. The Louisiana flock, reduced to the remnant thirteen birds in 1940, was nonmigratory. That the Texas Whoopers nested twenty-four hundred miles away in Canada's Wood Buffalo National Park would not be discovered until 1955. Their wintering territories were protected in 1937 when President Roosevelt signed an order establishing the Aransas Migratory Waterfowl Refuge on the Blackjack Peninsula in Texas. It was later renamed the Aransas National Wildlife Refuge.

Robert Porter Allen, research director for the National Audubon Society, began his landmark study of the Whooping Crane at Aransas in autumn 1946 and discovered that four birds had never migrated north the previous summer. Two were yearlings and two were crippled birds unable to fly. The following year the two flightless cranes again spent the summer at Aransas. Allen named them the Summer Pair. And he named the male Crip because of his injured wing. In March 1948, Crip's mate was shot. She died with a bullet hole in her trachea. One month later, when Allen was in Crip's territory, he saw Crip call to a lone Whooper flying north. She came down and they spent the summer together.

Back in Louisiana time ran out for the six cranes still living free on the marshes. By 1947 only one survived. The United States Fish &

Wildlife Service (USFWS), refuge personnel, and Allen all agreed the bird had to be relocated to Aransas. Though in poor condition after the capture and transfer to the refuge in March, the bird rallied. Upon release she wandered into territory held by a pair of cranes who attacked her. She recovered from those injuries and survived until the end of the summer. The refuge manager found her body. Cause of death: unknown.

That left Josephine as the sole genetic representative of the Louisiana flock. In the winter of 1947–48, thirty Whooping Cranes migrated to Aransas. Crip was waiting for them. Josephine still lived at the Audubon Park Zoo. Thirty-two Whooping Cranes in the world. Pete made it thirty-three. Blind in one eye, Pete had lived at the Gothenburg Gun Club in Nebraska since 1936. Allen wanted to put Pete and Josephine into a breeding situation. He wasn't absolutely sure they were male and female, but with only thirty-three Whooping Cranes on the planet it was certainly worth a try. The director of the Audubon Park Zoo, George Douglas, and the head of the gun club agreed to loan their birds.

Pete was sent to New Orleans in December 1947. But Allen felt the birds would be better off in a pen at Aransas that provided a natural environment. By October 1948, the 150-acre pen was ready and the birds were moved in. They danced in December and produced two eggs the following April. They were the first Whooping Crane eggs ever produced in captivity. Unfortunately both were infertile. Even worse, Pete died of natural causes two months later.

Crip was still on the refuge with his mate, but they hadn't nested. Allen wanted to put Crip in the pen with Josephine, who had proven herself a capable egg-layer. In October 1949, Crip was chased down and captured. His mate stayed with him until the last moment and then she flew away. Monogamy is the rule among cranes, but fortunately Josephine and Crip were an exception. They readily formed a pair bond. And though Crip's days of freedom had ended, his place in history had just begun.

Josephine and Crip produced the first Whooping Crane ever hatched in captivity on May 24, 1950. They incubated the egg themselves in their nest at Aransas. On Rusty's tiny back rested the hopes and aspirations of biologists desperate to help the wild flock. Four days later Rusty disappeared. Allen surmised that the chick had either died of natural causes and been scavenged by a Turkey Vulture or that a raccoon might have seized it.

The following year Josephine and Crip's single egg was lost when a storm brought strong winds and high water to the marsh and destroyed their nest. To make matters worse, the director of the Audubon Park Zoo wanted Josephine back. George Douglas showed up at Aransas on December 13, 1951, and demanded his bird. At that time the business of jurisdiction over endangered species was a new one for the federal government. Despite a flurry of calls to Washington for legal rulings on the matter, Douglas was allowed to reclaim Josephine. Not wanting to break up a mated pair, the U.S. Fish & Wildlife Service permitted Douglas to take Crip as well, on loan. So from a semiwild environment in the marshes of Aransas, the two Whoopers went to live in a small pen in a zoo. Four years passed before they nested again.

Back at Aransas in 1956, one pair of Whoopers got a late start on their northward migration. They left on May 3 but got only as far as Lampasas County, where one of the birds hit a high wire and injured a wing. Its mate joined it at a pond on a local ranch, but a few weeks later the pond dried up and the uninjured bird flew away. The other one walked to a water trough near a ranch house, where the owner caught the crane and called the San Antonio Zoo. Fred Stark, the director, immediately sent an employee to pick up the bird. Over the years Stark had been involved in valiant efforts to save other injured Whooping Cranes. The bird was named Rosie even though no one knew for certain that it was a female. Stark contacted the USFWS and was granted permission to keep the bird, on loan.

Rosie lived alone for nine years. In 1962 she was positively identified as a female. Roxy Laybourne, a biologist, had developed a new instrument for examining a bird's sexual organs while the bird was still alive. Previously, a bird's sex could only be confirmed during a necropsy or by observing a pair for conclusive behavioral data.

While Rosie waited for a mate, Crip and Josephine did all they could to help the cause of Whooping Crane conservation. From 1955 to 1965 they produced fifty-two eggs. Only about one-fourth of them hatched, and only four of those survived to maturity. There were two chicks from 1957, George and Georgette. Peewee hatched in 1958, and Pepper arrived in 1961. Both Josephine and Crip were already adults when they unwittingly joined the effort to breed Whooping Cranes in captivity. In 1964 they were thought to be at least twenty-six and twenty years old, respectively.

The wild Whoopers were still teetering on the brink of extinction, and with so few birds (only thirty-three cranes returned to Aransas in the fall of 1963) every individual represented a vital contribution to the gene pool. If Rosie, who was living at the San Antonio Zoo, didn't breed, her genes would be lost forever (she appeared to be an immature bird when captured so it was unlikely that she had any wild offspring). George Douglas at the Audubon Park Zoo refused to send any of Crip and Josephine's offspring to San Antonio and had denied Laybourne access to the birds for positive sexual identification. Since there was a possibility that one of the four young birds might be a male, Rosie was moved to the Audubon Park Zoo in April 1964, even though that meant the entire captive population of Whooping Cranes was in one location. The whole group could be wiped out by illness or a catastrophic event.

Later that year Douglas died. The new director allowed Laybourne to examine Josephine's offspring: George, Georgette, Peewee, and Pepper. She pronounced Peewee to be the lone female in the group. Rosie was then paired with George, whose name was later changed to Angus. Georgette became George II and years later was renamed Tony. Unfortunately Rosie and Angus did little more than coexist.

A year later, the one thing that everyone feared happened. On Thursday, September 9, 1965, Hurricane Betsy slammed into Louisiana. All the cranes were moved inside and survived. But three days later, when they were back in their pens, a helicopter surveying the damage lingered over the enclosures. Josephine repeatedly threw herself against the fence. By the time the zookeepers got to her, Josephine was bloodied but still standing. The next morning she was dead. The continued existence of the Louisiana flock, genetically speaking, depended on her offspring: Tony, Angus, Peewee, and Pepper.

Josephine's death left Crip alone—but not for long. Since Rosie and Angus hadn't demonstrated a strong pair bond, everyone agreed to see if Crip would pair with Rosie. He did. They spent one more year at the Audubon Park Zoo and were then transferred to the San

Antonio Zoo on January 5, 1967. Rosie laid two eggs in June, and the first chick hatched on July 6. Elation turned to sorrow when Crip accidently stepped on the baby and it died. Fred Stark was determined to protect the second chick from the bizarre misfortunes that seemed to haunt the Whooping Cranes. After it hatched, he removed the chick from the nest and put it in a cardboard box in his living room, with a lamp to keep it warm. For the next two weeks, Stark took care of the rare crane. Her name was Tex.

Stark hand-fed the chick and kept close watch on her. Did he realize that in the absence of other cranes and with almost constant human companionship the young bird would come to look upon people as her protectors and friends? That she would see in humans a reflection of herself? Probably not. But to Dr. Ray C. Erickson, the young federal biologist who came to get Tex when she was sixteen days old, the situation was immediately obvious:

"He was not behaviorally qualified to know that [there would be problems], which is no reflection on him. He did the best he could to try to save the bird and to raise it properly, nutritionally, and so forth. But raising [her] in such a situation, where she didn't have exposure to other birds, almost from the time she was hatched, didn't give the bird a chance to be imprinted on cranes, on her own kind."

Erickson had come to take Tex to the Patuxent Wildlife Research Center, a new federal facility in Maryland for the study and captive propagation of endangered species. The ultimate goal was to replenish the depleted wild populations of endangered animals.

The first leg of the trip went smoothly.

"I took her in a cardboard box, which was heated with a hot-water bottle under some padding on the floor. Just a small box about a foot square and maybe fourteen or fifteen inches high. On the flight from San Antonio to Dallas quite a number of people showed an interest in it because they could hear a peep every once in a while. So I showed it to some of the passengers because I felt it was in the public interest to let them see it. There was no handling or anything like that.

"Then when I got to Dallas, I had to transfer [to another airline], and so I started boarding and the crane let out a peep at the wrong time, just as I was going by the stewardess. And she said, 'Do you have a bird in there?' I said, 'Yes. But it's a Whooping Crane, a very rare, endangered species.' She said, 'I don't care what it is. You can't take a bird aboard where food is being served.' I said, 'Well, I better talk to the manager about this.' She said, 'Well, you can talk all you want to, but you're not going to bring that bird aboard.'

"So I went and talked to an officer in charge there and he said, 'That's right, you're not allowed to bring a bird in the same compartment where food is being served.' I said, 'Well, I'm very concerned about the welfare of this very valuable bird representing a nearly disappeared gene pool. It must be given the best possible care on the trip.' He assured me that the bird would occupy the tail section of the baggage compartment and there would be nothing to fall on it. He assured me that the temperature would be within five degrees of what it was in the passenger compartment. Well, I saw there was no alternative. I saw the bird safely into the [cargo] compartment. They sealed it. Then I went aboard and remained very nervous during the trip. I told the captain of the flight that I wanted to be allowed to supervise the unloading of the bird, right from the compartment. And he said, 'I can assure you that you will.'

"So we got to Baltimore. I got out of the plane and went [right to] the section where the unloading was taking place and went out to the plane. I asked about the tail compartment and they said it had already been unloaded. So I raced the length of the terminal to where the baggage was already coming out. Along the roller, bumping merrily along, gently, was the box."

Though it was several years before she was officially declared a female, to Erickson, "She always seemed to be a little bit more petite in her actions than you would expect from a male." As Tex matured her identity problems became more obvious. She showed no inclination to socialize with other Whooping Cranes and lived in her own pen. She could see and hear the other birds but welcomed attention only from her human friends. Erickson recalls her "stiff, aloof stance, almost trying to have the posture of a human. But she was a shameless flirt. She would dance with anyone." Well, almost anyone. According to Erickson, "Anyone with a dress was given a different reaction."

During Tex's first years at Patuxent the research center was beginning a captive breeding program for Whooping Cranes. Single eggs from several two-egg nests at Wood Buffalo National Park in the Northwest Territories were collected and flown to Patuxent for incubation and hatching. The cranes were hand-reared but had plenty of visual and vocal communication with others of their species. Eventually the new Whoopers all lived together in a very large pen. But no one knew which were female and which were male. Short of an internal examination of a live or dead bird, there still was no conclusive method for determining a crane's sex.

George, however, while studying the taxonomic relationships of cranes based on their unison calls for his doctoral thesis in the late 1960s, had learned that males and females of a species have different unison calls. At Cornell, George had shared this information with another young ornithologist, Dr. Cameron (Cam) Kepler. Cam went on to do fieldwork on the Puerto Rican parrot. In April 1973, he moved to Maryland as Patuxent's research behaviorist.

Cam applied the information from George's as yet unpublished thesis to Sandhill Cranes, and it proved effective in identifying males and females. And even though some scientists remained skeptical, he did the same with the Whooping Cranes and separated out several pairs. "I had to keep proving it," he remembers. "Every time something I said was a female laid an egg, that was a big success. And each time a female laid a fertile egg we had the other bird confirmed as a male. Every sex identification I did behaviorally worked out."

And then there was Tex. She gave unison calls and Cam knew the bird was a female, but "it was obvious to me that she was not going to be useful for any males," Cam recalls. He was able to spend a little time with her, and a few other people lavished attention on her when possible, but Cam knew it wasn't enough. So did George.

And while breeding all the Whooping Cranes in captivity was of paramount importance, getting chicks from Tex was imperative. On the morning of June 16, 1971, zookeepers found Rosie, Tex's mother, quite ill. The San Antonio Zoo veterinary staff worked all day to save her, consulting frequently with colleagues at Patuxent, but she died late that afternoon. The necropsy revealed a liver tumor. Tex, mixed-up Tex, was Rosie's only surviving offspring. If Tex did not produce chicks, Rosie's gene pool would be lost forever.

George was visiting Patuxent one or two times a year and usually stayed with Cam and his wife. "We spent a lot of time looking at all the birds and at Tex," says Cam. "And we thought, 'Here I am, getting these birds to breed, and here's Tex languishing away.' And there was also a bird in the Audubon Park Zoo in New Orleans languishing away. A male named Tony.

Tex at nest in a cornfield. *Photo by George Archibald.*

"We knew both institutions were highly territorial and protective of their respective cranes. But George said to me, 'Wouldn't it be wonderful if we could have Tex and Tony together at the International Crane Foundation?' And I said, 'yes, it would be wonderful'—I'm not very institutional in my thinking and that sometimes gets you into trouble—'but I don't think Ray Erickson will authorize transferring Tex to ICF.' Ray was protective of the Whoopers and ICF was an unproven institution at that time. And George said, 'Well, I know the people at the Audubon Park Zoo, and I know they're not going to authorize sending Tony to ICF.' George needed a male Whooper for Tex's artificial insemination. But George talked to the Audubon Park Zoo and I talked to Ray. As we expected, both flatly said no.

"The next time George and I got together, we hatched a scheme. We knew that neither institution would give us a Whooper. We also knew that each institution suspected the other would never give up a crane. So about two weeks later I went into Ray Erickson's office and said, 'You know, we've got Tex here and we don't have enough time for her. She's languishing away. We can cover her with artificial insemination but that doesn't do any good if she doesn't lay, and she's not going to get into reproductive condition to lay or even ovulate unless she has constant stimulation from people. It would be really nice if we could get her someplace where she could be stimulated on a regular basis, and George would do it, but I know that's not going to happen. But, if George can get Tony out of the Audubon Park Zoo, do you think we could send Tex to ICF?' And Ray said that if George could get Tony out of the Audubon Zoo, he'd send Tex to ICF.

"Well, George was doing the same thing down in New Orleans. And they said, 'If Cam can get Tex to ICF, we'll send Tony.' And that's how we did it because neither institution would make the first move. After all the fiddling around we did to make the move possible, the move itself was almost anticlimactic."

Almost.

By the time Ron and ICF researcher John Baldwin returned from their eight-hour round trip to O'Hare International Airport on April 15, 1976, quite a crowd had assembled at ICF. In addition to friends from town and reporters, there was a television crew from Louisiana whose story coverage had started with Tex's departure from Patuxent. The Audubon Park Zoo in New Orleans was sending Tony to Baraboo in a couple of weeks. Millie Zantow, ICF's administrator, led the group down the hill to the breeding unit.

Tex was assigned the first house on the right in the breeding unit. The indoor living quarters were already divided—half for Tex and half for George. Milly had placed a bed and desk in George's half. Tex had a water bucket, food bin, and wall-to-wall wood shavings on the floor. A small door gave her access to her yard.

Ron and Milly liberated Tex inside to let her acclimate slowly to her new surroundings. She didn't exactly walk around her new pen. It was more of an arrogant strut. She looked at all the strange people staring at her. Then, for the first time in nearly a century, the call of a Whooping Crane pierced the midwestern countryside.

Finally it was time for everyone to hike back up the hill and leave George and Tex alone. Ron and Milly paused to consider what George was getting himself into. He had committed to living twenty-four hours a day with a rather large bird who had amorous designs on him. Except for meals and calls (from nature), George was now another resident of the breeding unit. "But if anybody can get Tex to produce, George can," Ron observed. Then he and Milly continued up the hill and left George and Tex to their first night together.

Even though workers at Patuxent gave Tex special attention, no one had the time to develop a permanent relationship. Now, for the first time in her life, she had the opportunity to form a pair bond with what she considered to be her own species. It didn't take Tex long to warm up to George's devotion. When she wanted to eat, George was there to stand guard. When she tucked her head snugly beneath her wing to take a nap, George was there to make sure no predator surprised her.

Just who was protecting whom was not always clear. Tex quickly assumed a possessive attitude toward George. If a staff member approached the pair while they were foraging on the hill, Tex left George and strutted toward the intruder in a threat walk. The red skin on her head blushed bright red as she showed it off to her best advantage by pointing her bill to the ground. George found this highly entertaining. He enjoyed all of Tex's antics—well, almost all.

There was, George recalls, the "one day that I sat in my little shed and everything seemed pretty normal, when suddenly I saw her running. She was doing that galloping crane run across the field, chasing a big skunk. I thought, oh my gosh, I'm going to have to live with a bird that's been sprayed by a skunk. So I go tearing across the field and started screaming, 'Tex, Tex, Tex.' She started unison calling because she couldn't help herself. Then the skunk kept going and she came back."

During their first breeding season together George often wore a red knit cap when he danced with Tex. Whether this made him more attractive to Tex is not certain. And though he lived with her, foraged with her, and danced with her, George could only contribute so much to the Whooping Crane cause. That's why Tony was shipped to ICF from New Orleans two weeks after Tex's arrival. The plan was to artificially inseminate Tex with semen collected from Tony. Even though the staff knew Tex wouldn't respond to him, for his sake, Tony lived next door to Tex so he could see and hear another Whooping Crane. He knew he was a crane. Part of his beak was broken off and he had crooked toes, but Tony had no identity problems.

Tony did have another problem, however. He didn't have much sperm. And what sperm he had weren't too exciting. They just kind of lolled around in the ejaculate. Tony was a dud. But a contingency plan was already in place. Cam Kepler and Ray Erickson at Patuxent had agreed that if Tony was unable to provide satisfactory semen, they would send semen from their birds to Baraboo. But during that first season in 1976, Tex was inseminated with Tony's contributions. And though she clearly bonded with George, Tex did not lay any eggs that year.

In 1977, the ICF staff began the regimen of artificial insemination while patches of snow still littered the ground. This gave the birds a chance to get used to the handling again before they reached peak breeding condition. As the season progressed, biologists at Patuxent arranged for Whooping Crane semen to be flown to Baraboo two or three times a week.

Perhaps it was an omen when on March 26, ICF's only Siberian Crane, Phyllis, laid an egg for the first time in her life. She had been in captivity for twenty-four years.

Two weeks later, Saturday, April 9, began like every other day at the Crane Foundation. The office staff had the weekend off, but everyone else maintained their daily work routine. I was at ICF that year to study the Hooded Cranes. After my observations that morning, at about ten o'clock, I watered and fed the birds in the barn and the nonbreeder flock. George asked if I would help him with the breeding-unit birds. We filled the water trough on the trailer hitched to the truck and drove down the hill.

The first house we stopped at was Tex's. Naturally, I waited outside while George went in to get the bucket. When he came out Tex was right behind him. George dumped the old water, scrubbed the bucket, and dipped it in the trough for fresh water. He and Tex went inside to put the bucket back and George came out again. Tex was right behind him.

"I thought she might like to come with us," he said. I knew Tex had already declared war on women and wasn't too thrilled. Before we moved on, George decided to bestow some attention on Tex by putting her through the stimulation part of artificial insemination. He barely stroked her when her tail went up and revealed a greatly enlarged cloaca. Then the three of us set off for the next house. I was careful not to get too close to George and incur Tex's wrath. George promised to keep an eye on her. Tex kept her eye on me.

Three immature Red-crowned Cranes lived in the last house in the breeding unit. They were only a year old and still had their brown plumage of youth. George let them out for a brief reconnaissance flight around the property. (The days of free-flying cranes ended soon thereafter out of concern for both the cranes and the unsuspecting people they sometimes landed next to.)

While I enjoyed the sight of young cranes effortlessly soaring on seven-foot wingspans, George kept an eye on Tex. She was getting farther away from him and closer to me. Suddenly I caught a flash of white in my peripheral vision, but it was too late. Tex chased me clear around the truck and trailer. On our second pass by the passenger door, I dove head first into the truck and slammed the door behind me. Tex still managed to get in a solid jab with her bill. George was doubled over in laughter. I moved over into the driver's seat and glared at George: "You can walk back." Then I drove up the hill leaving George behind with a triumphant Tex.

George returned Tex to her pen, but when he checked her soon after she was pacing at the east side of her enclosure. He opened the door and Tex headed straight for the cornfield. She quickly built a haphazard nest of corn stalks. George kept her company. As the hours passed he tried to leave her but she followed him up the hill. By now George knew that she was going to lay. He could feel the egg inside of her. So he put a chair next to her nest and sat with her. Six hours later Tex laid an egg, the first of her life. She was ten years old.

George retrieved the egg and put Tex back in her pen. When George walked into the incubation room, I was checking on some other eggs. He placed Tex's egg in my hand. It was still warm. And it was kind of narrow at one end with a series of funny little wrinkles. It certainly was one of a kind.

Unfortunately the egg was infertile. But Tex and George proved to everyone that they could do it. And they would do it again.

Logistically, the next breeding season would be a little easier. The Audubon Park Zoo agreed to send Angus to ICF. The staff hoped he would provide better semen than his brother Tony. Angus took up residence in the same complex as Tex and Tony on

September 14, 1977. Unlike Tony, who had a few physical deformities, Angus was a beautiful crane.

Tony and Angus were the last surviving offspring of Josephine and Crip. There were only two other chicks that lived into adulthood. Peewee was twelve years old when she died in 1970. Pepper was almost thirteen when he died in 1974. Crip, father to Tex, Angus, and Tony, was living with his third (captive) mate, Ektu, at the San Antonio Zoo.

The 1978 breeding season following the epidemic was a tough one. Of the fifty-two eggs produced, only twenty-seven were fertile and seventeen hatched. Some of the chicks were weak and did not survive. But one egg in particular held everyone's attention.

Tex laid again on April 27. And again, there was only one egg. Most cranes usually lay two eggs, but Tex was not like most cranes. Her egg was carefully monitored during incubation. After three weeks a dark mass was visible below the air cell. The embryo was growing into a Whooping Crane chick. When George "floated" the egg in a bowl of water, the developing embryo responded by moving, and the jiggling egg was cause for elation.

As the incubation period drew to a close the chick began the arduous hatching process by breaking into the air cell at the top of the egg. In the morning George heard it peeping inside the shell. Everyone on staff was alerted. The chick would be out within a day. But later that afternoon there was only silence. It didn't hatch. An examination by the National Wildlife Health Research Center determined that the embryo was malformed. If the chick had hatched, it probably wouldn't have been normal. George was crushed: "The biggest disappointment of my life."

Cam Kepler describes breeding endangered species as "one part biology, one part art, a certain amount of luck, and a fair amount of politics." Apparently the luck hadn't kicked in yet. There was another major setback for the species in 1978. On May 24, several hot-air balloons passed over the foundation and frightened the cranes. Angus ran frantically in his pen, crashed into the fence, and broke his beak. With part of his upper mandible missing, he was unable to eat by himself and had to be force-fed. In August, during one of the stressful feeding sessions, Angus broke a leg. Still he endured. He was suspended in a sling in an attempt to keep weight

George and Tex in the field. *Photo by Kyoko Archibald.*

off the leg. Finally, the once beautiful bird, now crippled and weak, could fight no longer. Angus died on October 7.

That left Tony as the sole male Whooper at ICF. Once again Patuxent stepped in to help. For the 1979 breeding season frozen Whooping Crane semen was sent to Baraboo. It was shipped and stored in liquid nitrogen at −196°C and used as needed to supplement Tony's donations to the cause. On May 9, Tex laid an egg. But the shell was soft and it broke. The staff was unable to determine if it was fertile. It was, of course, her only egg that year.

Had the egg hatched, and had the afternoon of March 27 several weeks before been different, Crip would have been a grandfather. On that day at 1:55 P.M., Tex's father died of a heart attack. The reliable old bird was at least thirty-five years old. The survival of Crip and Rosie's genetic line and that of the Louisiana flock through Josephine depended on their only surviving offspring, Tex and Tony.

Though George lived with Tex only in 1976, he continued to spend substantial amounts of time with her in the succeeding seasons. But in 1980 his responsibilities as codirector of ICF and the need to help other crane species through fieldwork kept him away from ICF during the breeding season. In his absence a Japanese colleague, Yoshimitsu Shigeta, danced with Tex. But Tex put Asians right behind women and redheads on the list of people types she detested.

The breeding program suffered another blow at three o'clock on an August afternoon in 1980 when Tony was found dead in his pen. The necropsy showed an abdominal hemorrhage. He was twenty-three years old.

Oblivious to the ominous developments around her, Tex continued to endear herself to people who took care of her. Aviculturist Lisa Hartman says Tex was generally well behaved, but "she was curious. Tex always had that look in her eye as she watched you. You knew you had to keep an eye on her, too." Tex's characteristic strut only intensified that feeling. "One of my favorite things about her," remembers Lisa, "was when she came out of her house in the winter. You know how anger is always characterized by smoke coming out of someone's head? Well, she'd come out of the warm house into the cold and you'd see steam rising from her head as she walked around."

As the 1981 breeding season approached, George realized that other commitments would again prevent him from spending time with Tex. So head aviculturist Mike Putnam, a Caucasian man with dark hair (Tex's dream human), agreed to dance with her. Tex liked him and responded to his attention. But despite Mike's effort—he danced with Tex three times a day, seven days a week—Tex did not lay.

Everyone regrouped for 1982. On April 1, George spent the day with Tex. Between dawn and dusk he never left her side. And he did the same the next day. And the next. They danced in the morning and the evening. He walked with her as she foraged in the field near the breeding unit and helped her defend their territory against anyone who dared to approach. She, in turn, stood guard while he typed or read in a small shed that was his office. Often they just kept each other company.

Biologists at Patuxent had also made a strong commitment to Tex. After Tony's death in 1980, Patuxent sent another male Whooping Crane, Tux, to ICF. Tux had physical deformities and could only be used in an artificial insemination situation. But the bird died from trauma suffered in a freak accident in his pen in April 1981. With no male Whoopers at ICF, Patuxent was the only source of semen to cover Tex. Dr. George Gee, research physiologist at Patuxent, usually coordinated the collection of semen and its shipment to Baraboo. A large team of people was involved in the project. It was too expensive to ship fresh semen all the time so the Patuxent team sent a substantial amount of frozen semen stored in liquid nitrogen. All the samples were "donated" by Killer, who was, unfortunately, aptly named. He killed two mates at Patuxent. They were bizarre incidents in that he had lived with each of them for several years and gave no indication of aggressive behavior. His breeding efforts were now restricted to artificial insemination.

The plan was to inseminate Tex with the frozen semen until she neared ovulation and then give her fresh semen, also from Killer. Biologists knew that inseminating a crane before she ovulated increased the chances of fertility.

By mid-April, George determined that Tex was coming into breeding condition. The Patuxent team collected a fresh sample from Killer and put it in a tube placed inside a plastic Thermos bottle. A worker rushed it from Patuxent to the Baltimore airport and hand-carried it to the ticket desk. The Thermos bottle rode in the cockpit with the pilots. The semen had to be used within ten hours. When the unusual cargo arrived in Madison, an ICF aviculturist was waiting for it. The aviculturist drove back to Baraboo (a forty-five-minute trip), transferred the semen into a syringe, and inseminated Tex. Two or three days later everybody did it all over again.

It didn't take long for George's friends and colleagues to find out what was happening, and they soon gave up trying to reach him during the day. For the staff, it was business as usual. Lisa, though, would sometimes stand at the top of the hill, look down, and "there would be George, lying on the ground, and Tex foraging nearby. Or I'd see Joan sitting in a chair, having a meeting with George. I always wondered what anybody walking by would think about that scene."

Joan Fordham, administrator of the foundation since 1979, took it all in stride. "Working with George was often unusual, so talking with him in the field was only a little more unusual than normal."

But Tex's animosity toward women, more acute during the breeding season, was an inconvenience. "Although I did not go into crane pens on a regular basis, I had done so often enough to be able to read her behavior and anticipate it most of the time. My only real problem was George. He used to stand back and laugh at my efforts to ward off Tex. He could control her with just a few words, but preferred to watch her give me a run for my money. But only once did she really jab me." (It was important that Tex be dominant in her territory and unfortunate that the women of ICF paid the price of her success.)

Holding executive meetings in a cornfield, rushing to the airport every two or three days, helping a big white bird look for earthworms—it was just another season at the Crane Foundation. Until May 1.

On May 1, George noticed that Tex was behaving differently. Her food consumption dropped drastically and she was lethargic. He thought she was probably forming an egg and stayed close to her all day.

By dawn the next morning Tex had resumed her activities. At noon George palpated her and felt an egg. They built a nest. At sunset, Tex was still holding on to her egg.

On May 3, George and Tex spent a quiet morning together. At 1:30 in the afternoon she sat on her nest. George sat next to her and waited. At 3:00 P.M., Tex laid the egg. One end was exceptionally narrow and had a series of funny little wrinkles. George removed it immediately and replaced it with a "dummy," a Sandhill Crane egg filled with plaster of paris. He put Tex's egg under an incubating pair of Florida Sandhill Cranes. Natural incubation is always a better option (but not always an available option in captivity). True to form, Tex did not lay a second egg, and by mid-May she began straying from her territory. George moved out of the cornfield on May 20.

The Sandhills took care of Tex's egg. Whether they were incubating a developing embryo, no one knew. George and Mike Putnam waited two weeks before they candled the egg. By holding the egg next to a high-intensity light in a darkened room, they could determine whether the egg was fertile. A visible network of blood vessels belied the secret within the shell: it was fertile. But everyone's elation turned to concern when Mike discovered that it was losing weight at almost twice the normal rate. Perhaps the shell was thin. If the pattern continued, the chick would surely die.

They gave the Sandhills a swimming pool in the hope that the birds would bathe and then cover the egg with their wet feathers. They tried spraying the nest with water in an effort to hydrate the egg. But the loss of precious fluids continued. On the eighteenth day, the egg was removed from the Sandhills and placed in an incubator set at the usual temperature, 99.5°F, but with a higher than normal humidity. The egg continued to lose weight. And time was running out.

Dr. Bernard Wentworth of the Department of Poultry Science at the University of Wisconsin in Madison received an urgent phone call on May 24. The egg was due to hatch, if indeed it would, in about one week. Dr. Wentworth had a suggestion: submerge the egg in cold water. When an egg is put in cold water, the cold temperature causes the egg's volume to decrease and a vacuum is formed. This pulls water into the egg. He had first used this technique in 1958 during a research project with chicken eggs. In the mid-1970s he used it to get antibiotics into duck eggs that weren't hatching because of bacterial contamination. In his lab that evening, Dr. Wentworth made up an antibiotic solution for the first soak of Tex's egg. He wanted to cleanse the shell so that no bacteria would be pulled in along with the water during succeeding soaks. It would be like an alcohol swab before a shot. Dr. Wentworth was in Baraboo the next morning knowing that "the best we could hope for was for the weight loss to level off."

Five minutes in 40°F water would nearly suck the life out of a human being. But it was the only for hope for sustaining the life within Tex's egg. On succeeding days Mike or George soaked the egg in 50°F water. It worked. Where before the egg had lost nearly two grams per day, it now lost barely a half-gram in a week. Now that the egg was stabilized, the staff anticipated the next stage: hatching, an exhausting event for the chick.

On May 30, Mike moved the egg into the hatcher. He could hear the chick tapping inside the shell. The next morning Mike and George also heard the chick peeping. It was in the air cell at the top of the egg. By 3:25 P.M., the chick had pipped—there was a tiny hole in the egg. The chick had already labored for hours, and it still had a long way to go. On the morning of June 1 the pip hole was larger. The chick worked throughout the day to crack the cap off the top of the egg. Late in the afternoon, Mike put a piece of tape across the opening to force the chick to rest and wait for more of the blood vessels in the egg's membrane to dry up. Finally, at 6:40 P.M., Mike looked in the hatcher and saw a Whooping Crane. In the breeding unit at the bottom of the hill, away from all of the excitement, Tex foraged quietly in her yard.

The chick was named Gee Whiz. The name both honored George Gee from Patuxent for his personal and professional support and expressed everyone's amazement that the chick even existed. Gee Whiz's weight of 104 grams was at the low end of normal hatching weights for Whooping Cranes and he was weak. The staff organized into shifts for round-the-clock care. Most birds usually don't eat during their first day of life, but after forty-eight hours Gee Whiz still showed no interest in food. On June 3 George force-fed him a small amount of food to stimulate him. His condition improved slightly. The hours dragged as the staff watched and waited for Gee Whiz to rally. By 1:30 A.M. on June 4 they could wait no longer for fear he would die. They began an aggressive program of intensive care to get nourishment into the chick. His food pellets were moistened and molded into capsule-sized portions for force-feedings every few hours. Fortunately Gee Whiz could be encouraged to drink water on his own. He gained seven grams by the end of the day but suffered a major setback on June 5. He began vomiting and his weight dropped to 87 grams. The staff injected him with antibiotics to ward off infection in his weakened state. Because Gee Whiz had trouble swallowing, the staff switched from force-feedings to tube-feedings so the nourishment went directly into his stomach. He also received subcutaneous fluid injections. He responded.

The next day he weighed 101 grams and began to eat pellets on his own (with a lot of encouragement from the staff). The antibiotics and tube-feedings continued until gradually the improvements surpassed the setbacks. On June 11, a simple notation on Gee Whiz's health chart said it all: "Outside all day, eats by himself."

Between the constant attention he needed to survive and the adoring attention of the media, the staff walked a fine line. The publicity was important both for the foundation and the conservation of endangered species. But they were determined to ensure that Gee Whiz knew he was a crane. There weren't any young Whoopers for Gee Whiz to socialize with at ICF, but there were other young cranes that he met in the exercise yard. Genetically, Gee Whiz is half Killer and half Tex. And since Tex's parents were Crip and Rosie, Gee Whiz ensures the survival of those gene pools.

Most of the attention centered on Gee Whiz, but the indifferent mother and the proud "father" were not totally ignored. George received an invitation to tell his and Tex's story on "The Tonight Show" with Johnny Carson. He was booked for June 23.

Before he left for Los Angeles, George took a walk around the foundation. "It was a beautiful day and I went to walk around the birds down below like I always did. One of the interns was making a film about ICF and she asked if I would dance with Tex for the film. So I let her out along the road. She was molting and looked awful. But we danced and they filmed it. I went out to L.A. feeling really good about everything." George flew to Los Angeles on the afternoon of June 22. "I stayed at a beautiful hotel. I had my dinner and went to bed."

Back at ICF, Lisa checked the birds at the end of the day before she went home, just like she always did. Mike was on vacation in Connecticut. Ron retired to his house just a short walk down the road from the foundation. Joan went home to her family and a quiet dinner. Tex foraged in her yard for awhile. Then she tucked one leg up into her belly feathers, turned her long neck to lay her head on her back, and went to sleep.

On the morning of June 23, Lisa and the rest of the staff arrived for work at 8:00. In Los Angeles, George was still sleeping.

As Lisa and the avicultural staff were getting the truck ready so they could feed and water the birds, Joan was looking over the day's paperwork in the office. A short while later Lisa and the others drove down the hill to the breeding unit. "Tex hadn't come out of her shed that morning, which was unusual because she usually came out when we arrived. But I knew she was molting and often the cranes stay in their sheds when they're molting." Still, Lisa was uneasy and went to check on Tex.

George woke up and tried to decide whether to go out and do some fund-raising or stay in his room and prepare for his appearance on "The Tonight Show," which would be taped later that afternoon. He decided to stay in and read his Bible. He was nervous about the show. "I thought that if I read the Bible I would have peace and would find a scripture to help me. I found my favorite scripture and this wonderful feeling of peace came over me."

Lisa opened the door to Tex's shed. "I saw parts of her trachea lying on the floor. I looked around and found more parts of her. She had been disemboweled. We checked the pen and there was a big raccoon in there, hiding in the Christmas trees we put along the fence for visual barriers." Near the roof of Tex's house, the raccoon had torn a hole in the nylon netting that covered the top of the pen. A shaken Lisa appeared in Joan's office with the news. Ron was notified. Local authorities were called and they killed the raccoon. The sheriff warned them, "They'll be back tonight." The staff hoped it was an isolated incident.

George was scheduled to tape the show in a few hours. The staff discussed whether to tell him. Joan felt it wasn't fair for him not to know. In his hotel room George was writing down a scripture when the phone rang. Joan told him Tex was dead. He assured her, "I'm okay. I'll do the show."

George wasn't quite sure what would happen during the taping. But he explained about Tex's need to bond with a human because she was imprinted and showed some film of her. Then Johnny Carson quietly asked George, "Should we tell the audience the sad news?" And he did. In Connecticut, Mike Putnam leaped to his feet, stunned. Ray Erickson, two years into retirement, sat quietly in Oregon: "A lot of times it's hard to anticipate some of the problems you're going to face."

But now the problem of raccoon predation at ICF was real, not just a possibility. By the morning of June 24, the office was inundated with telegrams from around the country expressing condolences over Tex's death. When a second bird, a young Eastern Sarus Crane, was found killed, the staff set live traps along the pens and strung electrical wire around the breeding unit. They organized a twenty-four-hour patrol. Every crane that had an indoor shelter was locked inside. Meanwhile the press clamored for details of Tex's death, and life.

Just after midnight, George arrived back at the foundation to find Ron and the others patrolling the perimeter of the breeding unit. As he briefly described his experiences in Los Angeles, they heard a strange call from the other section of the property. Ron called it "a hair-raising, macabre sound to anyone who knew cranes." Everyone ran up the road toward the pens. George climbed a nine-foot fence to get there quicker. Ron ran around and met him in the pen of "I Presume," a one-year-old Blue Crane. George knelt over the dying bird. Its jugular vein was ripped open. In a few seconds the bird was dead.

It would take time to predator-proof the rest of the pens. The cranes had to be protected in the meantime. There was only one option, and it was not a popular one. The necessary permits were obtained along with the services of a local hunter and his dogs. ICF caught some bad press over the raccoon hunt. Several people criticized ICF for preaching conservation while endorsing the killing of raccoons. Ron handled the situation in the next newsletter: "We believed then, and we believe now, that our responsibility to the rare and endangered birds in our custody was the paramount consideration, and our decision to hunt the animals raiding our facilities was inescapable. To further jeopardize the lives of our cranes, some so rare that the entire world's population could fit into one of our 60' × 60' pens, in an attempt to avoid killing a few members of a widespread and abundant species seemed illogical and an abrogation of the stated purposes of ICF."

One of those pens was empty now. The first one on the right as you came down the hill. And no one walked in the field nearby. No one sat typing in the shed that was suddenly there for no reason. Women and redheaded men were safe.

But in another pen at the top of the hill lived a young crane with a lot of growing up to do. And a lot of life to give. Gee Whiz is more than a hope for his species, the sole hope for continuing two genetic lines that exist only within him. For while many cranes have come into this world by artificial insemination, no other crane had as much devotion, determination, and effort put into its creation as did Gee Whiz.

And no individual crane touched so many people over so many years as did Tex. She went from Fred Stark's living room to a cardboard box on Ray Erickson's lap, to the Patuxent Wildlife Research Center, and then to the International Crane Foundation. Finally, they even discussed her on a national television talk show. Like her mother before her, Tex gave the world one descendant. Along the way she left a few occasionally frustrated biologists, some bruised behinds, and a few broken hearts.

George and Tex on an afternoon stroll. *Photo by Kyoko Archibald.*

NINE

Time to Move on

By the late 1970s, ICF's bond with the Sauey farm was loosening. Research, experiments with new chick-rearing techniques important to future reintroduction programs, and proper medical care for the cranes were difficult if not impossible to conduct on-site. The 1978 epidemic had rendered the nonbreeder field, roadside pens, and main barn useless for future captive propagation plans. Down below, the breeding unit was full and there was no room to expand. Ron and George believed strongly in the prairie restoration and had big dreams for an expansive program. The number of foreign scientists and students who wanted to study at ICF was steadily increasing. Thousands of people now visited ICF each year, and improved facilities for education programs and even public restrooms were desperately needed. Even if the Sauey farm had been big enough to accommodate all of the expansion plans they still would have searched for a new site. After all, Norman and Claire still made their home next door. They never figured on being part of a tourist attraction. In the latter part of 1978, Ron, George, and the new board of trustees all agreed it was time to move on.

While George was overseas that winter, Ron, along with Mary and John Wickem, searched for a new site. Woody Zantow, realtor and husband of ICF's first administrator, Milly Zantow, had learned that Eunice Erickson, an old school friend, was selling her 160-acre farm. One afternoon Woody met Ron and the Wickems for a tour of the farm in the only manner possible in the middle of winter, on cross-country skis. Even under a foot of snow Mary could see that the farm "was a beautiful piece of land. We knew immediately that this was the place." Equally important was Eunice's delight when they told her why they wanted the land.

Eunice and her brother bought part of the farm in 1949 and the rest in 1953. She had been left a widow with a six-month-old baby, and her brother returned from the service with physical disabilities.

"He couldn't do much, but he liked farming, so between the two of us we made one. Kept it going. We raised crossbred beef, corn, oats, and grasses in rotation."

Eunice is still going. The first thing you notice about her is not necessarily that she's a tall woman, but that at seventy-three her posture is ramrod straight, her gait steady and strong. Close-cropped gray hair frames a face lined not from age, but from years of honest farming, physical labor, and perhaps all the cigarettes she smokes.

Many of Eunice's contemporaries drained wetlands to increase their agricultural acreage. But not Eunice.

"It's not the way I do it! We used to have a big Blue Heron in the west pond and all kinds of stuff in that east pond. We gained more by leaving it as it was. We loved our wildlife."

She decided to sell the farm when her brother died in 1975.

"I toyed with the market for four years. I didn't waste my time with anyone who wasn't serious or didn't have backing. I talked [with the ICF people] from January until the deal was completed in May. You just don't sell it like a bag of potatoes or a pair of shoes."

Eunice remained on the farm until her new house was built. It took her six more years to sell all her cattle. She ate the last one. Eunice is now ICF's neighbor. She lives on a one-hundred-acre spread across the road. "I'm used to having elbow room," Eunice explains.

ICF's new site is just off County A Road on Shady Lane Road five miles north of the foundation's old City View Road location. It's close to but not on a busy road, and it's only a short drive from the interstates for easy access by tourists. It's near the old ICF site, which eased logistical problems of moving, and large enough that the breeding cranes who require privacy can be placed far back from Shady Lane Road and the public facilities.

Owen and Anne Gromme and Mary and John Wickem provided the down payment, with the rest to be paid on a fifteen-year contract. Additional major financial support came from another old friend and supporter, Wolf Brehm of Vogelpark Walsrode in Germany. The local Baraboo National Bank provided the mortgage. It was barely a half-dozen years since George and Ron had sent letters to anyone remotely interested in cranes, and some who weren't, explaining over and over who they were and what they were doing up on the hill on City View Road. With the help of a few old friends who had always shared their dream and the assistance of new trustees who brought their diverse talents and personalities to the task at hand, George and Ron worried a bit less about ICF's mere survival and allowed themselves to plan their foundation's future.

Their years at the Sauey farm had taught them much about captive management of cranes, such as what types of pens worked best and what species-specific features an enclosure needed to promote the breeding condition of a crane pair. The bitter lessons of the epidemic and the marauding raccoons would greatly influence the new facility's design. The entire operation would attain a new level of sophistication.

It would take millions of dollars to develop the new site, and ICF solicited funds from major private and corporate donors and the general membership. Because there were a half-dozen components in the site plan, the new ICF could be built in stages as the financial base slowly expanded. But no one realized in 1979 that from purchase to the final construction it was going to be a ten-year odyssey. The first building was to be a facility for public viewing of cranes who were not involved in propagation. Concurrent with that would be a visitor's center with a small theater for the slide show that began each tour.

As details of the land purchase were being finalized Konrad Liegel appeared. He had been invited by Charlie Luthin to assist with a ten-acre prairie restoration at the Sauey farm. In short order he discovered that Charlie was leaving and the prairie was moving to the new site.

"We wanted to learn something about the new site," says Konrad. "We had to understand the land before we could restore it." Konrad was soon joined by his friend Scott Freeman. "In 1979 and 1980 we prepared the herbarium collection, a guide to the plant communities of the new site, a history of the site, and a topographic soil map of the restoration area."

The site is perched on a terminal moraine deposited by the retreating Wisconsin Glacier. Kettle holes, rolling topography, and soil diversity from sand to silty clay are all calling cards left behind by the glacier.

Konrad also directed surveys of the small mammal and nesting bird populations on the site. Konrad recruited Darrel Morrison, then chairman of the University of Wisconsin Landscape Architecture Department, to join the project. Morrison, Konrad, and Scott divided the site into three sections: the restoration area, the public area, and the breeding area. The team expanded to include Evelyn Howell, another UW landscape architecture professor, and her class. They figured out which plant communities should be included in the restoration area. The final design spanned sixty-five acres of prairie, oak savanna, wetlands, and forest. The goal was not to lay out display plots for the various plants but to re-create complete (if small) ecosystems. ICF had long preached the need to preserve wild lands for wild cranes. The restoration afforded an opportunity to show visitors the beauty and importance of prairies and wetlands. It was not an offshoot of the foundation, but an integral component of crane conservation.

Konrad and his army of interns and volunteers fanned out in a fifty-mile radius of the Shady Lane Road location and collected native prairie-plant seeds from along old railroad beds and remnant prairies. It took hundreds of hours to collect the seeds, clean, and store them for future planting. One gathering season might yield two hundred pounds of seed from more than 125 species of plants. The eventual ten-acre Federation Fields Prairie—named in honor of the Wisconsin Garden Club Federation, whose members were generously supporting the project—was situated in the middle of the restoration area, which was itself the middle third of the property.

On May 23, 1980, each prairie person carried a bag of premixed seed to a designated location on the one-and-a-half-acre inaugural planting site. Each bag contained precise proportions of ten grasses and seventy-four forbs (prairie flowers). At the appointed moment Konrad joined his "stalwart volunteers [as they] began scattering the [bags' contents], shouting words of encouragement to the seeds as they fell into place. Good luck. Go for it. Grow baby grow." But what had taken months to gather now took only one hour to dispense. Through their fingers passed big and little bluestem, Indian grass, asters, blazing stars, sunflowers, black-eyed Susans, goldenrod, and lupine. Then "all hands joined in a furious rain dance." Thirty days later the first seeds germinated.

As the prairie slowly expanded, the crew cut down nonnative pine and black locust trees, leaving the tallest, straightest oaks to tower over the native grasses. Oak savanna, a balance of open grassland and forest trees, took its place among the plant communities.

The Owen Gromme Marsh (Eunice's west pond) was planted in 1983 and 1984. A second kettle marsh (the east pond) is on the John Stedman Prairie, restored from 1984 to 1986 under the auspices of Patricia Stedman as a memorial to her late husband.

The diversity of plant communities provides habitat for a variety of different species. Butterflies have become so numerous at ICF that they rate their own guidebook. Least skipperlings favor the marshes, wood nymphs and eastern tailed blues enliven the prairie trails, spring azures and tiger swallowtails prefer the forest edge, and brown satyrs await hikers deep in the woods. Butterflies of the prairie and savanna rely on fire, a natural part of prairie life, to prevent invading woody plants from crowding out their food sources. Here, too, ICF provides. Controlled burns are an essential tool of the foundation's management.

Establishment of native plant communities is not limited to the prairie acreage but extends throughout the entire facility, with grasses and wildflowers along footpaths leading to the Johnson Exhibit Pod and surrounding the buildings and the parking lot. A forested depression that separated the east and west public areas was left intact except for a footpath laid down to connect the two sections. Despite the restoration's prominence in the site plan, ICF still had no budget for an ecology department. As had been done ten years before for the cranes, donations of money, plants, and supplies were eagerly sought. When construction began at the new site, Konrad was finally put on the payroll as site manager, more than two years after he arrived at ICF.

All of the restoration areas were devoted to native North American plant communities, but an African savanna, or grassland, was planted at ICF in 1982. Actually, it was a superb North American imitation of the African Crowned Cranes' habitat. Interns and volunteers planted native tallgrass and shortgrass species in the one-and-a-half acre exhibit to conjure up images of the African tallgrass marsh and shortgrass veld. A few acacialike trees were added to complete the mirage. It became the home for two female Grey Crowned Cranes and one pair of Black Crowned Cranes. A footpath circles the savanna, and what became known as the Sandy Knoll rises up beyond the north arc of the trail. On the knoll, perhaps the most authentic prairie land on the site, you can view more than twenty-five prairie plants at close range, including Junegrass, pasque flowers, wild lupine, prairie dropseed, azure aster, prairie dock, coneflowers, butterflyweed, prairie blazing stars, and leadplant.

In addition to students, interns, and volunteers, the Wisconsin Conservation Corps (WCC) played a vital role in the habitat restoration and development of the new site. The WCC is a team of young adults funded jointly for one year by the state of Wisconsin and organizations that request their services, in this case ICF, the Nature Conservancy, the Upham Woods 4-H Camp, and the Sauk County Natural Beauty Council, all of whom "shared" the crew. At ICF the WCC constructed the Chick Exercise Yard, helped collect seeds, built the overlook west of the Johnson Pod (which provides a panoramic view of the restoration), laid trails through the prairie, wetland, and oak savanna, assisted with signs along the trails and at various exhibits, and built the small benches designed by Aldo Leopold that were placed throughout the property to offer a comfortable seat for resting or daydreaming.

Konrad and his plant people had labored at the new site for more than two years when the official groundbreaking ceremony for the public section was finally held on a rainy September 25 in 1981. Nearly fifty people joined George and Ron at the southwest corner of the site. Architects, contractors, plumbers, carpenters, electricians, board members, and friends from Baraboo slogged through the wet hayfield to celebrate both the continuation of a dream and a new beginning. The first structure built as part of the twenty-five-acre public area was the Johnson Exhibit Pod, a circular building with twelve pens radiating out from a central core like spokes on a wheel. It was named after longtime ICF supporters Mr. and Mrs. Samuel C. Johnson of Racine, who supported its construction.

Moving Gee Whiz from Johnson Pod to Crane City. *Photo by George Archibald.*

After ceremoniously moving a shovel of dirt at the pod site, the entire group moved one hundred yards east to the center of the planned African Crowned Crane savanna exhibit. There Ron and George planted a nine-year-old burr oak to commemorate their years at the Sauey farm beginning in 1972, a full year before ICF was incorporated. They chose the sturdy burr oak because "its resilience against prairie fires and life span that hurtles centuries represents the ICF spirit."

Increased activity at the new site now made it desirable for the staff to begin maintaining a full-time presence at the Shady Lane Road location even though the administration building was still just a designated black rectangle on the site's master plan. The staff was slowly expanding and continuing to evolve. Jim Harris, who wrote several freelance articles for the ICF *Bugle*, was hired to replace Scott Freeman in the education department. Marion Hill, an ICF volunteer, worked one season part-time as Jim's assistant and then became a full-time employee. Two aged government surplus house trailers were purchased and moved onto the property in March to house the office staff. Along with the Johnson Pod, construction of the Cudahy Visitor Center, funded by the Richard and Anna M. Cudahy Fund, was under way. The unusual arch on the visitor center was the roof from Eunice's old barn, which was still standing when ICF purchased the land.

The Johnson Exhibit Pod was completed in late 1982 and the aviculture staff made plans to move twenty-one cranes to the new ICF in February 1983. During their minimum three-month quarantine, each crane had to test negative twice not only for the dangerous IBDC virus but also for parasites. The long quarantine put a strain on the aviculturists' daily routines. Since the cranes had to be locked inside, birds and humans had to tolerate each other in close quarters.

So it was a relieved staff that lined their cars up in a caravan on February 1. Many of the cranes merely sat on someone's lap and gazed out the window for the five-mile ride to the new site. Nervous birds were placed in shipping crates. After several trips over two days, all twenty-one birds were safely settled in at their new home. The group included five pairs of White-napeds, one Brolga (Olga), one pair each of Siberian, Sarus, Red-crowned, and the Blue Cranes Killer and his lovely Priscilla, one Sandhill, and Gee Whiz. Three cranes from other institutions brought the total to twenty-four. Since these cranes were for public display, they were all either young birds or not endangered and therefore not involved in ICF's captive breeding program. For the next six years, until all the crane facilities were built at the new site, the aviculture staff had to commute between the two ICFs.

Each of the four aviculturists took turns working the pod. Even the excitement of a new facility didn't override the inconvenience of two ten-mile round trips a day, in all kinds of weather, to check on the cranes. Sometimes the pod person made extra trips because all the tools and equipment were still at the old site, and if you discovered you had to fix something with a Phillips screwdriver and all you had in the truck was a regular screwdriver, you had to go all the way back to the old ICF and retrieve it.

At the Johnson Pod the public can see a working captive propagation facility rather than a static display of penned birds. Some pens are equipped with a sprinkling system for rainy season nesters, and other enclosures have floodlights for the extreme northern species in order to provide the best physical environment possible for each crane. Flight netting stretches across all of the pens to accommodate full-winged birds, and each enclosure at the pod has two outdoor runs. But a few years later it was apparent that public viewing at the front of the pens and aviculturists entering the rear to feed and water prevented the cranes from establishing a secure territory for their nests. When the staff serviced the birds through a gate near the public area, three females who had lived at the pod for several years and never produced eggs began laying.

Automatic waterers in the indoor shelters were rated highly by both staff and cranes, but for different reasons. The cranes pulled the plugs out of the water basins and created their own private wetlands. The laborsaving waterers were subsequently replaced by old-fashioned but crane-proof rubber buckets.

By summer 1983, the pod cranes were well adjusted to their new surroundings, the Cudahy Visitor Center was completed, and on June 26 ICF officially opened its new facility to the public. In three hours more than fifteen hundred people toured the site. But it was just a modest beginning for ICF's new era. Amid the excitement of planning the opening day activities, ground was broken for the Norman and Claire Sauey Hatchery and Chick-Rearing Complex.

Completed in 1984, the first floor of the two-story hatchery was the old barn, renovated and expanded but minus its roof and relieved of a foot of manure left behind by Eunice's cattle. In the public section on the west side of the complex is the Schroeder Exhibit Room, supported largely by the Walter Schroeder Foundation. It has a small movie theater and educational displays that explain artificial insemination and chick development from the earliest embryonic stages to the moment of hatching. Near the entrance in a wooden booth sits a ceramic crane chick next to a food dish. A child can put his or her arm into a crane puppet and "feed" the chicks through a hole in the side panel to simulate costume-rearing, the recently developed method for raising chicks.

On the second floor are offices for administrative staff, a combination kitchen-lounge-meeting room, and a small library. The R. D. & Linda Peters Research Laboratory on the ground floor's east side contains rooms for incubating and hatching eggs, a large laboratory for research, a photographic darkroom, and a surgery/treatment room with an adjacent recovery room. It's hard to imagine that the work carried out on the first and second floors once fit into three horse stalls and a tack room. The aviculture staff finally moved to the new site, but the breeding pairs still remained at the Sauey farm.

In 1986, construction began on the new breeding facility, and the staff slowly began to wind down the operation at the old site. Although the old breeding unit was still being used, occasionally the staff removed equipment from a pen as birds were shifted or their housing needs changed. In one case this involved removing a divider fence in a yard to allow Richard, a Sarus Crane, more exercise room. Richard is not a crane you'd care to meet in a dark pen at night. He's a huge, dominant, aggressive bird who has never hesitated to defend every inch of his enclosure against even the most peaceful, kindhearted aviculturist.

On this morning a new employee, Doug, whose job was divided between maintenance and aviculture but who never quite got the hang of the bird stuff, pulled up Richard's yard partition and rolled the fence up for easy removal from the pen. As Doug dragged the coiled fence behind him, he was unaware that Richard had jumped on board and was hitching a ride out of his yard. When Doug turned around to close the gate, he was horrified to find Richard staring at him. Then, without so much as a single step, Richard took flight.

In another section of the breeding unit, Assistant Curator of Birds Scott Swengel was checking on some birds.

"I looked up to see the largest flying bird I'd ever seen. As a birdwatcher I concluded it could only be a Sarus Crane, but what was it doing flying over ICF? The bird flew west and crashed into a tree. I watched it fall to the ground, hitting limbs on the way down. It was so stunned that it just stood there when I ran over to catch it and discovered it was Richard. He was okay, physically, but for about four months he was a wimp, real mellow. Then he became a meany again."

Not until veterinarian Dr. Julie Langenberg was contracted in summer 1987 to work ten hours a month was the potential of ICF's modest health care facility finally utilized. A wildlife specialist with experience at the National and Philadelphia Zoos and a graduate and former faculty member of the University of Pennsylvania's veterinary school, Julie moved to Madison in spring 1987 with her husband, a USFWS veterinarian who worked with cranes at Patuxent and was recently transferred to the National Wildlife Health Research Center. She was in the right place at the right time.

Claire Mirande, ICF's curator of birds since 1984, was looking for someone to provide regular veterinary care on a part-time consulting basis. Julie was available, had experience with exotic species, and most important was willing to take a medical program that had been somewhat sporadic (despite the annual crane health checkup each autumn) and develop a preventive health care program. She knew going in that it would be a long process.

Analyzing that early period Julie says, "It was evident from the beginning that you don't do that on ten hours a month. What you do on ten hours a month is deal with the most critical health problems. I wasn't interested in doing just that."

Budget constraints hampered the program's development, but Julie worked around that.

"I put in a tremendous number of hours that I didn't get paid for, but I don't think that's atypical for ICF people. It was my choice, primarily because of the institution and the kind of work that was being done."

The staff might have thought that what they needed most was simply consistent veterinary care, but Julie's experiences told her otherwise. Her consulting status lasted two years and then she became a half-time employee. Getting acquainted with the various health concerns of the different crane species and individual birds was only part of Julie's mission. The other part was assuring the staff that her presence and input would not interfere with their management program.

"The staff was good at recognizing problems and they took the birds' health problems seriously, but they were so used to having to deal with them on their own that some staff members had very strong feelings about how things should be done. What I had to do was diplomatically work with them, convince them that there are veterinarians who have background in conservation biology and captive propagation and will work with people and not try to take over the program [and] that I respected their experience because they had a lot more experience with these birds than I did at that time, but that I had knowledge they didn't have and we should work together."

A half-dozen years later Julie now finds herself consulted about numerous nonmedical issues, such as moving a bird, by a doting staff concerned about every aspect of their birds' environment.

"At times I've told them my input is not important on a particular issue, but it's better that way than the other. That they do talk to me about little things is a positive reflection on my having established a relationship of trust."

With Julie's guidance, ICF began to acquire basic diagnostic equipment. Previously the only on-site diagnostic work was fecal evaluations. The lab is now equipped for blood-cell counts, complete blood counts, cytology studies, and radiology. A fiber-optic scope is used to visualize internal organs through a tiny incision, and a laparoscope allows Julie to examine a bird's sexual organs through a similar small incision and make a positive identification. ICF purchased gas anesthesia equipment for surgical procedures (safer than injecting drugs) along with a cautery unit and a wide array of surgical instruments.

In 1989, ICF hired Patty McCourt, a combination aviculturist and licensed veterinary technician. Since Julie can't always be on-site, Patty's ability to handle basic emergency treatment and perform diagnostic tests means the cranes always have access to medical care. Dr. Tom Curro, a resident at the University of Wisconsin's School of Veterinary Medicine (SVM), where Julie is on the faculty, is on staff quarter-time. Tom's presence means as much to Julie as to the cranes: she is no longer on call twenty-four hours a day, 365 days a year.

Julie brings groups of fourth-year veterinary students to ICF for a few days throughout the year. They do not play junior veterinarian, although they do learn about being a crane doctor. Their mornings are spent helping the aviculturists feed and water more than one hundred cranes, even if it's pouring rain outside or a body-numbing five degrees.

"I want to expose them to how critical it is to understand the basic management of any animal, whether it's a zoo animal or somebody's pet. So many medical problems we have with captive wild animals are related to management concerns," is Julie's explanation to any befuddled future vets. "The feedback from the students is universally positive. They're surprised about what kind of an institution this is and are usually overwhelmed by the kinds of things going on and the complexity of the way we run the place. I also tell them it's the best chance they'll have to get close to these birds. That's exciting to them and they don't mind if they're picking up crap while they're doing it."

ICF also hosts students from all over the country who are studying at the NWHRC. Individual requests to spend time with ICF's health care program come from around the world as well as the United States. The time and energy spent by ICF staff on educating young veterinarians and ornithologists is an investment in not only the cranes' future, but that of all endangered species and captive wild animals. More and more conservationists are looking beyond their personal projects and seeing themselves as part of a global community, with the attendant responsibilities of any good citizen, including passing on knowledge and experience to future generations.

Some of ICF's visiting students contribute significantly to the body of information on crane biology. For one young researcher's project, ICF raised several Sandhills so she could collect blood samples weekly and examine how the various blood-cell populations change as the bird grows. Determining normal cell counts for chicks of different ages is vital information. According to Julie, "A young bird's blood is different from an adult's and no one had ever described it."

Raising healthy and mentally well-adjusted chicks took on, if possible, an increased sense of urgency at the new site. It is the chicks that hold the hope and promise of returning free-flying cranes to the wild.

Next to but physically separate from the laboratories and offices is the chick-rearing complex, with a brooder room for very young chicks still learning to feed themselves. Plexiglas partitions between the brooder boxes allow the chicks to see each other but prevent physical contact, which may lead to aggressive chicks injuring more submissive ones. Anyone without a next-door neighbor has a mirror to view his or her own reflection. Extending off either side of a corridor are twenty-five pens, each with an outdoor run, for self-sufficient youngsters. Half of the chick pens are completely shut off from public view. The staff must observe the young birds in these enclosures through one-way mirrors, and in that corridor no one speaks above a whisper. This is the venue for costume-rearing chicks in isolation.

Chick exercise yard. *Photo courtesy of International Crane Foundation.*

Costume-reared chicks have plenty of contact with other cranes. It's people that have no place in the isolation setup. Like all chicks at ICF, the costume-reared birds are taught to eat by a hand puppet modeled after an adult crane head with a red spoon affixed to the bill. This is so the chicks associate feeding, a behavior important to the imprinting process, with cranes and not humans. Birds in isolation never see the human protruding from the puppet. They have brood models (taxidermied cranes) with hidden tape recorders that play adult crane calls and, when they leave the brooder room, a live adult or subadult crane in an adjacent pen for a role model. Any human who enters a chick's pen or takes one out for exercise must always wear a crane costume that disguises their human form.

Costume-reared cranes are more difficult to manage in captivity because of their apprehension toward the people who administer medications, collect blood samples, and place identifying bands on their legs. Costume-rearing is time-consuming, expensive, and somewhat inconvenient. So why do it? Because a costume-reared crane has a better chance to survive in the wild.

Release experiments with juvenile, yearling, two-year-old, and three-year-old Greater and Florida Sandhill Cranes in the 1970s and early 1980s indicated that "soft" releases are better than "hard" releases. Soft releases involve gradually acclimating the cranes to their new surroundings in the wild. In a hard release, the birds are taken from their captive situation and left to meet the challenges of the wild with only the briefest period of acclimatization to a natural environment. Even parent-reared cranes, much wilder than their hand-reared counterparts, cannot overcome the limited experience of growing up in a pen with no opportunity to forage for natural foods and learn what to eat and where to roost at night. Solving that problem with parent-reared chicks involves allowing the juveniles a longer acclimation period at the release site, placing brailles (plastic straps) on their wings to prevent them from flying away during this time, and baiting wild birds into the release area who can teach the juveniles how to live in the wild. But since a pair of cranes usually raises only one chick each year, using parent-raised birds severely limits the number of chicks available for a release program. In captivity, a female will produce four to eight eggs in a single breeding season if each egg is removed as soon as it's laid. Costume-rearing, which is simply a variation on hand-rearing, provides a way for aviculturists to raise the additional chicks in a semiwild state suitable for release. The adult cranes are allowed to raise a chick from a later clutch.

ICF's first attempts to raise a "wild" crane were in 1981 at the old site. Two Blue Crane chicks were reared in enclosures that prevented them from seeing people. A local schoolteacher was recruited to create a puppet of an adult crane's neck and head complete with a movable bill. Either a volunteer or Dr. Hiroyuki Masatomi, a Japanese ornithologist studying at ICF that summer, donned the arm-length puppet, stuck their arm through a curtain shielding the chick, and manipulated a spoon to teach the baby crane how to eat. It was an imperfect system because, as the chicks grew and were moved into larger quarters, they did see people. In this embryonic stage the procedure was more often referred to as puppet-rearing instead of costume-rearing.

In 1982, as a fellow of the Aldo Leopold Fellowship Program, Kyoko Archibald, George's wife, was forced to use the technique on two wild Sandhills when their parents abandoned their nest only a few days before the chicks hatched. Normally, late in the incubation period cranes have a strong bond to their nest and are not easily disturbed. But when Kyoko moved her blind into a marsh on the Aldo Leopold Memorial Reserve to observe the crane pair raise their young, the adults left the area. She had to adopt the eggs or the chicks would die. The first night, still hoping the parents would return, Kyoko wrapped the eggs in her down jacket and returned to her blind, where she balanced precariously in silence on a bush just above the frigid marsh water for hours. But by morning the cranes had not returned.

After several days of incubation at a house near the reserve, the chicks hatched and spent a few weeks in semi-isolation during which they saw mostly the crane puppet. Then they began spending their days in a pen near the marsh and eventually lived there all the time. By then the chicks knew Kyoko as a person, not just an arm-length puppet, and became rather tame. But they grew up in a wild setting, foraged daily for natural foods, and slept under the stars. Kyoko's chicks, named Leo for Aldo Leopold and Ter for Frank Terbilcox, then the reserve's manager, were as well prepared for a free life as possible given the current knowledge about soft releases.

As the chicks neared fledging, the time when they would be capable of flight, Kyoko placed metal numbered leg bands on Leo and Ter. When their parents returned to a nearby alfalfa field to feed late in the season, Kyoko set up an introduction. After several false starts and aggressive posturings by the adults (while the chicks were safe within their portable pen), the pair calmed down considerably. The chicks fledged on August 9 and were given their freedom on August 12. There were a few more interactions between the youngsters and their parents before Kyoko decided that her presence was a negative distraction for Leo and Ter and decided to leave them on their own. But when she later discovered the chicks alone, she moved them back to the marsh where the adults roosted at night. One evening at the reserve in late August, Kyoko saw four cranes flying. She wanted to believe it was the family. Perhaps it was. But on August 30 the chicks were alone once more. Soon after they disappeared from the reserve. There was nothing more Kyoko could do. She had to let Leo and Ter find their own way in the wild.

A year and a half later, in February 1984, Kyoko received a letter from Steve Nesbitt of the Florida Game & Fresh Water Fish Commission:

"I'm happy to be able to tell you that we have seen one of the two birds you raised. We've seen it in flocks of 600–1000 cranes west of Gainesville. . . . It appears to be a normal subadult member of the flock."

Clearly, puppet-rearing as a tool to prepare cranes for release to the wild was something worthy of further investigation. To develop the concept of costume-rearing George recruited Dr. Robert (Rob) Horwich, an ethologist who had been studying young birds and mammals, especially infant development in primates, for twenty years. Horwich's research had shown that young mammals go through behavioral periods during which they intensify particular behaviors at specific ages. Rob felt that if he "could introduce crane chicks to the experiences they needed at the correct times during their development, they would be more apt to develop and learn the normal skills needed for survival in the wild."

But the young birds also needed a proper imprinting model to encourage normal social relations with other cranes. Contact with humans needed to be drastically reduced, perhaps even eliminated. In 1985, ICF obtained permits to collect wild Sandhill eggs for Horwich's project. During the five chicks' first few weeks of life they lived in individual brooder boxes. Some had a stuffed crane for company, while others had a cloth model with feathers attached. Speakers built into the models broadcast recorded Sandhill Crane brood calls.

For the next stage of their development, Horwich designed a crane costume to transform him into a "mother crane." He didn't look much like a crane when he wore it, but more important, he didn't look like a human. A sheet covered his head and body. Over his face was a dark screen that hid his features but permitted him to see where he was going, more or less. On one arm he glued some feathers so he could brood his little "offspring" with his "wing." On the other arm he wore the head puppet. Under the costume he carried a tape recorder to play crane calls. The chicks became quickly enamored of their bizarre mother.

The expansive new ICF property, with its burgeoning prairie and kettle marshes, provided an ideal field school for the chicks.

Horwich, assisted by Marty Moore, Cathy Owen, and Linda Hasselbock, was able to raise his cranes at ICF for ten weeks before moving them to the release site at Necedah National Wildlife Refuge, a staging area for migrating cranes fifty-five miles northwest of ICF. At Necedah the chicks lived in a large pen for a month. At about one hundred days of age they were banded and fitted with radio transmitters so that another assistant, John Wood, a graduate student at the University of Wisconsin at Stevens Point, could track their movements by telemetry. Then the fence was removed and they were free.

"Almost immediately we saw short and temporary liaisons with wild birds," Horwich reported. "Sometimes wild cranes would join our chicks and interact with them. Sometimes the flights and flight calls of the wild cranes would stimulate our chicks to fly after the wild flocks. . . . Once they had joined this wild flock, the chicks would fly away when we humans came closer than one hundred yards. . . . The chicks had accepted their own species and had learned fear of humans from them."

But there were a few rough spots as the wild cranes geared up for their fall migration. The chicks regressed and hung around Horwich's tent, waiting for "mother" to appear. So Rob had to break camp and leave. His "tough love" approach worked. The chicks once again became self-sufficient. But then three of them headed southwest instead of southeast to the wintering grounds in Florida. Rob went after them and with radio telemetry located one on a turkey farm. Dressed in his costume, Horwich caught the crane, put the bird in his camper, and headed back to Necedah where, upon seeing wild Sandhills pass overhead, the wayward crane gave it another try, this time heading in the right direction. The other two remained somewhere along the Mississippi River. Two of the cranes, including the one rescued from the turkeys, were later sighted at Jasper-Pulaski State Fish and Wildlife Area in Indiana, a major staging area. The whereabouts of the fifth crane, who had socialized into a wild flock almost immediately upon release, were unknown.

John Wood and his advisor, Dr. Ray Anderson, surveyed the wintering flocks in Florida during the winter but couldn't find any of the release birds. Months later, in spring 1986, observers in

Wisconsin waiting for the cranes to return spotted four of Rob Horwich's five released cranes, a remarkable success rate.

In 1988, Dr. Richard Urbanek of the Ohio Cooperative Fish & Wildlife Research Unit repeated the experiment, working out of Seney National Wildlife Refuge in Michigan's Upper Peninsula. Of sixteen chicks released, fifteen migrated to Florida and back to Seney the following spring. Several were sighted later on their second fall migration. Thirteen more chicks were costume-reared at Seney in 1989 and nine of those successfully migrated that fall and the following spring. But the release birds weren't the only Sandhill Cranes whose activities ICF was monitoring in 1990.

That summer Dick Meal, from the Briggsville area, only about five miles from the Leopold Reserve, informed ICF that a rather tame crane family was hanging around his house eating raspberries from his garden. The red plastic band identified the male as one Steve Nesbitt had banded for his project in Florida, but it had slipped down and obscured a second, metal leg band.

Kyoko Archibald drove out to Dick's house to have a look for herself. Naturally she wondered if the male was Leo. But could a crane, costume-reared for only a few weeks and then conventionally hand-reared, even if it was in a wild setting, compete successfully with wild birds for a mate and reproduce? Kyoko recorded the events of her visit:

"The male was eating corn Dick had scattered in his back yard. As I approached him, the crane walked away from me and went back to where his mate and chick were standing. When the male reached the chick's side, he turned around and walked toward me. I felt a little threatened by his bold confrontation—I stopped and stared. Then surprisingly, he picked up a dead small animal, turned, and fed it to the chick. He was ignoring me completely!"

Later that summer while Kyoko was vacationing in Nova Scotia, ICF's field ecologist, Jeb Barzen, enticed the male crane into a walk-in trap with corn, caught him, and read the number on the metal leg band. It was Leo. He became the first puppet-reared crane to be set free and breed in the wild. Leo was outfitted with new bands and a radio transmitter and left to live out the rest of his life, however long that might be, wherever it might take him.

Costume-rearing, once a novel experiment, has become a part of ICF's crane management. It is an accepted fact that the technique produces cranes who "know" they are cranes and relate better to their own kind than to humans. In 1992, ICF costume-reared four Siberian Cranes for several weeks before slowly introducing them to people. Siberians, especially females, readily form attachments to people. The hope is that by eliminating contact with humans during the critical imprinting period shortly after hatching, these Siberians will be better breeding birds who will form strong pair bonds and copulate naturally.

The staff also initiated an experimental costume-rearing demonstration in 1992. Daily at 11:40 A.M. visitors are led by a tour guide to a gentle slope overlooking a field behind the hatchery. As the guide explains the costume-rearing technique, sharp-eyed observers can pick out an odd-looking humped form in a white sheet walking slowly through the parking lot 150 feet away, turning every now and then to look back and down at the ground. The apparition disappears behind the service building for a minute, and when it emerges around the north end of the garage the downy eight-inch chick trailing behind is clearly visible. They walk into the field and stop about fifty feet from the entranced onlookers. Actually, the chick kind of trots, runs, doubles back, circles around, grabs a bug here and there, battles a particularly offensive blade of grass, and then plops down on her hocks for a well-deserved rest. The chick is not in total isolation, because she sees the visitors and they do nothing to frighten her. Previous "chick walks" involved one or two imprinted Sandhills who walked along a trail with a tour group. New birds were used every year, and finding homes for them at the end of the season became increasingly difficult. Perhaps the costume-reared chick can be used in demonstrations for years to come. She may be outfitted with a radio transmitter and conditioned to fly between designated locations on the property. In that case, visitors will also be able to experience the field technique of radio telemetry. A receiver will pick up a distant signal as the Sandhill waits near the breeding area, Crane City, for her cue. The beeps will sound louder as she flies across the prairie and on to the field where her "mother" is foraging.

Crane City is the avian metropolis on the back third of the property with sixty-one enclosures and roads with names like

Tancho Terrace, Sibe Street, Whooper Way, and Brolga Boulevard. The new breeding unit was completed in 1989. Each enclosure is actually two separate outdoor pens connected to an insulated house. The outdoor runs are used on a rotating schedule so the soil can rest and pathogens have less chance to accumulate. Some yards and houses are subdivided for incompatible birds or unsocialized birds. Gates connecting the pens and the two halves of the house allow the staff the option of maintaining the cranes individually or as a pair. Some enclosures are equipped with photoperiod floodlights and others with sprinklers. Every pen is covered with flight netting, and dark fabric covers fences between each complex to provide visual barriers. Because at least half of each crane's enclosure is empty at any one time, and empty pens separate adjacent birds, each individual or pair has the illusion of owning a much larger territory than they actually do. An electrified perimeter fence, buried four feet down in the ground and three feet out, surrounds Crane City, with its crane homes laid out neatly in rows like a planned suburban neighborhood, a neighborhood with residents from around the world.

Though ICF's international role as leader and partner in saving cranes and their habitats has not changed over the years, except to expand, internally there have been some inevitable changes. When ICF moved to their new site, former ICFers talked longingly of the old days, the intimacy of the workers, the spontaneity, the free spirit. No one ever suggests that things were better in the early years, just different. One person who made the transition from City View Road to Shady Lane Road is Scott Swengel:

"When the staff was really small, it was more of a team because there might be one person in a department and we'd [aviculture] help them if they needed help and they'd help us. I really liked it the old way, but I also like having more people to work with. We've added a lot of interesting people to our staff and gained a lot of diversity by getting bigger. I think our international program is getting more diverse because we have more people sticking their noses into it. With more people, you get more ideas."

The "new" ICF may have a different style, but the spirit is the same. How many veterans from the old regime didn't know quite what they were getting themselves into? It's still happening. When

Crane City. *Photo by David H. Thompson.*

Bob Hallam came to work for ICF in 1982, he noticed a lot of shot glasses laying around.

"I thought, 'these ICFers party hard,' only to find out they were for semen collecting."

In an informal survey of the staff, from administrators to aviculturists to office support staff, they revealed their feelings about working at ICF. They told me how exciting it is to meet people from all over the world. There is a sense of amazement and appreciation for how so many people can work together toward a common goal with minimal conflicts. Some confessed to wasting time gazing out their office windows at the chicks in the exercise yard and delighting in their antics. Some staff mentioned the opportunity to travel, to learn from leading experts in conservation, and to share their own knowledge with interns and visitors.

Julie Langenberg: "The main thing that makes me want to stay here is that ICF is probably the first zoological institution that I've worked at whose mission I really believe in. And I really agree with their approach to their mission."

Secretary Teresa Searock: "The world has become both larger and smaller to me."

One small part of that vast world resides in a house that sits off by itself on the west side of the breeding unit. Its own perimeter fence isolates it within the confines of Crane City. The Black-necked Cranes live there. They almost didn't.

TEN

Treasures of a Marsh

O n a frigid March morning in 1985, after thirteen years of correspondence and negotiations, the world's fifteenth and most mysterious crane species arrived in Baraboo. George and Ron were joined by television crews, reporters, several trustees, and the mayor of Baraboo at the old breeding unit where the two cranes would be quarantined. Also present that day was Prakash Gole from India and Wu Yikang, counselor for science and technology from the Chinese embassy in Washington, D.C.

Lan Lan (which means "flower"), the male, had been captured as a chick years ago and hand-raised, so he was quite tame and the obvious choice for all the publicity photos. He calmly walked out of his crate and into his new home. Yang Yang (Chinese for "sun"), the female, had been wild-caught as an adult and was still frightened of people, so the crowd walked back up the hill before she was uncrated quietly by the staff.

There were so many questions to be answered by these two rare birds. What did their unison call sound like? What was their repertoire of behavioral displays? Were they compatible and would they breed? What temperament would their chicks demonstrate? Would they be shy and wary or aggressive?

George had persisted through the years in his quest to bring Black-necked Cranes to ICF. Despite Ron's contacts among Indian conservationists, the chances of obtaining eggs from the few Black-neckeds that still nested in India were slim to none. The dismal outlook from the late 1970s, when only two pairs were sighted in Ladakh, brightened somewhat when Prakash Gole discovered fourteen birds, including six nesting pairs, in 1980. He even saw two newly hatched chicks in one nest. But even an optimist would have to concede that there are no surplus eggs among a breeding population of twelve. George had also kept up his contacts in China, where scientists estimated the population at around seven hundred cranes, all on the Tibetan Plateau.

In 1981, George met with Chinese government officials to request twelve Black-necked Crane eggs from the Tibet region. The Chinese were agreeable but there was the matter of the Tibetan expedition's cost, which ICF would have to pay and which the Chinese said would cost $150,000. All hopes of receiving eggs were dashed. But ICF maintained a working relationship with Chinese scientists and government officials through other projects.

From 1983 to 1985, ICF led sixteen Earthwatch teams to the Zhalong Nature Reserve in northeastern China. Earthwatch is a private organization in Massachusetts that recruits volunteer researchers (who pay their own expenses) to help professional scientists with their projects. The Earthwatch group helped collect data on Zhalong's six species of cranes and other wildlife. They also pumped money into the local economy and promoted goodwill. With each session ICF brought equipment and supplies for Zhalong's research and education center. As ICF's relationship with their Chinese colleagues grew stronger and friendships were forged, George made another proposal. He would give them several species of cranes for the Zhalong research center in exchange for one pair of captive Black-necked Cranes. They were finally here.

But on day twenty-nine of the quarantine, everyone's dreams and hopes for these cranes collapsed. Lan Lan showed signs of respiratory distress. The staff consulted several avian veterinarians who advised testing him for a respiratory parasite (this was two years before Julie Langenberg was hired). By the evening of the following day his condition had deteriorated. The next morning Lan Lan appeared a bit stronger, and the staff decided to take him to the School of Veterinary Medicine in Madison. But when Claire Mirande returned to his pen to crate him, Lan Lan was dead.

The necropsy revealed a lesion on the tracheal wall that had developed a mucous plug. It was an unusual condition, difficult, perhaps impossible, to diagnose and treat in time even if a vet had been present. Often animals in captivity don't show signs of illness until the problem is so advanced that treatment becomes a futile race against time. The Chinese were sympathetic and agreed to send another male, but it was another three years before the bird was shipped. In the meantime, ICF's Black-necked Crane problems were mounting. Yang Yang tested positive for IBDC, the herpesvirus.

The staff upgraded their quarantine procedures from routine to extraordinary. In addition to using footbaths, the aviculturists had to shower and change clothes after each contact with Yang Yang to avoid possible infection of the other birds.

In November 1988, a new male Black-necked Crane, Xiwang, arrived from China. Though in captivity for years, Xiwang was a wild-caught bird and as difficult to work with as Yang Yang. It was the least of ICF's problems. Xiwang, like Yang Yang, brought to ICF from halfway around the world, also tested positive for IBDC. Destroying the birds was out of the question, and so was sending them back to China. It had taken years to get them. Their numbers in the wild were still estimated to be less than one thousand.

But ICF was able to work out a management plan with the advice of NWHRC biologists, approved by the Department of the Interior, that allowed them to keep the birds and transfer them to the foundation's new site. They had to build a facility separate from the main breeding unit in Crane City. The extra perimeter fence prevents bill-to-bill contact should a wild Sandhill fly in and land next to the pen. And even though Yang Yang and Xiwang cannot fly, their pens are covered with flight netting to prevent any wild bird from landing in the enclosure. The staff must tend to them last every morning, after they have visited all of the other cranes. In 1989, the Black-necked Cranes finally moved into Crane City.

Since both birds were extremely wild, the staff could only handle them for health checkups. There would be no artificial insemination for the Black-necked Cranes. Fortunately, Yang Yang and Xiwang proved to be a compatible pair. But would they copulate? Even though they were a new pair, Yang Yang had been at ICF for five years by the time the 1990 season began and everyone was anxious for them to breed. No one wanted to wait another year or two for them to settle down.

That year Ann Burke was conducting behavioral observations of the Siberian Cranes. By April she began hearing extremely loud precopulation calls from the west side of Crane City, often at about 5:30 in the morning and between 6:30 and 8:00 at night. Other aviculturists also heard the vocalizations during their shifts. They had all heard precopulation calls before but never that particular one. That's because it was the call of the Black-necked Crane.

It was a great start, but territoriality is an important component in developing a confident breeding pair. Because they were tested positive for IBDC and had to be kept isolated, the Black-neckeds were deprived of crane neighbors who might stimulate territorial defense. Then George remembered a Brolga at the old site who used to attack the window when he saw his reflection. He put a mirror outside the Black-necked's pen so they would defend their yard against their own images.

If Yang Yang did lay an egg, how would they retrieve it? The birds became highly stressed and agitated in the presence of people. In order to acclimate them to a regular egg check and (everyone was thinking optimistically) an egg pickup, each day a staff member stood in their doorway of their house and simply looked into their yard. Sometimes the aviculturist on duty walked around to the side of the pen and looked in. This routine went on for weeks. No one ever saw an egg. But everyone was being conservative with regard to how much disturbance the cranes should be subjected to.

According to Ann, "Scott used to joke that one day we'd go to the pen and a chick was going to run out."

The vigil continued until one day Scott, making his rounds in Crane City, observed that Yang Yang and Xiwang seemed to be, well, just different. He entered the gate of the outer perimeter fence and stood at the inner gate, looking into their yard. Xiwang and Yang Yang walked toward him.

"Now I knew something was going on," recalls Scott. "They never walked toward me before. I walked down the fence line and they kept coming. As I stood at the end, near the corner of the yard but still outside their pen, one of them did a distraction display. I looked down and saw I was only a few feet from their nest."

Costumed chick parent with young Whooping Crane in ICF's
Gromme Marsh. *Photo by David H. Thompson.*

Scott quickly retrieved a plaster-filled Common Crane egg from
the van to replace Yang Yang's egg. When he entered the yard, the
Black-neckeds charged him once and then backed off when they
saw Scott was not going to retreat. They behaved like a wild pair.
Hand-raised birds are not as afraid of people and often persist with
their aggressive displays.

Trung Trung hatched on July 10. Her name means "crane" in
Tibetan, and she was the second Black-necked Crane to hatch
outside of China. The first was to the only other pair of captive
Black-neckeds outside China, hatched in Wolf Brehm's Vogelpark
Walsrode a mere six hours before. Yang Yang laid two more eggs in
1992 (none in 1991), and both of those hatched.

Even though there is no apparent transmission of IBDC from
females to their eggs, ICF takes extreme measures to ensure the
safety not only of Yang Yang's eggs but also the eggs and chicks of
other cranes. The Black-necked Crane eggs are removed from the
pen, disinfected, and given to another pair of cranes, proven

"sitters" who are IBDC antibody negative, for incubation. The eggs cannot go in the incubator with those of the other birds. Trung Trung was incubated by Florida Sandhills, and the 1992 eggs were cared for by White-naped Cranes. A couple of days before hatching, the eggs are placed in their own hatcher, which is completely disinfected after being used. Once Trung Trung learned to eat on her own in the brooder box, she was given a yard completely isolated from the other chicks. She now has a female Common Crane for company, is on display in the Johnson Exhibit Pod, and has, as expected, tested negative for the virus. But despite Trung Trung's negative IBDC status and the lack of viral transmission to eggs, ICF took even more stringent measures with the 1992 chicks and constructed a completely separate chick-rearing facility in Crane City that will be used for all future Black-necked Crane propagation. Both 1992 chicks have also tested negative for IBDC.

And what of the wild Black-necked Cranes in their remote wetlands? Are they still holding steady at seven hundred? In 1989, ICF initiated the first winter count of Black-necked Cranes in China, the Kingdom of Bhutan, and Vietnam. It was organized by Dr. Mary Anne Bishop, an experienced crane researcher who had studied Whooping Cranes in Texas. George visited the Red River Delta in Vietnam, a historical wintering area for Black-neckeds, but didn't find any cranes. Mary Anne and Dasho Paljor Dorji, president of Bhutan's Royal Society for the Protection of Nature, searched four valleys and found 286 Black-necked Cranes. Another Royal Society member reported 11 at a fifth location for a total Bhutan count of 297. Observers in China, including a team of ICF member-volunteers, reported 408 Black-neckeds in Yunnan and Guizhou provinces. The 1989 winter count yielded 705 cranes. But that did not include southern Tibet, where scientists assumed at least several hundred cranes resided.

Mary Anne coordinated a second count in 1990 that involved many more observers. The previous year only five areas in China had been included, but in 1990 an additional twelve sites were surveyed. While the Bhutan count held fairly steady at 299, the China census jumped to 1,255 cranes, including the first report from Tibet of 516 cranes. In India 3 pairs were found, for the first wintering record since 1976. That left the world total at 1,560. But southern Tibet had yet to be fully explored.

The 1991 count sent a shock through crane watchers around the world. Sponsored by the Brehm Fund for International Conservation of Birds, scientists from the Tibet Plateau Institute of Biology and ICF surveyed the barley fields and sandbars of several south central Tibet river valleys and found 2,800 Black-necked Cranes. In just a few years the known population of the endangered Black-necked Crane had more than quadrupled!

ICF's expanding global commitments to saving cranes, wetlands, and grasslands have been made possible in part by the foundation's impressive new facility, expanding financial base, and departmental specialization by the staff. In just the first three years of ICF's International Training Program, established in 1985, forty-five foreign fellows and interns from seventeen countries studied at ICF for periods of three weeks to three months. Fellows, often professional conservationists and university professors, use their time at ICF to plan programs they can implement in their native countries. Foreign interns are younger people on the threshold of their chosen life's work. The cranes of the world have cut through mountains of bureaucratic red tape to bring people together.

If there is one theme that runs through ICF's twenty years of conservation work it is that ultimately the success of a project rests with the individuals who must do the population census or planting or educating. Development Coordinator Bob Hallam says, "The real idea of ICF is not solving the problems of the cranes. It's [helping] other people solve their problems . . . in the wild. We're the catalyst."

In the fall of 1988, four Vietnamese arrived in Baraboo to study at ICF, followed a year later by two more of their countrymen. In the second group was Nguyen Xuan Truong (Muoi Nhe), a former leader of the resistance against the French and U.S. military who had started an improbable chain of events with a simple desire to heal his homeland.

Muoi Nhe's home in the Plain of Reeds on the Mekong River delta was once nourished by floodwaters from the Mekong River. During the war French and U.S. forces dredged huge ditches and drained the Plain of Reeds of its water and life. The heavily acidified soil left behind was useless for wildlife and agriculture. After the war the government of Vietnam moved people into undeveloped areas to try and reclaim the land. Muoi Nhe became the first leader of Dong Thap province, which is part of the Plain of Reeds. His plan to restore native plant species in the early 1980s, particularly floating rice and rear mangrove, for food and cash crops was hindered when fire destroyed the mangroves on the desiccated land. So Muoi Nhe supervised construction of dikes around four-teen thousand acres to impound the monsoon rains. The man-groves, source of rot-resistant timber, fuel, and other products, thrived. Then, in 1984, some rather tall birds of a species that many of the villagers had never seen before began frequenting the restored wetland. Muoi Nhe recognized them, though he hadn't seen them since before the war ravaged his country. The Eastern Sarus Cranes had come home. In 1986, ornithologists from the University of Hanoi confirmed the cranes' existence for the scien-tific community, and that was the only opening George needed. He visited the region in spring 1988, laid plans for an education center in the local village, Tam Nong, to be financed by the Brehm Fund for International Conservation of Birds, and extended invitations to the Vietnamese to visit ICF and study wetland and crane ecology at ICF's own living laboratory with Jeb Barzen.

Jeb then went to Vietnam in 1989 and, assisted by Rich Beilfuss (a former field ecology intern who was later hired by ICF), began working on a plan to restore the wet and dry seasons in the Plain of Reeds that were once a natural consequence of the Mekong River's periodic flooding. Next, George led Earthwatch teams to this newest conservation hotspot (as far as ICF and the cranes were concerned) to collect data on the wetland the people call Tram Chim ("bird swamp"). After several other trips to Vietnam, Jeb and Rich returned in 1991 accompanied by Huong Payson, a U.S. citizen who emigrated from Vietnam in 1965. Huong was translator, field conservationist, and indispensable guiding spirit, and she skillfully bridged the language and cultural gap between ICF and the local people. ICF honored Huong for her contributions at the annual member's meeting in 1991. Unbeknownst to Huong and much to her delight, Jeb had studied hard to deliver his tribute in Huong's native language. Then Huong, petite and resplendent in her áo dāi, the national dress of her homeland, thanked ICF for giving her the opportunity to return home and help her people. Tram Chim is now a national park. The restoration process continues and is a delicate endeavor because the goal is to benefit not only wildlife but also the local people, who must earn a living from the land.

In March 1991, a management meeting for the wetland convened at Tram Chim and was attended by Jeb, Rich, Huong, and Vietnamese scientists, district leaders, provincial leaders, and local people. An agreement was reached to allow some canals for transportation and rear mangrove farming. But the Vietnamese also wanted a major canal down the middle of the core reserve to control water levels. Jeb and Rich felt the cost in terms of drainage and disturbance to wildlife such as the Black-necked Stork would be too high. They wanted the water to move freely. Huong put forth their proposal that if natural management didn't work, the canal could then be constructed.

After much deliberation, the Vietnamese agreed to try this new idea of letting nature control the ecosystem because Muoi Nhe remembered another marsh. A marsh that only a few of his colleagues at the meeting had seen and one that the villagers would never visit. Muoi Nhe had visited Wisconsin's Horicon Marsh and had seen the ditch that crosses that vast wetland. He saw the management problems that arise from such a disturbance. Jeb and Rich, with all their years of experience and education, could not convey the simple lesson that Muoi Nhe learned at Horicon. One afternoon in a Wisconsin wetland spawned the common vision for a marsh half a world away.

Not long after Muoi Nhe came to Baraboo, ICF received some other long-awaited visitors. In May 1990, twelve wild Whooping Crane eggs from Wood Buffalo National Park arrived. All but one were fertile and the seven surviving cranes are now part of ICF's program.

Captive propagation remains a primary activity as biologists continue their struggle to establish a second wild Whooper flock in the United States, geographically separate from the 150 or so birds that migrate between Wood Buffalo National Park in Canada and the Texas gulf coast. A second flock will help ensure the species' survival in the wild if a disaster such as a hurricane or oil spill wipes out the Texas–Wood Buffalo birds. But captive flocks are subject to their own brand of catastrophic threats. ICF lost twenty birds in

1978 to the herpesvirus. In 1984 at the Patuxent Wildlife Research Center, where all of the captive Whooping Cranes lived, Equine Encephalitis Virus (carried by mosquitoes) killed seven of the rare birds. In 1989, the USFWS and the Canadian Wildlife Service decided to move half of the birds (twenty-two Whoopers) to ICF so that the flock would not be as vulnerable to any single threat.

It was the increased work load from the Whooping Cranes that necessitated changing Julie Langenberg's status from consultant to half-time staff veterinarian and hiring a veterinary technician and one more aviculturist. Another street, Whooper Way, with twelve more enclosures, was added to Crane City with financial backing from the National Fish and Wildlife Foundation.

Northwest Airlines donated air transportation for some of the Whooping Cranes and the U.S. Marines brought the rest of the birds in two shipments aboard a Marine Corps Reserve KC-130 in November and December 1989. The last flight, on a bright but cold December 7, was a festive occasion that ICF shared with friends and neighbors. Four hundred local schoolchildren came to the airport with homemade signs welcoming the Whooping Cranes. Where once George and Cam Kepler schemed to get ICF just two Whoopers who were poor breeding prospects, now the Crane Foundation was being asked to accept a major role in the conservation of the world's rarest crane species.

In 1990, an eight-year-old female named Riva, and Rattler, a twenty-one-year-old male, both from Patuxent, produced the first Whooping Cranes in Wisconsin since Gee Whiz hatched in 1982. The chicks were appropriately named Wisconsin and Baraboo. Unfortunately, Baraboo was a weak bird and did not survive. Wisconsin was parent-reared so she could participate in the USFWS Whooping Crane Recovery Team program to establish a nonmigratory Whooper flock in Florida's Kissimee Prairie. But the 1991 release was tabled for logistical reasons and Wisconsin has joined the new breeding program in Calgary.

Somewhere among the twenty-two new Whoopers was a mate for Gee Whiz. He was seven years old and still had no offspring to continue his genetic line. His semen had been collected and frozen every year since he attained sexual maturity. This ensured the continued existence of Gee Whiz's genetic pool in case he died and also conditioned him to tolerate the AI process. Gee Whiz's intense and unavoidable association with people due to his ill health during his critical imprinting period had likely affected his ability to socialize with other Whooping Cranes. He looked great, though. Gee Whiz grew to be a tall, feather-perfect, glorious respresentative of his species. To encourage normal crane behaviors, he lived with a female Red-crowned Crane for a few years. Gee Whiz, however, was already demonstrating a preference for blond women and strong aggression toward men, including George.

The arrival of the Patuxent birds gave Gee Whiz his first introduction to another Whooping Crane. He intimidated his first partner, Faith, a hand-reared bird. They lived next to each other for two years and never developed a pair bond. He wasn't drawn to a second female, Mousse, either, except to display aggression. But he did continue to assert his dominance over men and enjoy visits by women, especially Claire Mirande, Ann Burke, and Marianne Wellington (all blonds), even when the visit was only to feed and water him.

By spring 1992, Gee Whiz still wasn't inclined to pair with another Whooper. The staff was still mixing and matching Whoopers to establish pairs, and leaving a female next to Gee Whiz when she might bond with another male wasn't helping the species. Since there weren't any "odd females out" in 1992, Gee Whiz was alone once again.

Concerned that his breeding condition might diminish (even though he didn't pair with any of the females, they had provided some behavioral stimulation), the staff agreed that Claire, Ann, and Marianne would allow themselves a few extra moments with Gee Whiz during the course of routine maintenance. Perhaps they would indulge in an extra dance every now and then. Gee Whiz responded with voluminous amounts of top-quality semen loaded with morphologically perfect, highly motile sperm.

Riva, a proven layer, was chosen to receive Gee Whiz's semen, and Scott Swengel monitored her behavioral and physical development throughout the breeding season to ensure maximum fertility of her eggs. He walked a fine line between the need to examine Riva and the desire to minimize disturbance. Riva laid five eggs. The last four were fertile. All hatched. All fledged. Because Gee Whiz's offspring are the only genetic representatives of Tex and Killer (his mother and father), the chicks were hand-reared and will be part of future captive breeding programs. The day may come, however, when Gee Whiz's descendants will be free-flying cranes, wild once more.

For now, all hopes are with the Florida release, rescheduled for early 1993. ICF's work on the project began in early spring with efforts to breed other pairs whose offspring, unlike the Gee Whiz/Riva progeny, could be raised for release. There were eleven additional eggs—one was broken by the pair immediately after laying, four were fertile, and two hatched and fledged. Both chicks were raised as potential release birds; one was parent-reared until fledging, when it joined its sibling, who had been costume-reared. Also in the isolation pen were six 1992 Whooper chicks from Wood Buffalo National Park eggs. All eight will be sent to Florida along with six chicks from Patuxent. For the first time in ICF's history, a group of chicks remained nameless, known only by their band numbers. The USFWS doesn't want the staff or the public to become emotionally attached to the release birds.

Marianne Wellington is the aviculturist responsible for the Chick House and, with the help of interns and staff, she guides the isolation birds through their paces. As soon as the chicks are able to trek down to the Gromme or Stedman Marsh, usually at one month of age, they begin their evening explorations of the world beyond their pens.

In the morning Marianne posts a sign on the office door alerting everyone to the "Marsh Walk Tonight!" Throughout the day announcements are issued, "We're going out tonight. Better be gone by 6:00 P.M." The chicks are not allowed to see people as nonthreatening objects or even be aware of a person getting into a car and driving off, so everyone must vacate the premises before the session begins. Otherwise, you're stuck in the building until the chicks return to their pens. Aviculturist Ann Burke once narrowly missed making her departure on time. She was about to start her car's engine when the isolation pen door opened and the chicks bounded out with their costumed "parent." She slid down out of sight and was stuck in her car for the next two hours.

The emerging personalities of the chicks become readily apparent on the marsh walks, and it's one of the joys of watching the birds grow up.

A marsh walk/fly with young Whooping Cranes. *Photo by Jim Harris.*

"The first time out," Marianne explains, "they really stick to you. Some will forage right away but others just stay close. After a couple of times in the marsh they start moving away from you.

"Some will chow down any new food. But others, especially with live food because they're not used to something squirming in their mouth, might drop the bug. I've watched adult cranes keep offering a new item to their chick so I know to keep presenting it until they accept it."

In the isolation yard attached to the Chick House, the young cranes have a swimming pool, but it's a poor substitute for a real marsh.

"The first time we took the Whoopers to Gromme Marsh I waded in where there was lots of water and the chicks were hesitant to follow. They would delicately touch the surface of the water with their foot as though trying to figure out what it was. One touched it and walked away. A couple of others touched the water and let their feet sink to the bottom before pulling them up and backing off. A few finally followed me in, the rest stayed in the high grassland. But the second night everyone went in."

When the Whoopers were about two months old, a couple of them required minor medical attention. It was an opportunity to introduce the chicks to humans in a negative context so that, in the wild, they would recognize people as dangerous intruders to be avoided. Marianne, as a human instead of their parent, went into the yard to catch the chicks. A costumed parent was waiting with the birds to act alarmed and teach them fear in case they didn't react negatively. But the baby cranes took command of the situation.

"The chicks freaked out on their own. They were up against the fence trying to get away. The [person in the] costume made sure they didn't hurt themselves. I cornered them, and these teeny little birds were taking me on. A couple of them spread their wings and hissed."

Usually costume-reared cranes learn their "fear of humans" lesson in the field. As the chicks forage peacefully with their costumed parent, a human pops up out of the grass and chases them, often yelling just for added good measure. Since the Whoopers reacted so strongly to people in their pen, it wasn't necessary to conduct a field session. But the staff did decide to conduct a "predator lesson" on the ICF prairie to prepare the chicks for any such interactions that might occur in Florida.

Everyone agreed that a dog was the safest animal to use for the demonstration. Calie, Jeb Barzen's four-and-a-half-year-old Gordon Setter, got the assignment. Gordon Setters are pointers, they don't retrieve. If the Whoopers allowed Calie to get close, she wouldn't try to mouth the cranes or jump on them. Still, the staff put themselves and Calie through a practice session with a Sandhill chick before proceeding with the Whoopers in late July.

By then most of the Whooper chicks had fledged, so Marianne decided to work with only two at a time. For the first lesson she chose a pair who had not yet attained flight. Intern Rebecca Dellinger led the chicks out to Stedman Marsh while Marianne, in costume, hid in the grass. Claire Mirande, also in costume, waited back by the hatchery in case the chicks got so frightened that they ran off in unexpected directions. As Jeb and Calie made their way through the prairie, Marianne poked her head up to see where they were. Calie pointed Marianne. The costume, because it is stored in the Chick House, held the scent of cranes. Jeb redirected Calie and she zeroed in on the real birds. One chick immediately took off running toward the buildings and found comfort in the form of costumed Claire. The other one disappeared into the tall prairie grass and, while Marianne and Rebecca searched for her, the chick quietly made her way to Claire, the one costumed parent she could clearly see. The entire episode had taken an hour.

The next session that evening involved two Whooper chicks who could fly. They were reluctant to walk to Stedman, so while they stood on a high ridge in front of the marsh, Marianne called Jeb on her walkie-talkie with instructions to release Calie. Instead of fleeing, the cranes watched Calie approach to within one hundred yards before they took off. One chick landed at Stedman Marsh.

Meanwhile, on the west side of the property, George was in Gromme Marsh wearing a crane costume and waiting to begin a special evening program. Eric Scott, George's assistant, was at the overlook waiting with the guests. He was about to call George by radio, at which point George was supposed to walk out of the marsh and up to the overlook to present his lecture. As Eric stood facing the group, with his back to the marsh, a large bird flew by.

"What was that?" someone asked.

"Well, we know it wasn't a crane," Eric replied before he turned around completely. Then, "It's, it is a crane!"

For the next hour, four costumed parents and two humans whispered into their radios and played Whooper brood calls on tape recorders while the chicks waited patiently for all their moms and dads to find them.

By summer's end all the Whooper chicks are accomplished fliers and the sign on the office door announces the time of the day's "marsh walk-fly." In late September, I join Marianne, Claire, and the chicks for one evening's adventure.

Shortly after 5:00 P.M. we meet in the Chick House to put on our costumes. The bottom piece is an ankle-length dresslike garment. It's really nothing more than an ill-fitting piece of white sheet with the ends sewn together that wraps around my body and is supported by inch-wide shoulder straps. On top I wear a hood that extends down over my torso and has two sleeves for my arms. On my right arm I place the crane-head puppet. There are only two black-billed puppets that resemble adult Whooping Cranes, so I use a pink-billed model normally reserved for the Siberian Crane chicks. My left hand clutches the bottom of the other sleeve so the birds won't see my hand. Marianne and Claire are similarly attired. The dark mesh that covers our faces prevents normal visual communication and we cannot talk when we are with the chicks, so we use our puppets to get one another's attention like children at play. On my feet I wear black rubber knee-high boots. It's a cool night, temperature in the fifties, and beneath my costume I have on my best wool sweater. Around my waist, inside a nylon fanny pack, is my personal cassette recorder which contains a continuously playing tape of Whooping Crane brood calls. We will play the calls on the way to and from the marsh to keep the chicks with us. I leave the pack unzipped so I can easily reach the controls. Marianne cautions me, "When you get to the marsh, be sure you zip up your pack so the recorder doesn't fall in the water."

At 5:30, Claire and I walk out to the prairie just beyond the parking lot and about fifty yards from the isolation pen hidden behind a stockade fence. Marianne opens the door and silently, swiftly, each chick steps across the threshold. Behind my dark face screen I gasp slightly as each bird runs several feet, pumps its seven-foot wings a few times, and is suddenly cruising north across the prairie. They circle back and come in for a landing, legs dangling, wings held steady in a slight arc, ready to put on the brakes. With Marianne in the lead and our recorders playing the brood calls, we run over the ridge toward Gromme Marsh, encouraging the chicks to soar again. Some fly above our heads but a few just skim over the grasses.

The shoulder straps of my costume slip almost immediately, and I trip over the hem of my dress. It's a long run to Gromme, and as we approach the wetland I'm short of breath and feeling overheated in my wool sweater. I try to watch the cranes and try not to fall on my face. Each of us carries a plastic 35-mm film canister containing chopped smelt. Should a chick fly off on a private mission of exploration elsewhere on the property, we will reward the bird upon its return with this special treat. Unlike the more experienced Marianne and Claire, I turn my back to the birds when I retrieve a piece of fish so the chicks won't see me struggling to get my huge bill into the one-inch canister opening and hear my exasperated sighs.

At last we arrive at the marsh. The chicks wade right in and begin looking for food. I place each foot carefully and hope I don't sink too deep. The costume dangling around my ankles is quickly soaked in the icy water. The moisture spreads up the dress to just above the tops of my boots, where my blue jeans become saturated. In minutes my knees are wet and cold to the point of numbness. Crane conservation is truly a glorious occupation.

We turn off our recorders. Except for the gentle sounds of probing crane bills slapping against the water, the marsh is silent. All around us is prairie. The marsh's low vantage point in the kettle depression has made Crane City, the hatchery, and the parking lot disappear from view. Marianne and Claire begin pulling up young cattails and feeding the tender bases to the chicks. A few of the birds stick their heads under the water and try to pull up their own cattail. But it's late in the season and most of the plants are too tough for their liking.

I observe the proceedings for much too long. I need to forage and act "crany" so the chicks don't think I'm a statue. I poke my puppet head amongst the plants as if I, too, am searching for a meal. When I reach toward another plant, I hear something plop into the water: my cassette recorder. I never zipped up my fanny pack. No time to lose. It's right between my feet. But I can't push up the left sleeve of my sweater because I'm wearing a puppet on my right hand. I plunge my expensively clad left arm into the freezing (by my standards) marsh. After a few gropes I find my recorder, put it back in the pack, and dutifully zip it shut. It's only 6:30 P.M. We have another hour to go.

No experience I have ever had with cranes, whether watching wild ones or hand-raising babies in the days before puppets when we used to run across the Sauey lawn with chicks eagerly following us, has prepared me for this night in the marsh. Interactions between a conventionally hand-reared crane and a human resemble two individuals who speak different languages. They manage to communicate but each remains firmly in her or his own world, reaching out but not quite connecting.

In the marsh, I can venture into the cranes' realm. Not only am I physically in their domain, but the costume-rearing process makes me just another wetland creature. For these two hours we are a cohesive unit, not a keeper and captive birds. There are things the cranes must be concerned about in the marsh such as predators and humans, but I am neither. The Whoopers forage around me, turn their backs to me, stand beside me. I feel accepted to an extent I could never achieve in human form. Despite my lumbering gait, awkward costume, soggy left arm, and chilled knees, I feel rather peaceful wading with the birds. Looking up I see that Marianne and two chicks have moved about fifty feet away. Suddenly the young cranes begin dancing, leaping into the air and then bowing until their sinuous necks almost break the water's surface. Just as quickly, all is quiet again.

At 7:15, Marianne signals with her puppet head that it is time to head back. We trudge out of the marsh with the birds effortlessly following us. Three of them take off and disappear over the ridge beyond, although still on the property. The other four walk back with us. Claire motions to her recorder and shrugs her shoulders as if to ask me, "Is your tape on?" It is, but on my waterlogged cassette player the brood calls sound about five miles away. One by one the three flying chicks return. Claire gives the first two a piece of smelt. Marianne mimes to me, "Do you have any smelt left?" I shake my head no. I'll have to confess later that I dropped my canister in the marsh.

It is nearly dark when we reach the high ridge and head back to the isolation yard. All the birds take off for a final flight around the Stedman Prairie. I stop and turn to watch them, not wanting to miss a second of the spectacle as the evening winds down. They make their final turn at Crane City and prepare to land. One touches down five feet away, and the wingtips of two others nearly brush my shoulders as they glide past and alight a few feet beyond.

It seems the birds don't want the evening to end either. They walk slower and take smaller steps as we get closer to their pen. We finally usher all seven back into their yard. Marianne brings in the last chick, gently nudging the reluctant youngster from behind until the last twenty feet, when she firmly grasps the bird on either side, puppet head and all, and escorts him all the way into the pen. We try to make amends with two dozen minnows we dump in their swimming pool.

These chicks will carry a greater burden to Florida than just their individual struggles to survive a season in the wild. They must grow up. They must reproduce. They must grow old. Will these young Whooping Cranes usher in the next phase of Whooping Crane conservation?

Diane Pierce

ELEVEN

"People Live like Birds in a Wood; When the Time Comes, Each Takes Flight."

. . .

(Chinese Proverb)

Ottawa, Canada, June 1986. Ron and George enter the rear of a huge auditorium where hundreds of people are listening to a solemn German paper on ornithology. A tall older man with graying hair and beard leans against the wall. The older man sees his youthful colleagues and rushes to embrace them. Between hugs and laughs the men talk excitedly and exchange news of their lives from the past few years. People in the back of the lecture hall admonish them to be quiet, but they will do nothing of the sort. Ron, George, and Vladimir Flint are together again.

But their reunion lasts only as long as the conference. Ron must return to Wisconsin, and Flint will remain in Canada only one more week with George before returning to Russia. At the airport terminal Ron shakes George's hand and turns to Flint. The older man finds the moment difficult.

"Do you mind if I kiss you goodbye because I am afraid I will not see you again?"

But Ron assures him, "Of course we'll see each other again. You're not so old and your health is okay."

"Just the same, I would like to kiss you."

Flint wraps his long arms around Ron, who returns his embrace and then boards the plane.

It was the last time they saw each other.

Six months later, on Christmas Day, Ron suffered a cerebral hemorrhage while preparing dinner in his parents' home. He died on January 7. He was thirty-eight years old.

A sudden death, especially of one so young, is never easily accepted. Ron's death hit his family, friends, and the conservation community particularly hard. It took several days for word to reach Ron's friends in North America and beyond. His parents received telegrams of condolence from all over the world. Many of Ron's friends made their way to Baraboo to pay their final respects. For some, even those who had known Ron for twenty years, it was the first time they met each other. He forged strong friendships throughout his life with a lively variety of people and devoted himself to maintaining those bonds. One of the eulogies was delivered by Jim Greenhaulgh, who first met Ron in kindergarten.

Ron was an unpretentious man. He was content not to be the center of attention, and many in the general public and the media barely knew who he was. More than once Ron came face to face with an intern or a new employee who didn't recognize him. He always accepted their ignorance with his usual good humor, though surely it must have bothered him at least a little.

I once tried to throw Ron out of his own barn. It was 1977 and I'd been at ICF for several months. I knew who Ron was but I'd never seen a picture of him. Suddenly this strange man walked into the barn without a tour guide. He ignored all my (increasingly) stern admonishments to wait outside, looked at me, smiled, and said, "Hi. I'm Ron Sauey."

Throughout ICF's early years Ron was often in India or at Cornell. Even George didn't see too much of him. In 1974, Ron made his first trip to India's Keoladeo Ghana Bird Sanctuary near Bharatpur in the state of Rajasthan to study the Siberian Crane. His home each field season was a tiny bamboo cabin behind the forest rest house, Shanti Kutir. Shortly after Ron's arrival that first season,

Habib, the cook, brought news of Keoladeo's new visitor to Belinda "Blue" Wright and Stan Breeden, photographers on assignment for *National Geographic* who were staying at Shanti Kutir.

"There's a new sahib here! He doesn't speak Hindi but he thinks my cooking is first class."

Habib also told them that the new visitor sat in the marsh all day and, like Blue, was having difficulties with a local official. That evening Blue went to the bamboo cabin to meet her "comrade in arms" and commiserate about the official. She and Ron talked until morning. "I have a found a soul mate," he declared.

Blue often met Ron in the morning, accompanied him to his blind, and returned six hours later when he emerged. Leaving after Ron entered his blind made the birds think that all the people who came were now gone (cranes can't count). In the predawn chill they rode their bicycles along the tops of the bunds, or mud mounds, that divide the marsh into sections. At the marsh Ron held his spotting scope, binoculars, notebooks, and dry pants safely above his head and, Blue recalls, "unhesitatingly stepped off the dike into the cold, sinister-looking water" for the one-hundred-yard trek to his blind, a rather un-steady platform hidden by a bamboo shell and mounds of vegetation.

Once in the blind Ron delighted not only in the Siberian Cranes but the Indian Sarus Cranes, geese, and multitude of bird life in the sanctuary. His research was concerned with both the Siberian Crane's current status and also with the bird's future in all parts of its range. From 1981 to 1982 he served on a committee evaluating Keoladeo whose findings prompted Prime Minister Indira Gandhi to declare Keoladeo a national park. Ron's engaging smile and genuine interest in the people and culture of India made him a welcome guest in that faraway land.

When Ron began to spend more time in Baraboo, he set about remodeling his house, the old White House. He equipped his kitchen with a stove and convection oven worthy of the finest restaurant. There was one compartment just for warming plates. His father, Norman, an accomplished woodworker, made all of Ron's kitchen cabinets in his garage workshop. Ron bought an old round table and six chairs and his guests sat and swapped stories of cranes and dreams and distant lands. Howard Ahrensmyer refinished the chairs for him. Herb and Helen Malzacher's old bedroom on the first floor was converted to a study with floor-to-ceiling bookshelves. His literary collection ran from cookbooks to books on Chopin. He read philosophy and silly humor. A double sliding glass door off the north end of the living room opens onto a small porch overlooking City View Road. There was supposed to be a greenhouse on the other side of those doors, but that was a project that slipped away from him. A spinet piano sits against the east wall. When Ron really wanted to do justice to his adored Chopin he went to his parents' home next door. In a room his mother added to the house just for Ron's grand piano, he played the master's études and waltzes.

He laid cream-colored carpeting in the living room and established the house rule, "No shoes in the house." No one minded. It was sort of a rite of entry, a symbol of being in Ron's home, a place you very much wanted to be. As in the old days, he cooked and baked tantalizing treats for his guests and they washed the dishes after dinner.

Ron's most ambitious project was building a silo on the old barn in back of the White House. There he kept a breeding pair of Barn Owls for Wisconsin's Department of Natural Resources restocking program. His freezer was always stuffed with dead mice, as a few surprised houseguests discovered. He was an active conservationist and a member and past president of the Citizen's Natural Resources Association. His admiration for pheasants never wavered, and shortly before he died he was making plans to reclaim his old coop at the farm.

Each year after the Christmas Bird Count in December, friends who birded quadrants all over the area crowded into Ron's kitchen for a delicious home-cooked breakfast. Ron's creative culinary juices flowed better when he cooked for twenty or thirty people. He was a gracious host, always ready with a smile and a laugh.

His easygoing nature worked against him when it came time to write his doctoral dissertation. It took him years. Perhaps his impassioned attention to detail and his desire for perfection slowed him down. Friends, however, understood that Ron just wasn't driven by the same factors that motivate most people. He had loved his work in India, made significant contributions to the conservation of the Siberian Crane, and found new friends that enriched his life. Having a few initials after his name wasn't going to make him a different person or alter that experience. But Ron persevered, and when he did complete his thesis in 1985, he was immensely proud.

At ICF Ron left the crane management to George. He was always more comfortable with wild birds observed while cramped in a blind

Ron and George, summer 1986. *Photo courtesy of International Crane Foundation.*

or hiking through a mountain pass. But Ron remained active in ICF's fund-raising and dabbled in the administrative responsibilities of their growing institution.

Sometimes, especially in the beginning, Ron and George's widely disparate styles and ideas for ICF caused conflict, and at times their friendship was strained. ICF's creation happened so quickly, and they were so inexperienced, that they never actually did any long-range planning or talked about exactly who would do what. Over the years, as each grew into a stronger individual, they once again became a team.

In his eulogy George spoke of their relationship.

"In June of 1986 Ron and I drove together to eastern Canada to attend two international conferences. For two weeks we had a chance to deeply share many things that we formerly just hadn't found the right moment to express. Despite all our years together, our relationship . . . seemed to be only fledging.

"[In the past fourteen years] Ron and I learned to understand and accept each other and thus became closer and closer friends. Many people thought Ron and I looked and acted alike, and yes, we did have much in common. But, for those who knew us well, they knew we were quite different. Ron was a perfectionist who wanted ICF to be a limited but beautiful jewel box. I was a compulsive generalist who wanted ICF to be a shabby castle whose turrets would be seen by the cranes in earth's remotest wetlands. Were it not for the weekly meetings with the third director of ICF, attorney Forrest Hartmann, ICF might not have survived those turbulent early years."

Several months after Ron's death ICF established the Ron Sauey Fund for International Conservation. Donations flooded in and the fund grew to nearly a hundred thousand dollars in just four years. The fund supports projects in countries where financial resources are limited and is used for wildlife management, field research, public education, and to assist foreign interns who come to Baraboo. Proceeds from the Crane Foundation's annual Bird-a-thon, initiated in 1989, are divided equally between ICF's operational needs and the fund.

But Ron's family wanted a personal memorial to keep his presence and contributions a part of everyday life at ICF. Trustees Chappie Fox and Fred Ott thought a library might be appropriate and began a series of discussions with Ron's family. Everyone agreed that a library was the most fitting tribute for Ron. He loved books and learning and sharing that knowledge. The library would replace the White House as a gathering place for researchers with their own dreams of saving the world's cranes. People coming from and going to exotic locales would stop there to recharge their spirits.

ICF raised funds for the furniture, equipment, lower level, and landscaping, but construction of the building itself was supported by Ron's parents, Norman and Claire, and his twin brother, Don. Norman, Jr., presented an unusual fund-raising gift to ICF of a complete set of Owen Gromme prints to sell. In September 1990, after several years of careful planning, the Sauey family broke ground on a site set back slightly from Shady Lane Road where the land rises gently.

During the next eight months Norman was at the construction site nearly every day, observing every detail of the building's progress. Herb Fritz, who had designed several other ICF buildings, was the architect. Another veteran ICF collaborator, Ken Decker of Kendon Construction, was the builder.

ICF and the Sauey family scheduled the dedication for May 26, 1991, Ron's birthday. But they planned an entire weekend of events for the occasion. An early start was needed to get them all in.

Five o'clock in the morning, Saturday, May 25, at the Aldo Leopold Memorial Reserve. Several dozen determined individuals, Ron's friends, family, trustees, and old ICFers, brave the early spring onslaught of mosquitoes and gather at the shack. Trousers are stuffed into the tops of socks to guard against deer ticks, and insect repellent has been liberally splashed on every inch of exposed skin. A few unlucky souls, unprepared for the ravenous mosquitoes, are covered with welts in minutes, but no one retreats to their cars. Everyone speaks in hushed tones punctuated by the slap of hands on bare necks and faces to squash the gluttonous offenders. At 5:19, George, in a yellow windbreaker with the hood pulled tight around his face in desperate defense against the mosquitoes, plays a tape. We listen to the loud raucous notes of a Sandhill Crane and a moment later hear Ron's gentle voice as he explains the call. Then Nina Bradley, Leopold's daughter, begins reading her father's "Marshland Elegy" from *A Sand County Almanac*.

The sunrise is gray. A heavy mist hangs in the air. I sit under a large, graceful oak on a bench designed and built by Leopold. Nina rests her copy on a lectern fashioned from a downed tree limb. She must be wearing the Chanel of insect repellents, for she is serene as she speaks and everyone is focused intently on Leopold's words.

"The ultimate value in these marshes is wildness and the crane is wildness incarnate."

Ron loved to bird at the reserve, and so at the conclusion of Nina's reading we split into three groups and head off on various trails to see who is about. By now, 5:45, the mist is a light drizzle. It's a perfectly miserable day for birding, but so what. Besides, everyone is talking so much that any warbler that might be hanging around is surely long gone by the time we approach. Old friends who have come to Baraboo for this special weekend find each other through the haze of mosquitoes. New relationships are forged.

"We are all connected because of Ron, and although I have never met many of his friends, I feel as if I know you all," wrote Marge Winski not long after Ron died.

When my group comes crashing out of the woods, we meet trustee Abigail Avery silently standing on the road listening to a solitary bird singing energetically. Someone tells her it's a Song Sparrow. She is not impressed. His song was just as beautiful before the bird was identified. I feel certain Ron would have concurred with Abigail.

We pile into our cars and head off to ICF, the old ICF, where Norman and Claire are hosting a buffet breakfast under a red-and-white-striped tent. There are many more people here than I saw at the reserve. They are well rested, have dry shoes and socks, and no telling welts from aggressive biting flying things. The line of guests waiting to check in and receive name tags keeps breaking and reforming, moving like a humanoid amoeba as familiar faces are sighted and friends rush to embrace. Vladimir Flint and his wife Tatiana have come from Russia. Photographer Sture Karlsson has made the long journey from Sweden. ICF is a great equalizer. Staff, volunteers, visiting members who don't know anyone, trustees, all mingle freely.

Shortly after 10:00 A.M., George turns on a portable PA system and the stories begin. Former researcher Barbara Brownsmith recalled the first time she met Ron. She and her husband drove from Ohio to see ICF and ran into Ron, who had just that moment returned from India. Ron simply put down his suitcases and gave them a tour. Gerald Scott talks about the eagle nest Ron saw on his first camping trip. Ron's sister, Mary Anne, remembers the time Ron told her not to run from an aggressive crane. Of course, she couldn't help herself and Ron had to rescue her from the bird's attack. His ten-year-old niece, Mindy, wants everyone to know that Ron took her to see his Barn Owls one day and she saw the babies in their nest.

Ron had a lively sense of humor and a penchant for practical jokes. Frank Femali warns everyone that his story might not be too pleasant considering we all just ate breakfast, but since Ron always enjoyed it he's going to tell it anyway. Some of us know what Frank is about to say and remember that Ron was so amused by the incident that he wrote about it for a *Bugle* article in 1983.

"My cousin found his namesake, a hopelessly lame Sandhill chick, dead in its water bucket with only the poor bird's legs emergent. Unfortunately he discovered the accident while leading a large and immensely interested group of elderly ladies through the foundation. 'I had to think fast,' he later recalled, 'so I proclaimed the bird to be bathing and not to be disturbed and hurried them to the next pen!' "

Ron's close friend Mark McCleod recalls a rather disturbing incident. One evening when Mark settled into bed at the White House, he felt a hard lump on his mattress under the sheet. He pulled the sheet back and found a small plastic skeleton.

"I knew that Ron had guests from all over the world. Maybe this was part of some bizarre ritual. But why was it in my bed? What did it mean? Was it a curse? I was too upset to get back in bed so I wrapped myself in a blanket and slept on the floor."

In the morning he told Ron about the eerie artifact. Ron was intrigued and as puzzled about it as Mark. Then Mark relayed how he spent the night on the floor and Ron laughed until he was out of breath.

The next time they were together Mark put a trinket in Ron's bed. Ron never mentioned it. From then on their visits were marked by similar gifts left in each other's rooms that neither ever mentioned the following morning. It remained a private joke until the afternoon when Ron served luncheon sandwiches to Mark and several guests from India. When Mark tried to take a bite from his sandwich, he pulled out a rubber skeleton.

But there was another side of Ron. Peg (Loomis) Ridgely recalls a birding trip with him during which she saw her 499th life bird, a Bell's Vireo. They had gone to dig up wildflowers doomed by a road-widening project west of the town of Verona, heard a bird's call, and tracked down the vireo.

"I told him I wanted number 500 to be really special. Ron said we should go see the Kirtland's Warbler. Then he immediately set about making the plans. He wanted me to have that bird."

The morning is almost gone when the last story ends. Most of the guests return to their motels in town, but some drive over to ICF and hike the nature trails. A few of us walk over to Ron's house just down the road.

The house, minus some furniture, artwork, and books that are now in the library, is almost just as Ron left it. Norman and Claire have invited Ron's close friend Belinda Wright to stay here during her visit. The boisterous mood of the breakfast is gone. We take our shoes off and walk quietly through the house. Barbara Brownsmith sits at the kitchen table. Marge Winski stands in the study. Friends Ron met through the Citizen's Natural Resources Association rest on the sofa. Some time passes before we engage in conversation.

Outside the sky has brightened to a lighter shade of gray. There is little breeze to disturb the clammy, moisture-laden air. Through the kitchen windows comes only the promise of more rain. When everyone has left and Blue and I are alone in the kitchen, she tells me about Ron, Marge, and the aphids.

Marge often stayed in Ron's house when he was away for long periods. The only responsibility he put upon her was the care and nurturing of his plants. Once he returned from India and discovered hundreds of aphids crawling over his precious flora, in his house! Ron was amazed that Marge had never noticed the crisis. While frantically washing and dusting his plants, he dubbed her "Queen Aphid." Still, he invited Marge to watch over things the next time he went away. When he was safely out of the country, Marge sent him a phony press release.

"Baraboo, Wisconsin . . . A massive aphid infestation was reported today at the Ronald T. Sauey residence on City View Road. The catastrophe was first reported by a passerby who heard the horrific sounds of masticating resounding from the structure. No word yet on the whereabouts of Mr. Sauey's (ex) friend, Marge Winski, who was last seen heading north riding on a Almet chaise lounge pulled by a chain of loyal aphids."

But Ron returned from that trip to find all his plants in good health. However, there was an aphid infestation. Hundreds of aphids in his books, drawers, pots, furniture, and cabinets. When Ron used his typewriter, they popped out with each keystroke. Marge had cut out green paper heart-shaped aphids, drawn blue eyes on each, and hid them throughout the house. Years later Ron was still finding aphids. There was the afternoon he poured tea for a Chinese ornithologist and an aphid popped out of the spout.

Later, Marge finished the story for me.

"On my birthday a package arrived from Ron. Inside was a nest of boxes, each container opening to reveal another inside. When I at last opened the final box, I discovered a necklace with a silver heart. It had eyes and a minuscule crown."

Blue goes into Ron's study and comes back with a plastic box that contains paper clips. She removes the lid and dumps the contents on the table. There, among the metal clips, are several aphids, faded now to a dull green after so many years. But one catches our attention. It is bright green. A brand-new aphid.

Sunday morning the sun at last breaks through and the clouds melt away when we gather at ICF. Several rows of chairs are placed between the library and the Chick Yard for the guests. Gerald and Gladys Scott have front-row seats. Some of us sit on the grass, others stand farther back, lost in private memories.

Several speakers address the crowd. Ron's grade-school music teacher has come from Canada. Sture Karlson presents several of his photographic books to the library's collection. Vladimir Flint, who lost a brother at a young age, speaks knowingly of the difficulty of accepting the death of one so young. Then Belinda steps to the microphone.

"I know that I speak for a number of us when I say that much joy went out of our lives when we lost Ron. Thanks to the Sauey family and the help of a number of others, we have this library in Ron's memory, so suitably a place of learning, of beauty, and tranquility. It gives me a real thrill to think of all the thousands of people who will use this library, most of whom will not have known Ron, but they will surely think that he must have been one helluva guy for this library to have been built in his honor! Long after we, his family and friends, have gone, his memory will live on."

George and Belinda pull back a green curtain to reveal the sign pronouncing ICF's newest structure as the Ron Sauey Memorial Library for International Conservation. His family cuts the ribbon. The vaulted canopied entrance has a black walnut door that Norman made in his wood shop. Inside, directly opposite the front door, hangs Owen Gromme's "Salute to the Dawn." When ICF vacated the Sauey farm, Ron, lacking the space to properly display the masterpiece in his own house, asked his mother to watch over the painting. It had hung in his parent's home ever since. The painting says much about the man who commissioned it. Gaze upon it and you see Ron's love for nature, wild things, and fine art. You see a friendship between a young man and the master artist. Because "Salute to the Dawn" makes such a strong statement about Ron, Claire wanted dearly to keep it in her home. For the same reason, she decided to loan the painting to the library.

To the right of the entrance is the reading room with tables and comfortable upholstered chairs, an office for the librarian and education coordinator, a room for storing the photographic collections, a second office for the education director, and a large area for stacks. All of the interior wood, including window sashes, door frames, and office doors, was hand-finished in Norman's shop during the quiet winter months by Rob Ferdon, the Sauey's caretaker for their property. The reading room's south windows face Shady Lane Road, and the north view looks out on the Chick Yard and hatchery complex. Beyond that you can see part of the prairie and all the way to Crane City. After sunset during the breeding season, the Siberian Cranes' photoperiod floodlights illuminate the distant darkness.

When the library was still in the early planning stages, the Sauey family decided that one section of the building would be "Ron's room." As the building took shape, Norman realized it wasn't right to hide the room away behind walls. Everyone else agreed, and the room was left open to the entrance and reading room. It is a place where people who never knew Ron can gain a sense of who he was through personal photographs of his friends, a place where visitors can view artwork Ron collected, sit in chairs from his home, and pick up a magazine from the coffee table that his father made for him. It is a place where a new generation of ICFers can imagine what it must have been like to be welcome in Ron's home, a place where old friends can remember.

Ron's room is augmented by a new sofa that sits in front of the eleven-foot-tall windows. You can sit and watch the young cranes run about in their yard. Or just sit. Behind the sofa is a magnificent cherry-wood conference table donated by Mary Wickem's family in honor of her husband, John, who died suddenly several months after Ron.

The aesthetics and atmosphere of Ron's room are due in large part to his friend Belinda Wright, who came from India to oversee the finishing touches in the library's interior design. On the walls around the conference table hang prints and original artwork from Ron's home that show a variety of birds. Owls, one of Ron's special passions, are well represented.

A recent (1991) painting by David Rankin showing the world's fifteen crane species is on the south wall. Rankin had originally created the painting for educational posters. Like Ron, his own travels in India gave him an enthusiasm and love for the country, and Keoladeo National Park in particular. Rankin never met Ron, but he wanted to donate his painting in honor of the man who "helped put Keoladeo on the map." It hangs above a display case that contains a rare 1897 book about cranes opened to an illustration of the Siberian Crane, the bird to which Ron devoted his professional life.

Other display cabinets have some of Ron's owl collectibles, a copy of his dissertation—*The Range, Status, and Winter Ecology of the Siberian Crane*—and photographs of Ron with the Indian ornithologist Salim Ali, Vladimir Flint, and the old White House gang. The White House guest book is there, too, open to an entry by his cousin Frank Femali:

"Thank you for letting me take refuge at this quiet and peaceful place. I think all the stress is gone now, which makes it that much harder to leave."

Ron's room quickly becomes crowded. Over on the other side of the library I look out toward the hatchery and Crane City. Next to the hatchery is the trailhead for the Ron Sauey Bird Trail, laid by his friends at Madison Audubon in 1989.

From the hatchery Ron's trail meanders through the upland prairie past Canada wild rye, rattlesnake master, daisy fleabane, and rough blazing stars. Then it joins the wetland trail down to the Gromme Marsh, circling tantalizingly close to the one-acre wetland.

Beyond the marsh, Ron's trail enters the Walter Scott Oak Forest. For ten minutes the footpath leads me deeper into the woods. It's cool in here, at the bottom of the forest. The sun's warmth penetrates sparingly through the oak canopy. Up ahead is a

Ron with a Red-crowned Crane. *Photo courtesy of International Crane Foundation.*

bench built by Ron's friends. This is a fine place to rest. I feel driven to this small clearing by the words of a teenage boy:

"If I ever should end my life early upon this planet, I would hope my grave would be placed not within a graveyard but upon some lonely ground where the owl hunts and the chipmunks play."

—Ron Sauey, August 24, 1966

DIANE PIERCE ©

TWELVE

One More Dance

A round the time that Rob Horwich was beginning his costume-rearing work at ICF, a young woman who once read something back in her home country of India about George and a dancing crane came to Baraboo. Meenakshi (Mini) Nagendran took one look at the cranes and ICF and decided to join the crane conservation movement. Her ultimate goal? To restock Siberian Cranes in India and learn the migration route.

More than half of the Indian population of Siberian Cranes had perished between 1974 and 1984. Only thirty-seven birds returned to Keoladeo National Park in 1985. Despite protection on the wintering grounds and the security of the remote breeding territories discovered in 1981 by Sasha Sorokin, the cranes' tenuous grip on survival was quickly slipping away. The migration route, a perilous journey, was still an educated guess. From historical literature and scattered sightings, Ron had pieced together the presumed path:

From late February to early March, the cranes leave Keoladeo National Park and fly northwest across Pakistan to Lake Ab-i-Estada in southeast Afghanistan. The birds might be stopping to rest and feed in various river valleys in central Pakistan. If they are, they could be in great danger. Demoiselle and Common Cranes are routinely hunted in Pakistan, where hunting is an important cultural tradition and the local people, more concerned with their sporting customs than wildlife conservation, are not likely to make an exception for a bird they probably don't even know is endangered.

After resting at Ab-i-Estada, perhaps for several weeks, the cranes move north through a valley formed by two southward extensions of the Hindu Kush Mountains, the Koh-i-Baba Range on the west and the Spin Ghar Range on the east. This path takes the Siberians and thousands of other migratory birds over Kabul, Afghanistan, where some of them, including Siberian Cranes on occasion, can be found in the open-air food markets, their once ivory plumage now tattered and soiled, piercing yellow eyes now sunken holes.

The valley narrows north of Kabul until it runs into the Hindu Kush Mountains. Here the cranes and their fellow winged travelers must make their way through several passes, particularly the Salang Pass at nearly twelve thousand feet. Once through the pass they continue north along a valley formed by the Qonduz River until they reach central Asia's longest river, the Amudarja, which for more than six hundred miles forms the border between Afghanistan and the Soviet Union.

Ron surmised that the cranes probably fly west along the Amudarja only briefly before turning north again, perhaps following the Surchandarja River north through the Gissar and Zeravshan Mountains to the Zeravshan River. From there the cranes might travel west to marshes near the city of Samarkand or fly north over the Turkestan Mountains of Tadkshik to the plains of Uzbek and Kazakh, steadily making their way northwest to the Aral Sea through the vast interior of the Asian continent.

From the Aral Sea the cranes begin the last leg of their journey by crossing a desert for almost one hundred miles. North of the desert is the Turgajskaja Valley, with numerous large lakes that may be important stopovers for the cranes. Observers have reported the cranes' presence in this region with regularity over the years.

When the birds leave the Turgajskaja Valley they enter Russia and western Siberia's mesmerizing tangle of rivers, lakes, swamps, and marshes that signals the nesting grounds are near. The cranes can follow any of a number of rivers downstream to the juncture of the Ob and Kunovat rivers near the town of Gorki.

About thirty-seven miles south of Gorki, in the Kunovat River Basin where open tundra marshes are interrupted by taiga forest, where temperatures are still below freezing in May and ice coats the cranberry bogs, is where Sasha made his historic discovery of eight Siberian Crane pairs in 1981. But the sixteen birds were far fewer than the total Indian population count that year of thirty-eight cranes. Were the eight pairs really members of the Keoladeo flock? There were only eight cranes counted at Feredunkenar in Iran during the winter of 1981–82 so it was unlikely that the Kunovat cranes originated in that country, even though the two migrating populations might be meeting in the Turgajskaja Valley.

In his 1985 dissertation Ron suggested two explanations for these discrepancies: "The number of Siberian Cranes in Iran is larger than currently known, or there is a third, currently unknown, wintering population. While both alternatives seem improbable, it must be remembered that the Iranian population was only recently discovered at Feredunkenar (1978); if this group had escaped detection for so long, why not another group in Iran or in some other area of southcentral Asia? Until banding studies are conducted on the birds along the Kunovat, the question will remain unresolved. For the present, however, the most probable hypothesis is that the Kunovat breeders winter in India."

Four years later only seventeen Siberian Cranes emerged through the Salang Pass in the Hindu Kush and returned to India. If the remaining birds could still be helped by conservation measures, the first step had to be procuring precise information about the migration route. Second, because so few birds remained, biologists had to bolster the flock through reintroduction of captive-bred cranes.

There had been three attempts at restocking through cross-fostering Siberian Crane eggs into the nests of Common Cranes. In 1982, Russian ornithologists tried the procedure with Common Cranes in the Kunovat River Basin. The Siberian chick hatched and they observed the Commons taking care of it for several days, but it later disappeared. Cause of death was never determined.

The next two attempts were at the Oka State Nature Reserve. Since banded Common Cranes from that area had been found wintering in Turkey (and had thus avoided the hunting threats in

Afghanistan and Pakistan), biologists hoped that the Common Cranes would lead their foster Siberian chicks over a safer migration route to a new winter haven.

On May 17, 1983, George took four Siberian Crane eggs from ICF on a nine-thousand-mile journey to the Oka Reserve. Captive Siberians at the Oka Reserve's Rare Crane Breeding Center, established in 1979, were not yet old enough to breed. Thirty-two hours after George left Baraboo, all four eggs were nestled in an incubator at Oka. After a brief rest (for the eggs and George), the oldest egg was placed in a small box with a hot-water bottle to keep it warm during the next part of its trek.

Dr. Yuri Markin had only been able to locate one Common Crane nest after an exhausting search on foot through the mosquito-infested marshes. George, Yuri, and Vladimir Flint set out by boat and then hiked several miles to the nest. They removed the two Common Crane eggs and replaced them with the Siberian egg and a plaster-filled Sandhill Crane egg so the nest would appear undisturbed. It was a historic expedition because this was ICF's first attempt to reintroduce an endangered crane species.

Back at Oka, Dr. Vladimir Panchenko, director of Oka's breeding program, discovered the remaining three Siberian eggs were infertile. It was a shattering disappointment, but the Russians understood the difficulties of breeding cranes. George explained that ICF's male Siberians had produced sporadic semen samples of sometimes dubious quality. But everyone wondered whether the egg in the Common nest was viable. In their excitement no one had checked.

A final inspection of the Common Crane nest several days later revealed that the adults had pushed the dummy Sandhill egg to one side but the Siberian egg was warm. They were incubating their foster egg. When George placed it in the surrounding water, the egg floated high and bobbed around—to everyone's delight, it was fertile. After the egg hatched, biologists monitoring the situation observed the parents lead the youngster away from the nest and into the surrounding alder thicket. They never saw the chick again. The experiment was repeated in 1985 with the same results.

The evidence from the experiments indicated that cross-fostering in its current form was not going to augment the dwindling Siberian Crane flock. Even if the chicks had survived, they might not have contributed to their species' survival. In a 1986 study by ICF aviculturist Tom Mahan and intern Brenda Simmers, cross-fostered cranes demonstrated a preference to socialize with the species of their foster parents instead of their own kind.

Each of four Greater Sandhill chicks was kept with its foster parents (White-napeds, Siberians, and Red-crowneds were used) for one year. Then the chicks were penned individually between two cranes of the same age but opposite sex. One neighbor was the cross-foster species (same as the chick's adopted parents) and the other was conspecific (same as the chick). The cross-fostered chicks spent more time foraging, preening, and walking along the fence nearest their neighbor of the foster species. Although the sample size was small, the results were not encouraging for future cross-fostering experiments.

Cross-fostering of Whooping Cranes into Greater Sandhill nests at Grays Lake National Wildlife Refuge in Idaho, which was implemented in 1975, had yet to produce a breeding pair of Whooping Cranes. Indeed, the project was later abandoned in 1991. Only 11 Whooping Cranes remain from the 288 Wood Buffalo and Patuxent eggs cross-fostered into the Sandhill nests. Four of the eleven survivors are females—they scattered widely across both the wintering grounds in New Mexico and the Idaho breeding territories, and it was difficult for the Whoopers to establish pair bonds. In 1992, a male Whooper and a female Sandhill produced a "Whoophill" hybrid at Grays Lake.

While cross-fostering as a conservation tool was losing popularity at ICF, Rob Horwich was developing costume-rearing, and several subsequent soft releases of Sandhill Cranes were successful.

After her 1985 visit to ICF, Mini Nagendran became a doctoral candidate at North Dakota State University and returned to ICF in 1986 for a three-month internship. The following year she costume-reared Siberian Cranes, the first time the technique had been used on that species, to be sure they would respond as well as the Sandhills. Since it would be much easier to work in India than the remote marshes of western Siberia, she wanted to release the cranes in Keoladeo National Park. How would she learn the migration path? By putting satellite transmitters (platform terminal transmitters, or, PTTs) on the birds and tracking them north to Siberia.

After discussions with the ICF staff, everyone agreed that first Mini needed to conduct an experimental winter release with Sandhills and test a PTT on a free-flying crane.

In spring 1988, Mini costume-reared seven Greater Sandhill chicks at a wildlife refuge in Texas. An untimely drought forced her to move the release site several times in an effort to stay near wild cranes who were also moving in search of marshes for safe roosting. Three chicks survived long enough to be released in early January wearing radio transmitters (the others had been killed by predators). Despite apparent associations with wild cranes who migrated north and were later found on the Platte River in Nebraska, and though they were observed flying in a northerly direction (after being driven in closed boxes over one stretch of the route to the Platte), the chicks returned to Texas. There would be no winter release of Siberian Cranes in India. The release would have to be carried out on the breeding grounds.

In May 1990, George went to the Kunovat River Basin, where he was part of a team of Russians and Americans that laid the groundwork for the rescue of the western population of Siberian Cranes. The plan was simple on paper: build a chick-rearing facility near the breeding territory of wild Siberian pairs; take eggs from ICF, Vogelpark Walsrode, and Oka and costume-rear the chicks on the marsh; put PTTs on the chicks at fledging; and release them and track the migration route.

Before PTTs could be deployed on endangered Siberian Cranes, however, the equipment had to be field-tested. The transmitters had been placed on cranes at St. Catherine's Island Survival Center and Patuxent during the design phase, and Mini tested them once in the field in 1989 on a Sandhill. But how well would the PTT function over the rugged Asian terrain? Would it hinder the crane in any way? To answer those questions Dr. David Ellis of the United States Fish & Wildlife Service joined the team meeting on the Kunovat River. With Yuri Markin's help David planned to put PTTs on wild Common Cranes and track their fall migration.

David and Yuri managed to catch two male Common Cranes with anesthetic-laced bait. A molting female was also caught and fitted with a transmitter. David returned to the United States on June 25 and not until mid-August did the Tyros satellite relay information indicating the three Common Cranes, named Boris, Ivan, and

Katya, were moving. By the end of August all three had moved south of the Kunovat and were in the marshes near the Ob River. Katya was the first to leave the region entirely. She was followed in mid-September by Boris and Ivan. But starting on September 24 all of the satellite's location points for Boris came from the same area near Tjumen, about 500 miles south of the summer territory along the Kunovat. Then, on October 10, Ivan's signal went silent. He had traveled about 650 miles. Katya was tracked all the way to her wintering grounds on the Iran-Afghanistan border near the Hari River, a journey of more than 2,000 miles.

There was no time to repeat the experiment with additional wild Common Cranes. In 1990 only ten Siberians wintered at Keoladeo. The 1991 field expedition would proceed as planned.

The season began on April 1 when George carried Tanya, a thirteen-year-old female Siberian Crane, past the gates of Crane City and into ICF's Stedman Marsh. There George hoped to establish a pair bond with Tanya and induce her to lay eggs that would be covered by artificial insemination. Tanya had never demonstrated an interest in other cranes. She hatched in 1978 from the eggs that Flint collected that year from the more plentiful eastern flock of Siberian Cranes. At the time no one realized how easily female Siberians imprint on humans, and since Tanya was hand-reared before the advent of puppets and costumes, she was often exposed to humans in a positive environment.

In the Stedman Marsh, Tanya gave little indication that she was not "all crane." She foraged in the wetland and took a nap in the sun when she got tired. With George by her side she danced, sending up sprays of water. As she came into breeding condition she feather-painted, poking her bill into the mud and daubing the base of her neck until she had a black necklace that contrasted sharply with her brilliant white plumage. She even solicited George for copulation.

Each night George returned Tanya to her pen with its floodlights that simulated the perpetual twilight of northern Siberia. Tanya's preference for humans wasn't her only quirk. She was terrified of the sliding entrance gate to Crane City. Twice a day she was stressed by its appearance and movement. So George decided to try camping in the marsh with Tanya. Everything went fine until a few deer meandered by for a drink and Tanya completely lost her composure. From then on George and Tanya continued their affair in her pen.

On the other side of Sibe Street from George and Tanya lived Ramsar, a nine-year-old female Siberian Crane and the only off-spring of Wolf, the geriatric crane. Despite being costume-reared for two months, Ramsar was not interested in the young male living next to her. Ramsar's behavior was an indication that cranes have several stages during which they solidify their identity with their own species. She was removed from isolation before she fledged, and later release experiments with Sandhills indicated that fledging and migration are critical periods during which the young birds re-establish their bonds with their parents and the wild flock. Ramsar was interested in George and would call to him when he walked by on his way to see Tanya. So George began dancing with Ramsar as well.

It was fortuitous that the deer traumatized Tanya out of her marsh, because she never came into breeding condition, while Ramsar, with George's help, produced three fertile eggs. One remained at ICF, where it hatched and was named Kunovat. The other two were carefully packed into an insulated box for the first leg of what everyone hoped would be a journey back to the wild.

The eggs and their personal courier, conservation biologist and volunteer Jim Bland, traveled to Frankfurt courtesy of Lufthansa, whose generosity toward the crane cause has made it ICF's official airline. At Frankfurt, Jim picked up four more eggs from Vogelpark Walsrode and joined his wife, Mini Nagendran, who would direct the costume-rearing in Siberia and teach the technique to the Russians. During her six weeks at Vogelpark, Mini had demon-strated artificial insemination and explained costume-rearing to the staff.

Jim and Mini flew to Moscow on May 15 and put the six eggs in an incubator at the Moscow Zoo. On May 17 they flew eight hours, with two stops, to the town of Salekhard on the Arctic Circle. Early the next morning they continued on by helicopter to Gorki, south of Salekhard. The vibrations from the helicopter were so intense that Mini couldn't put the box on the floor for fear of harming the eggs. She and Jim stood during the two-hour trip, suspending the box between them. When Mini peered out the window at the tundra wilderness below, she saw a pair of wild Siberian Cranes at their nest. In Gorki the six eggs from ICF and Vogelpark Walsrode were incubated along with two more from the Oka State Nature Reserve Crane Breeding Center.

Both ICF eggs hatched, and Mini named the chicks Bugle and Vodka. All of the Vogelpark eggs hatched, but one chick died six days later from a respiratory infection. The remaining three were dubbed Walsrode, Doinker, and Plastic. Neither of the Oka eggs hatched—one chick was malpositioned in the egg and unable to break out, and the other died for reasons unknown. On June 5 the team, consisting of Mini, Jim, and the Russians—including expedition leader Sasha Sorokin, Yuri Markin, Vladimir Panchenko, Tatyana (Tanya) Kashentseva, Lena Sotnikova, and Stanislaus (Slava)—took the chicks and embarked on the one-hour flight to the Kunovat River Basin. The oldest, Walsrode, was six days old, and the youngest, Vodka, had been out of his egg for just twenty-four hours.

The helicopter touched down briefly, and as soon as all the gear was unloaded (including an adult male Siberian Crane who would serve as the chicks' role model) it took off again, leaving only Mini, Lena, Tanya, and Slava. Surrounding the team for hundreds of miles was a peaceful wilderness of marshes and forest islands. No roads and scarcely a solid piece of ground to walk on. Silence. "A paradise," Mini called it.

Sasha, Yuri, Jim, and photographer Eduard Nazarov had set up the camp and erected pens for the chicks prior to the team's arrival. The pens were only used during warm days while the chicks were very young. At night Mini put them in pens in the choom, a tepeelike structure. Unfortunately the choom didn't provide as much protection from the elements as everyone had planned. The wooden frame was erected before the canvas covering arrived in camp. When the tarp was stretched over the poles, a gaping hole was left at the top. When it rained, which it often did, it rained in the choom. Heat from the fire escaped through the hole. Mini rigged protective shelters for the chicks, who had fresh hot-water bottles every two hours, but it was often cold and wet for the costumed chick parents, who spent long hours in the tepee.

Mosquitoes added their own touch to the ambience of life in the marsh. Even under her crane costume Mini wore her mosquito netting to protect her face. Two pairs of leggings were a must, and that didn't always shield her body from the assault. The chicks suffered miserably, too. They would tear their down out in desperate defense against the flying hordes. But after ten days they began to discover that mosquitoes were edible and readily partook of the movable feast.

The cold and rain that greeted the team upon their arrival at the Kunovat soon gave way to stifling heat. Mini's journal for June 22 notes the daily temperature: 113°F. But cold, rain, and heat were minor irritations compared to the health status of two of the chicks.

Doinker had hatched with all the toes on his left foot curled in. Each day Mini and Tanya wrapped fresh bandages around the toes to encourage them to grow straight. The problem was so severe, however, that Doinker walked with a limp. Then at two weeks of age Plastic's left leg began to turn outward. Despite continual attempts to stabilize the leg at the hock (the joint halfway up the exposed part of the bird's leg; it's the ankle, not the knee), Plastic's condition worsened each day. She and Doinker were finding it difficult to keep up with the others on the two-hour chick walks through the marsh. Curled toes occur from time to time among crane chicks and can often be corrected. The situation was far more serious for Plastic. Mini wanted to give the chick every opportunity to stay with the program, but each day she quietly confronted the reality that Plastic's deformity could not be overcome.

Everyone who raises chicks puts away their scientific objectivity at some point and enjoys watching the birds' different personalities emerge. Costume-rearing, unlike conventional hand-rearing, requires hours of nurturing and teaching. It's almost impossible not to become attached to the birds. Vodka was easygoing and never challenged Bugle and Walsrode when they robbed him of a delicacy he had foraged during a walk. Bugle was aggressive and dominant. Walsrode was independent. At just over four weeks of age she ran away from the group. Tanya found her later at a nearby lake. It was not the only time she blazed her own trail.

Meanwhile, Plastic continued to deteriorate. Mini knew she would have to euthanize the chick. "It will be," she wrote, "the most difficult thing I have ever done." On July 15, Plastic did not even attempt to walk. At 9:15 that morning, day forty-one of Plastic's life, Mini accepted in her heart what her head had known all along. The lethal injection was painless. The necropsy revealed a problem with Plastic's knee, which in birds is inside the body and not visible. The condition was not treatable.

Doinker struggled to remain part of the release program. One day she even caught a small frog, though she had to be convinced by her costumed parent to eat it. She still limped and sometimes had to rest during the group walks. On July 22 she tired so completely that Mini had to carry her. A week later Mini decided to remove Doinker from the program. Everyone on the team agreed that she would never survive in the wild. Doinker was penned near the base camp and tended to by a native Huntee man, Valodia, to ease her transition from costume-rearing to acceptance of humans. Valodia spoke no English, but Mini gave him a puppet and showed him what he had to do. "He listened with his eyes." A few days later the helicopter arrived and took Doinker to the Moscow Zoo.

There was no time to lament Doinker's departure. David Ellis and Yuri Markin had arrived in the helicopter with the PTTs. In less than three weeks Walsrode from Germany, along with Bugle and Vodka, both from ICF, would be released. Bugle was chosen to carry the solar-powered PTT because he was the biggest and heaviest and most likely to be unaffected by the transmitter. The PTT fit into a back harness, and it took several adjustments to be sure feathers didn't cover it and impede transmission of its signal. Later, a lighter, battery-powered PTT replaced the solar-powered model.

Finally, on August 17, the chicks were taken to the territory of a wild Siberian Crane pair that had their own chick. The "dummy" crane parent (a crane-costumed scarecrow), a fixture in their lives since they fledged and began spending nights outside their holding pens, was placed in the marsh to provide some emotional security for the chicks. On August 22, the dummy was removed. The chicks were on their own. Mini and the other team members took turns observing the birds from a blind. The wild Siberians made contact with the chicks on August 24. Mini recorded what happened over the next four days:

"This day [August 24], Walsrode, Bugle, and Vodka had gone over to the sleeping territory of the Sibe family and first the wild female flew and landed amidst our chicks and started unison calling. Then the male flew in and charged our chicks, but instead of attacking the chicks he did a drop-wing threat and ruffle threat.

Vodka and Walsrode stepped back a little and looked at him but Bugle decided to fly from the scene, reluctantly followed by his companions. That same afternoon the male Sibe again landed amidst the chicks while they were foraging and did a drop-wing. The chicks flew and landed less than one hundred meters east of the male and continued foraging. A few minutes later the female arrived with the their chick ("Spirit") and both families (ours and wild) were foraging in the open marsh separated by a quarter to half kilometer. An hour later when the wild family flew back to their sleeping territory, our chicks were alert and watched.

"The next couple of days were very interesting as well as very frustrating (both for us and the chicks). They would keep going to the Sibe sleeping territory, and during these times the wild family was in the forest feeding. Similarly, the Sibe family would come out into the open marsh, the male often would leave and be gone for quite a while (several minutes to [a] half hour), and the chicks would be feeding either in one of the many forest islands or some other marsh. On August 26, both families left their common territory for several hours. The wild family returned [in] early afternoon flying quite high from quite far, and three hours later the chicks returned from the exact same direction, also flying high. That night it appeared that the two families slept in the same territory.

"At 0413 hours on August 27, the two families were in the same territory separated by 100–200 meters. Walsrode, Bugle, and Vodka were foraging and at 0520 hours they went out of our view, behind an island."

Mini knew from previous observations that the wild family's morning regimen was to wake up, preen for a short while, and then commence feeding. On August 27, however, she watched a different scene unfold.

"It was a fairly cold morning (4°C). The male Sibe kept extending his neck in preflight posture and finally at 0546 hours he was airborne, closely followed by the female and chick, Spirit. At 0550 hours they disappeared over the south horizon, and at this time our chicks were still out of sight feeding somewhere. This was little Spirit's first migratory flight."

Walsrode, Bugle, and Vodka had only three days to integrate with the Siberian Crane family. Sandhill Cranes in the United States needed two weeks to assimilate into the wild flocks.

"Valodia Tyarov." *Photo by Mini Nagendran.*

When released Sandhills don't migrate with the wild cranes, or when they wander off course, they are caught and driven at night in closed boxes to the next staging area for another release attempt. Often this assistance is the difference between a successful release and grounded cranes. The marshes near Tjumen, the region's capital, five hundred miles south of the Kunovat River Basin, is the first staging area that wild Kunovat Siberians might use. When the Siberian Crane project began there had been an understanding by all parties that if the chicks didn't migrate, they would be transported to Tjumen. Even if there weren't any Siberians the chicks might be able to bond with the Common Cranes who rest at Tjumen and follow them south to the wintering grounds. That plan was changed at a high-level meeting in Moscow where good intentions put politics and biology on a collision course.

Through diplomatic channels the Indians had expressed a desire to participate in the project, a perfectly reasonable request since the Siberian Crane is also one of their native birds. The Russians were delighted at the prospect of a cooperative venture between the two nations. Since no one could guarantee that moving the chicks to Tjumen would ensure a successful release, a new plan called for releasing only Bugle at Tjumen. Vodka and Walsrode would return to Oka for several months and then be transported to India, even though the winter release of Sandhills of similar age had not produced encouraging results. Sasha's announcement of the new plan caught the entire team by surprise.

Mini was concerned that sending the inexperienced Bugle to Tjumen by himself would only increase his socialization problems with the wild flock. Sandhill releases had always involved at least two birds. So strong were her fears for his survival that Mini advocated returning Bugle to Oka along with Vodka and Walsrode.

The Russians, meanwhile, faced more than a disrupted expedition. On August 27, Mini heard her colleagues discussing some kind of trouble in Moscow. Her Russian wasn't quite proficient enough to understand all of the conversation and the Russians couldn't translate some key words. Two days later Mini picked up a BBC broadcast on her radio and learned there had been a political coup in Moscow.

On September 4 the helicopter touched down long enough to pick up the team and the birds. Two days later, after stops in Gorki,

Salekhard, and Moscow, the chicks were at Oka. Mini was ex-hausted. The team was profoundly disappointed.

At this early stage of the project, ICF was not ready to endorse a winter release. While the birds waited at Oka, George and Sasha discussed the situation. A consensus was reached to attempt another release next summer, when the chicks would be a year old. And if eggs from captive cranes could be obtained earlier, the 1992 chicks would be ready for release sooner and have more time to integrate with the wild Siberians.

At a wetlands conference in Karachi, Pakistan, in December 1991, twenty crane specialists from India, Russia, Pakistan, Afghan-istan, and the United States met to review the conservation efforts for the Siberian Crane. From India came news that suitable habitat would have to be managed carefully at Keoladeo National Park. Since grazing by water buffalo was eliminated in 1982, grasses had encroached on parts of the open marsh. This may have forced cranes to seek winter refuge elsewhere. Indeed, in the winter of 1989–90, two Siberian Cranes were found wintering outside Keoladeo.

In Pakistan conservationists had set up a crane reserve along the Kurram River Valley. Decoy captive cranes are used to attract the wild cranes much as the hunters use decoys to lure in the passing cranes. But at the reserve, the cranes find safe haven instead of the barrel of a hunter's gun.

Hunting of cranes, possibly even endangered Siberian Cranes, has been more difficult to control in Afghanistan. But Steve Landfried, who has monitored the situation and initiated educa-tional programs for the past ten years, announced he will continue his efforts with his Afghan colleagues.

Six Siberian Cranes returned to India in 1991, down from ten the year before.

The night sky over Sibe Street in Crane City was illuminated earlier than usual in spring 1992. By manipulating the photoperiod and giving the Siberian Cranes more hours of light, the staff was able to induce the birds to come into breeding condition sooner.

Ramsar, of course, needed more than lights. She needed George. But so did Tanya, and it was inconvenient for George to run back and forth across the street between Ramsar and Tanya. So a volunteer remodeled one of the crane house interiors into three compartments. Ramsar lived in one section with access to her own yard. On the other side of a visual and physical barrier installed to prevent fighting between the two female cranes lived Tanya, who also had an outside yard. The third area belonged to George. It was equipped with a desk, cellular phone, lap-top computer, and a carpet-covered wooden bench for his sleeping bag for those times when his "love life" left him exhausted. His door gave him access to Sibe Street and the human world beyond Crane City.

In 1991 Ramsar did not lay her eggs until May. The six eggs for the 1992 project were laid between April 11 and April 24 by three different females: Ramsar, Hirakawa, and Dr. Saab. Hirakawa's were particular cause for celebration—she had been barren for five years.

Spirits were running high when Mini arrived in Baraboo at the beginning of May to prepare for the field season. Less than a month before, lack of funding had put the whole project in jeopardy. Now it was a "go," and there was a frantic rush of activity to organize and pack the necessary gear. The unstable political situation in Russia had made communication with the team members difficult. No one at ICF was quite sure what additional supplies and equipment were needed at the Oka State Reserve. On Mini's departure day, May 7, the ICF van was loaded with 250 pounds of pellet crane food, assorted medical supplies for the birds, food for the team members including 15 pounds of sugar (a treat the Russians eagerly awaited along with the jar of peanut butter), Mini's baggage, and six crane eggs. The youngest egg was twelve days old, the oldest twenty-six days into its incubation. By the time everything was stowed for the trip to O'Hare International Airport, it was nearly 11:00 A.M. Mini's Lufthansa flight was at 4:00 P.M. Aviculturist Ann Burke and Mini climbed into the van and sped off on their four-hour drive to Chicago.

At the airport a customs agent stayed at Mini's side to facilitate the paperwork. A Lufthansa employee helped her carry the egg box all the way to the departure gate. In the final minutes before Mini boarded the plane, Ann reviewed the status of the eggs with her, detailing their ages, origins, and how they appeared the last time they were candled to check fertility. The twenty-six-day-old chick had appeared to move weakly in its egg.

A few passengers inquired about the large wooden box at their feet and Mini and Ann took turns explaining about the endangered Siberian Cranes and the release project that would increase the flock and help biologists map the migration route so they could better protect the birds. A final hug, "Take care of yourself, good luck," and Mini was gone.

In addition to the uncertainty of the Russian situation, Germany had been beset by labor strikes, and Mini wasn't sure what awaited her in Frankfurt, where she had to change planes. The airport was deserted when the plane landed at 7:30 the next morning. The strikes had ended less than four hours before. She had to haul her carry-on baggage, the egg box, and two large Thermos bottles (containing hot water to replenish the hot-water bottles that warm the eggs) across the airport to meet the Moscow flight.

In Moscow an Aeroflot flight attendant assisted Mini to customs, where Sasha Sorokin was waiting and eased her way through the line. The eggs rested overnight in an incubator at the Moscow Zoo before the four-and-half-hour drive to the Oka State Nature Reserve Crane Breeding Center the next morning. Mini balanced the box on her lap. The plan was to costume-rear the chicks at Oka until early July and then move them to the Kunovat River Basin.

The first chick due to hatch was the one that had seemed frail when it left Chicago. It never even made a pip hole. Upon opening the egg they discovered the chick was malpositioned, its head facing the small end of the egg, away from the air cell. But the next egg hatched on May 14. Mini named the chick Nadia, meaning "hope" in Russian. Losing the first chick was extremely disappointing but not devastating to the project. Some mortality is to be expected under the best of conditions. What happened over the next ten days, however, sent shock waves through the team that reached all the way to Baraboo. None of the remaining four eggs hatched. When the egg contents were examined they discovered that one embryo had died early in its development, one was probably infertile, one had suffered a high weight loss through a thin shell and had an abnormal yolk sac, and the last one was malpositioned and had fluid in its trachea and the right side of its head.

Sasha called a meeting to discuss what had gone wrong and determine the future of the project. It appeared that two of the eggs were not in prime condition when they left ICF. However, they were the only eggs available by early May when Mini had to leave. Everyone had agreed to start earlier so the chicks would have enough time to integrate with the wild cranes. The situation was further complicated by somewhat erratic incubation procedures during the egg's final days. The Russians had received a new German incubator and, as is often the case with mechanical equipment from any country, the instruction manual was ambiguous. It was several days before the turning mechanism was properly programmed. Finally, the incubation temperature was cause for much debate. Because older incubators had given erroneous readings due to improper calibration (but which were actually at the correct temperature, as evidenced by the previously successful hatching of Oka's chicks) those same readings on the new, accurate incubator were actually one-half to one degree too high.

What now? One team member even suggested that perhaps the project should be stopped. Others were stunned at the prospect of giving up. Yuri Markin spoke passionately for that contingent: "We must try everything." In the end, Sasha concurred. They had to go on. With still no funding for the Kunovat part of the expedition, their country in economic turmoil, unable to get their own money out of the banks, food and gasoline difficult to obtain except on the black market, and their own futures almost as uncertain as the Siberian Cranes', they decided to continue the release as planned, with a few necessary adjustments.

Though Oka had also lost a number of eggs, there was a successful Siberian hatch and that bird was added to the project. He was named "Hope." They also decided to costume-rear two Common Crane chicks as Siberians (using Siberian Crane costumes and vocalizations). The Common Crane chicks would, Mini said, "provide companionship to the Siberian Crane chick(s), and if the only alternative is to release Siberian Crane chicks in the company of wild Common Cranes, then these cross-fostered, costume-reared Common Crane chicks would serve as 'lead' birds for the costume-reared Siberian Crane chicks for the purpose of integration into a wild flock of Common Cranes."

Yuri caught a two-day-old wild Common Crane chick on May 23 and brought her to Oka, where she became known as "Espoir," the French word for "hope." Five days later a captive-produced

Common chick hatched and was named "Hoffnung," which is German for, what else, "hope."

On July 1, Mini, Sasha, the four chicks in their boxes, and two large crates containing the 1991 birds Bugle and Vodka who were scheduled for another summer release attempt, crowded into a small plane for a rough eight-hour ride to Salekhard then continued by helicopter to the Kunovat River Basin. There, where the sun would not set until mid-August, amid the tortuous swarms of mosquitoes and gnats, in Mini's "paradise" of wild cranberry bogs and pristine lakes, waited the last of the western Siberian Cranes.

Vodka was growing new primaries, and two new feathers were damaged soon after his arrival in Kunovat. His diminished flight capability mandated his return to Oka. Bugle was fitted with a leg-band radio transmitter to permit tracking of local movements and released on July 7. The transmitter was hardly necessary as during the next several weeks he was often observed near the chicks' holding pens, an area from which he was then displaced by their costumed "parents," or in a nearby marsh where the resident Common Cranes similarly displaced him. When the chicks got older, Bugle sometimes chased them for as long as an hour, though he never physically attacked them. He remained in the vicinity of the base camp and never found wild Siberian Cranes. When the leg carrying the transmitter appeared swollen at the hock on August 15, the team decided to recapture Bugle the next day.

Meanwhile Nadia, Hope, Espoir, and Hoffnung adapted well to life on the marsh. Hope, the Oka Siberian, was younger than the others, and when they fledged he was barely capable of sustaining a short flight. When they were about sixty-five days old the chicks spent their first night away from their holding pens in the company of a dummy parent. In early August they and their dummy parent were moved to the territory of a wild Siberian Crane family. Then on August 18, the dummy was removed and the costumed parents metamorphosed into their human forms and retreated to their blinds.

Nadia, the largest of the chicks, wore a leg-band radio transmitter. Espoir, the oldest Common Crane chick, was fitted with a backpack PTT. But what if the chicks didn't migrate? What benefit would the season produce? Time was running out for the western population of Siberian Cranes. How many more opportunities would biologists have to learn the migration route? After lengthy discussions between Mini and Yuri Markin, the consensus was that a wild Siberian chick would have to carry a PTT. A chick in the company of its parents stood a much better chance of a successful migration. The team wanted to use the PTT on the wild chick of a pair about ten miles from base camp, and not stress the family near the release chicks, which might possibly disrupt the integration process. But when Sasha surveyed the second family on August 12 their chick had disappeared. Sasha's concerns about disturbing the family near the release site were justified. They were also the first Siberian Cranes he discovered in Kunovat back in 1981, his most faithful pair. He and Yuri huddled for more discussions. If they were to have a reasonably secure chance to learn the migration path, the wild chick of the integration family would have to carry the PTT.

Since there were no funds for a helicopter to aid in running down the chick, Sasha and Yuri headed out one afternoon on foot to the sleeping territory. They waited seven hours for the birds to return to roost and settle down enough to give them an opportunity to catch the chick.

From the blinds, the team monitored the release. Hope, though eighty-two days old, was still not capable of long flights. He spent his days foraging where the dummy parent used to be and called to his companions when they flew off to feed. The wild Common Cranes regularly displaced the Siberian chicks and once even jumped on Hope, who appeared quite shaken by the experience. The wild Siberian male, however, seemed interested in Nadia and did not chase away the companion Common Crane chicks. On August 22, the wild male landed among Nadia, Espoir, and Hoffnung and they all foraged peacefully for fifteen minutes.

The next day the three older chicks flew off to feed and left Hope behind. His lack of flight and questionable physical condition had not gone unnoticed by the team or the hungry Golden Eagle nearby. Three days later the team broke camp and dispersed. The remaining three chicks were still on the marsh, but so was the wild family.

Some might question whether such enormous resources should be devoted to a population that appears to have little chance for survival. But if we do not act until the debate is settled, it will be too late. In the words of George Archibald:

"This project is a last-ditch effort that has to be undertaken, despite the risks. Our hopes are that the chicks will survive to join the wild cranes that fly to India for the winter. That hope is what keeps us dancing."

On August 27, Sasha could find neither the wild Siberians nor the released chicks in the Kunovat marshes. Radio tracking confirmed that the birds had left the area.

Epilogue

In late September 1992, satellite telemetry located the chicks south of Kunovat, on their way to Tyumen. Of the costume-reared chicks only Espoir, a Common Crane, carried a PTT. Nadia, the Siberian Crane, wore a radio transmitter, and Hoffnung, the other Common Crane, wore only his identifying leg bands. Biologists assumed that the three were traveling together.

In early October signals from the costume-reared chicks were picked up from an area south of Tyumen. A few weeks later the wild Siberian chick (and its parents) was located via satellite near the Amudarja River in Turkmenskaja, about fifty miles north of the Afghanistan border. This information, together with previous evidence that Iran's Siberian Cranes migrate along the western shore of the Caspian Sea, would seem to eliminate the possibility that this Kunovat family winters at Feredunkenar in Iran. The Amudarja River location is in line with Lake Ab-i-Estada in Afghanistan, a traditional rest stop for migrating Siberian Cranes traveling to and from India. But those were the last signals ever received.

While it appears that the Kunovat Siberians do travel to India for the winter, they might, instead, be part of a previously unknown wintering population. Ron considered the existence of a third wintering flock to be improbable but possible in his 1985 thesis.

The battery-powered PTTs contain an activity sensor. If the sensor indicates the bird has remained still for a long period, it may be assumed the bird has died. But since the transmitters were not emitting any signals, it was impossible to determine if, in addition to the equipment failure, the cranes had perished.

As of early January 1993, neither the release chicks nor the wild Siberian had arrived at Keoladeo National Park. Neither had any of the other Siberian Cranes from the western flock. The grim possibility that the wild India flock will never again wade through the marshes of Keoladeo is edging its way toward reality.

If the India flock has perished, can it be reestablished? Maybe. But first more information must be gathered on India's cranes. To that end the Indian Government has approved the capture of five wintering Common Cranes so they can be outfitted with PTTs. Then biologists can track cranes known to winter in India on their northward migration to their breeding grounds. Perhaps someday these Common Cranes can lead a new flock of Siberian Cranes to India.

The Common Crane project will be carried out by Indian biologists working with Mini Nagendran and Dr. Hiroyoshi Higuchi, director of the Research Center of the Wild Bird Society of Japan, who will supply the PTTs.

There is no neat and tidy end to the story of the Siberian Cranes. Wildlife biology is not a tidy enterprise. Success sometimes seems to be in inverse proportion to the best intentions. We may yet find the release chicks and the wild Siberian. We may not. The work with the Common Cranes might provide essential information to benefit the remaining Siberian Cranes, or it may simply help to ensure that Common Cranes do not befall a similar fate.

ICF hopes to host Sasha Sorokin in Baraboo in spring 1993 to discuss conservation plans for the Siberian Cranes. Future plans include addressing the problem of crane hunting in Pakistan, learning more about the Iranian flock's migration route, and developing Russian-Indian cooperative projects for the cranes.

International cooperation on global environmental problems is now possible on a greater scale than during the previous fifty years. During those decades precious time ran out for a number of endangered species. We cannot afford, the cranes of the world cannot afford, to let the difficulties of wildlife conservation alter our path toward knowledge, understanding, and preservation of the world's natural wonders.

The People

George Archibald was appointed the Rider in the Order of the Golden Ark on September 17, 1983, by Prince Bernhard of the Netherlands. It's a Dutch Order of Chivalry. In February 1984, he was named a Prize Fellow by the John D. and Catherine T. MacArthur Foundation. When the prize was announced, George was roaming the Australian outback.

At ICF an International Guest House was completed in 1993. A wetland habitat to house Whooping Cranes in a naturalistic environment is being planned.

Norman and Claire Sauey have reclaimed their farm. Horses roam the pastures once again.

Forrest Hartmann is an attorney in Baraboo.

Owen Gromme died October 29, 1991, at the age of ninety-five. During the graveside service, a flock of Sandhill Cranes flew overhead.

Anne Gromme died on August 4, 1991. She was eighty-seven. A year before her death, Anne established an endowment to help ICF pay operational expenses. She and Owen never doubted ICF's ability to raise funds for the exciting projects. They were always more concerned with the day-to-day costs of running the foundation, perhaps because they had stood by Ron and George through the early years when ICF's existence was so fragile.

Gerald Scott died in his sleep on December 10, 1991. He had been a high school biology teacher for forty-two years. He and his wife, Gladys, who still lives in Baraboo, were married for fifty-five years.

Chappie Fox has retired from the Circus World Museum but still helps out with the annual circus parade. He remains a member of the board of trustees.

Mary Wickem is still president of the board of trustees.

Howard Ahrensmyer died on November 17, 1983. His name means "ironsmith" in German, and in his honor ICF planted an ironwood sapling at the dedication of the Sauey Hatchery Complex in 1984.

Frank Femali lives in Lombard, Illinois, with his wife, Donna, and his daughters, Sarah and Leah. He programs computer-operated machine centers for the tool-and-die trade.

Barbara Brownsmith lives in San Jose, California, with her husband, Joe, and daughter, Mara. She teaches elementary school and includes conservation awareness in her curriculum.

Herb Malzacher still works at the Madison Zoo where he developed an expertise in elephants and orangutans. Helen helps companies utilize computers for management and administration. They live in Sun Prairie, Wisconsin, in an 1895 house they figure they will be restoring for the rest of their lives.

Diane Pierce maintains her home and studio in Florida.

Charlie Luthin is the program officer for Central America at Lighthawk, the environmental air force. They are a nonprofit organization that flies "key decision makers, media representatives, and fellow grassroots activists over and into endangered lands, giving them the first-hand experience they need to take action."

Milly Zantow lives in North Freedom, Wisconsin, with her husband, Woody.

John Taapken lives in Baraboo with his family. He owns the Ace Hardware store in town.

John Weissinger lives in Ithaca, New York, with his wife, Diane. He's a wildlife artist and produces a series of educational wildlife miniposters.

Joan Fordham left ICF in 1989. She lives in Baraboo and continues to do administrative work for nonprofit organizations. She works for Briarpatch, a teen and family counseling center.

Karen Voss and her husband, Marty, live in rural Eau Claire, Wisconsin, with their two daughters. Karen is a water-quality project specialist for the Wisconsin Department of Natural Resources. Marty is a physician.

Konrad Liegel has been an attorney in Seattle, Washington, since 1988. He specializes in environmental and conservation law.

Scott Freeman is director of public programs at the Burke Museum, a natural history museum on the University of Washington campus in Seattle.

Marion Hill lives in Madison and continues to volunteer at ICF.

Lisa Hartman works for the Wisconsin Department of Natural Resources.

Libby Anderson lives in Maryland.

Cam Kepler works for the USFWS Southeast Research Group

out of Athens, Georgia, a field station of Patuxent. He works on the Kirtland's Warbler and the Mississippi Sandhill Crane.

Rob Horwich is continuing his studies of black howler monkeys at the Community Baboon Sanctuary in Belize. The Sanctuary works with local landowners to preserve habitat for the howlers, which the native Belize people call baboons.

Belinda Wright makes her home in India and Ireland. She continues to combine her career as a filmmaker with concern for wildlife and conservation.

Vladimir Flint lives in Moscow and works on wildlife conservation issues.

Sasha Sorokin continues his efforts on behalf of the Siberian Crane.

Mini Nagendran returned home to California after the 1992 field season to write her dissertation.

Eunice Erickson still lives on Shady Lane Road and keeps an eye on ICF.

Marge Winski is the lighthouse keeper at the Montauk Lighthouse in Montauk, New York. She hid an aphid in the library.

The Cranes

Lulu, the sweet tempered and prolific Red-crowned Crane, died on January 4, 1978. She was twenty-five years old.

Phil died in September 1975, after surgery on his drooping wing.

Casey, the super-semen-producing White-naped Crane, lives at ICF. This wild-caught crane has lived in captivity since 1940.

Dr. Watson, who along with Casey introduced the Columbia County Sheriff's Department to the International Crane Foundation, died in 1983.

Killer and his lovely Priscilla, the Blue Cranes, can be viewed at the Johnson Exhibit Pod.

Pookie, one of the first Hooded Cranes ever to hatch in captivity, lives at the Bronx Zoo.

Olaf, the free-flying Common Crane, died in 1983.

Rusty, the Greater Sandhill Crane, was relocated to a private breeder because of exposure to IBDC. His pal, Freaky, died in the herpes epidemic.

Stella, the wild Sandhill, made several more visits to ICF and was never seen again.

Pat, the Florida Sandhill who built a nest outside my blind, died in 1983.

Won, the Red-crowned Crane found poisoned in Korea, lives at the Bronx Zoo.

All of the White-naped Cranes confiscated in Hong Kong are living. Four are at ICF and two were sent to another institution.

Vladimir, the Siberian Crane from the eastern population flown to ICF in 1977 as an egg, died in 1990. She produced twelve chicks.

Kyta, the other Siberian Crane from the 1977 expedition, died in 1987. She produced one chick, Hima, who still lives at ICF.

Icky, the Sarus Crane who lived at the White House, was transferred to another institution in 1980.

Dushenka, the first Siberian Crane ever hatched in captivity, lives at ICF.

Wolf, the Siberian Crane who was old when he arrived at ICF, died in 1988 of an injury. He was at least eighty-six years old.

Trung Trung, the foundation's first Black-necked crane chick, lives at ICF.

Tsuru, the Red-crowned Crane who was the first chick produced at ICF that fledged, lives in Crane City. He is huge and beautiful and has absolutely no fear of people. Tsuru is considered the most aggressive crane at ICF. He has fathered twenty-three chicks.

Leo, the first puppet-raised crane to be released and successfully breed in the wild, returns to Wisconsin each year.

On January 13, 1993, five Siberian Cranes arrived at Keoladeo National Park. None of the birds wore transmitters. Though the wild chick from Kunovat was not among the group, her parents, who were not banded, might be.

Index

Aanonsen, Linda, 69
AAZPA. *See* American Association of Zoological Parks and Aquaria
Ab-i-Estada, Lake, 116, 120, 121, 128, 239, 240, 261
Acadia University, 9, 12
Afghanistan, 83, 115, 116, 120, 128, 239, 242, 245, 253, 261
African Crowned Cranes, 14, 184
Agriculture Department's Animal and Plant Health Inspection Service (APHIS), 124, 128
Ahrensmeyer, Howard, 65, 66, 81, 140, 225, 263
Aldo Leopold Memorial Reserve, Wisconsin, 5, 29, 101, 105, 194, 197, 229
Ali, Salim, 62, 63, 131, 235
Allen, Robert Porter, 154
American Association of Zoological Parks and Aquaria (AAZPA), 146
Amin, Idi, 109
Amudarja River, 240, 261
Anderson, Allan, 73–74
Anderson, Elizabeth (Libby), 69, 117–18, 123–24, 128, 264
Anderson, Ray, 196
A-1 Tool & Die Company, 2
Apa Tani Valley, 62
APHIS. *See* Agriculture Department's Animal and Health Inspection Service (APHIS)
Aral Sea, 240
Aransas National Wildlife Refuge, Texas, 111, 112, 154

Archibald, Anne, 9, 10
Archibald, Don, 9, 10
Archibald, Donald, 8, 9, 12
Archibald, George, 8–17, 38, 43, 65, 98, 100, 179, 212, 223, 253, 263; and birds, early fascination with, 8, 10–13; and Black-necked Cranes, 203–204; and Brolga Cranes, 32–34; childhood home of, 8–9; and Common Cranes, 45–47, 81–82; and Conway, 39–40; diet for birds selected by, 96; fund-raising efforts of, 74–76; and graduate research at the International Crane Foundation (ICF), 102, 103, 104; on hiring personnel, 87; hybrid research conducted by, 52–53; and *The ICF Bugle*, 77; and the International Crane Foundation (ICF), planning of, 14–17; and the International Crane Workshops, 111–13; in Iran, 82–85; in jail, 44; management responsibilities of, 47–48, 54; and new site of the International Crane Foundation (ICF), 179, 181, 184, 185; personality of, 85; and Pierce, 70–71; and the prairie project, 73–74, 104–105, 179; on the public education program, 98, 101; and Red-crowned Cranes, 30–32, 34, 40, 41; and Sauey, relationship with, 227–28; and Siberian Cranes, 59, 117, 118, 124, 125,

If you are interested in becoming a member of the International Crane Foundation, write or call:

International Crane Foundation
E-11376 Shady Lane Road
Baraboo, WI 53913-9778
(608) 356-9462

Membership benefits include a one-year subscription to *The ICF Bugle*, free admission for yourself and a limited number of guests, and a 10 percent discount on all ICF merchandise.

ICF is open daily from May 1 to October 31. Guided tours are available at 10:00, 11:00, and 3:00 from Memorial Day through Labor Day and on weekends in May, September, and October. Group tours are offered from April 15 to October 31 and can be arranged by appointment.

The International Crane Foundation is located in south-central Wisconsin, a forty-five-minute drive from Madison via State Highway 12.

ICF is about 200 miles from Chicago via Interstate 90 or 94. Take exit 92 and follow Highway 12 east to Shady Lane Road. The foundation is on Shady Lane Road between Highway 12 and County A.